UNFULFILLED

a not so sparkling life

Also by Tiara King

SERIES

Poems Of A Musical Flavour: Volumes 1-6

MG/YA

#TEENBLOGGER: To Follow or Not To Follow?

NON-FICTION

How To Be A Jewel Diva
Closet Confidential
Dream It, Write It, Publish It!
Unfulfilled

Tiara also writes adult romances as *L.J. Diva,* and young adult horror as *T.K. Wrathbone*.

There is a full list of her works in the About section in the back of the book.

UNFULFILLED

a not so sparkling life

Tiara King

♛ Royal Star Publishing ♛

Notes on Life is an imprint of Royal Star Publishing
www.royalstarpublishing.com.au

All Rights Reserved, Copyright © Tiara King 2025
All poems by Tiara King Copyright © 2024

Trade Paperback ISBN: 978-1-922307-81-1
Large Print Paperback ISBN: 978-1-922307-93-4
E-Book ISBN: 978-1-922307-82-8
A catalogue record for this book is available from the National Library of Australia.

Cover design: Royal Star Publishing and ©Designed with Grace
Cover photos: Tiara King
Istock.com/catlane
Tomertu/shutterstock.com
Typesetting in Minion Pro by Royal Star Publishing

The right of Tiara King to be identified as the author of her work has been asserted.
This book is a work of non-fiction. Names have been omitted, and all recollections are the author's own.
No part of this publication may be reproduced, published, performed in public or communicated to the public in any form or by any means without prior written permission of Royal Star Publishing.
Requests to publish work from this book should be sent to:
authors@royalstarpublishing.com.au

CONTENTS

Dedication

Poem: How The World Turned ~ 1

This is Me ~ 3

Poem: Blood ~ 9

Blood is Not Thicker ~ 11

Poem: So Much to Come ~ 59

School of Hard Knocks ~ 61

Poem: Lessons ~ 99

Life is a Long Lesson ~ 101

Poem: What is Okay? ~ 141

Caring ~ 143

Poem: I Am A King ~ 209

My Sparkling Obsession ~ 211

Poem: Blog It! ~ 231

Keyboard Warriors ~ 233

Poem: The Creative Artist ~ 253

The Writing on The Wall ~ 255

Poem: My Reflection ~ 305

Reflections on Fifty Years ~ 307

Poem: Not Free ~ 315

Dedication

This book is dedicated to me and only me for all the goddamn hard work I've put in over the last fifty years.

How the World Turned

In the beginning it was all a dream,
what I might be, what I could be.
In the beginning how was I to know?
What I could be, what I would be.
So completely different,
oh, how the world turned
out to be so different
from the dream at the beginning of it.
The beginning is now the end,
never to start again.

This is Me!

I've been in my neighbourhood for almost thirty-one years, and while some still don't know my name, and others still get it wrong, all know me as the lady with the amazing clothes and jewellery. So, you would expect my life to be ever so sparkling all of the time. Right?

Wrong!

While the outside of me is sparkling on my days out and about doing the shopping, it isn't when I'm at home. Regardless of all of the sparkling, glittery, colourful things I buy and have and use to decorate my office and bedroom, my life is far from sparkling in the real world.

I've been here fifty years and I have an existence. I don't have a life. You'd expect someone who's just turned fifty-one (at the time of printing) to have one, wouldn't you? But alas, I do not, which is probably why all of my female characters in my adult novels are feisty independent women. They are what I cannot be, because in order to be that I would need the Universe to change the course of my life and it's clearly never going to do that. I would need to win the lottery, a house, or have my books go global and sell millions in order to make the millions I need to leave this shit hole of an existence and have the life I've always wanted, with two exceptions to that. No partner, and no kids. I'm too old to have children, and that has been sacrificed, and with no decent single men left anymore, I have no one to spend my life with. It looks like I'll be a single gal living in hell for the next fifty years of my life.

If I live that long.

Or until a particular person leaves the face of this earth. With luck, it's only another ten years. By then, I'll be sixty and even more out of luck and more depressed, and more alone and more emotionally fucked up, and more broke and unable to change anything once it happens.

Fuck the Universe and fuck life.

And now I'll tell you that there's swearing in this book, some of it strong, as you've just seen. I use it to punctuate the emotion of the situation. I also don't talk kindly about some people because they've done nothing to deserve it. And don't get me started on being the bigger person, or taking the high road, because that's just toxic garbage in itself. If you don't like swearing, don't read it. Really. It's okay, I won't mind. Because this book won't be for everyone.

The subtitle for this book was going to be *Fifty Stories for Fifty Years*, but I surpassed fifty stories and kept on going. And then I came up with the title *A Not So Sparkling Life*. Because, as mentioned, my life is not so sparkling most of the time.

These are stories about my life, silly trivial matters, serious heavy matters, school, family, life, jewellery, writing, business. They mean something to me and maybe one of them will mean something to you, or you'll laugh out loud and have some fun. The stories come from me sitting down in the last couple of years and writing down everything I could think of.

Then I realised I'd already written about some of the topics on my blogs over the years. I pulled them up and reworked them, added an old book I wrote about being a carer, and the introduction to my song lyric series as it describes my journey into writing songs so well. After all that, I had the bones of a book.

While some parts of my life have been exciting, that was when I was young and things were doable.

I didn't do them on my own. I couldn't. I was "too young" and "didn't know anything". My real life had yet to start, but little did I know it wouldn't actually be going anywhere but down, falling into the depressive pit of hell it was soon to be in. Which is what caring can feel like.

Through it all, across the last three decades, I struggled to do something for myself, which is why I was constantly making or writing something; songs, drawings, designing, signs for my walls or decorating other things. It moved into my jewellery business, blogging, writing, my publishing business and my books, creating for myself as an outlet to the shit life I had fallen into. I had no support at any point and did it all myself, which can be a good thing as you learn everything and don't become reliant on anyone who can waylay you. It can also be incredibly lonely and exhausting.

Looking back, with all of the cool clothing and jewels I wore, and the things I did and made, having a creative, sparkling life looked to be predestined, because I certainly didn't start out to head in the opposite direction and have a depressed and miserable life. Dealing with toxic people, users, abusers, family, and others…it all happened along the way. I'm also sure that all of the experiences I've had in my fifty years are how I've come to be as me, have made me the person I am.

But then, who am I?

Memoirs, in general, are supposed to have a theme and to have meaning. I tried to come up with a theme and considered those along the veins of life, dreams, creativity, and ideas. I decided to go with the theme of creativity, as I've been very creative since school, and I'm still creative now as a former jewellery designer and writer.

But there are other things involved on a bigger scale. A universal scale. How the Universe has other ideas for you and you're not always able or meant to have the life you want no matter how hard you try. No matter what you do, it just doesn't happen. No wonder so many people are depressed and hate their life. The people who have managed to succeed are constantly telling the rest of us how to live and how to do it, and it just doesn't work that way. We don't all get to succeed or have nice things. We don't all get to do what we want when we want. And while they live their life to the fullest, it's the rest of us schlepps who care for parents or children, clean bathrooms, and struggle to get by on minimum wages.

And that's probably how I came to the word *unfulfilled*, which I am. I'm living a life unfulfilled, because regardless of everything I did as a kid, a teen, and an early adult, it wasn't the normal stuff one gets to experience. I missed out on that and a lot of other stuff. And with everything that happened in my life in the last thirty years, my life became stagnant and grounded in mire.

A life unfulfilled, a life chained and bound to another without the freedom to be me. And it clearly doesn't matter about everything I've done, and do now and into the future—my life will still be unfulfilled, left behind, gone without.

My life will be unfulfilled unless something happens. And

that's not always down to the person to make that happen, especially when you're not in the position to make it happen. Sometimes, the Universe just wants to fuck with you and doesn't care what you think, feel or need.

Sometimes, life just sucks, and you have to suck it up and keep on moving regardless of how slow or how unfulfilling it is. And that sucks in itself.

But for now, let me tell you some stories about myself and the people who have come through my life. Those people aren't always great, in fact; I can't name one person who has said or done anything to change my life or who was amazing in any way. It would seem that ninety percent of the people that have come through have taught me the wrong lessons with their bad treatment of me.

Either way, have a laugh, have a cry, and have some fun with the stories to come. I've written and thrown in a poem between each chapter just for the fun of it. Because that's what I do. And because I can.

Blood

Blood is not thicker than water,
blood does not erase the pain,
of what is said and what is caused,
the trouble, the hell, the emotional drain.
Blood is not thicker than water,
I hate water but it's better than blood,
I can drink it or leave it, take it or keep it,
just like family, take it or keep it,
when I have my choice I'll leave it for good.

Blood is *NOT* Thicker

I hate my family.

Plain and simple.

For those who grew up, or who are growing up, in toxic families, you'll know what I mean. I've dealt with their shit for a good forty-six years of my life and it's fucking exhausting.

These are just a few stories from fifty plus years' worth— and believe me there are hundreds, and many will come to mind after this book is printed— about people who are full of toxicity, narcissism, hatred, anger, control, rage, and arrogance.

Toxicity can change you, destroy you, use you, and abuse you. Turn you into something you're not. Something you're not happy with. Decades of these emotions can change and destroy for the worse, unless you're mentally tough enough, and even then, it still changes and destroys you on so many levels that you may think you're okay but you're not.

Many people who come from great, loving families don't understand when we talk about the toxic narcissistic tendencies of our own. They have no clue how people speak to each other outside of their own and certainly can't walk a mile in our shoes.

In that case, don't make excuses, such as, *oh, but that's*

your sister, that's your mother. It doesn't matter how you're related, or what type of relationship you have with another, toxicity, narcissism, hatred, anger, control, rage, and arrogance should never be excused.

Why does the person who helped create you get given a free pass and forgiven for constant abusive behaviour?

They shouldn't and being related to these people should never matter because abuse is abuse, toxicity is toxicity, and narcissism is narcissism, and it doesn't mean as an adult that you should put up with it and pardon it just because one is your parent or sibling. Even in families.

It also doesn't mean our stories should be dismissed with even more toxicity. But they are, and that's a problem in itself.

There's a very long list of reasons why I hate my family. Lies, manipulations, dramas, bullshit, hatred, anger, resentment. The five of them are incredibly toxic and I'm glad we don't see three and barely see two. But add them to my mother, and this is a family I *do not* want to be in. On any level.

I've often said I hate my family, and I do, and Mum says she doesn't understand. When I remind her of all of the garbage they've spewed, and shit they've dumped on me, and us, she agrees, but then says I should let it go and move on. Nope. Not happening. As Dr Phil would say, *the best predictor of future behaviour is past behaviour.* And their past behaviour, which is also their current behaviour, is absolutely shocking. Mum forgives them everything, but blames me for everything, and it's very evident who she gives a shit about. Meanwhile, I'm just the one here looking after her…

If I lived my life my own way, I'd have nothing to do with any of them. Unfortunately, I'm not in that position. I'm in a situation not of my own making and can't avoid them no matter how much I try or want to. No wonder I want to get the hell out of Dodge and away from them. And, if the day does comes that I do, there will be no contact ever again.

In my family I was treated differently to my siblings. There were allowed out with friends, to have jobs, a boyfriend, or in my brother's case, a girlfriend. I wasn't, except for one small job in the snack bar three doors down. That was it, until I had to do what Centrelink told me to do and go for jobs. Then she had no choice.

Maybe that has influenced how a part of my life turned out. In fact, I'd bet on it. And it's not great.

I never got support to try new things. She grumbled at me wanting to take singing lessons and only paid for five, and then told me for several years she had "wasted" her money just because I didn't want to continue with the company I had gone to because they weren't actually teaching me to sing, and I wanted to change to someone else. She said if I wanted singing lessons I had to pay for them. I saved my money for months until I had $110 to pay for ten lessons with a lady in another suburb. Did she want to take me? No. Did she want to support me? Hell no. And regardless of me hinting at it at certain times through my life, especially when we got into country music gigs and line dancing, did she pick up on it? Did she offer to help or support? A big fat no.

Has she supported me with setting up my jewellery business, or my writing? No. She thinks it's all a waste of time and money. Except when I told her I'd earned thousands out of my books. The shock that rolled over her face. When writers ask about family reading and supporting their writing they're constantly told not to rely on it. Family and friends, nine times out of ten, will not support your dreams and visions. And you know what? They actually don't have to. That's why you need to rely on yourself.

One thing I realised, from the stories my mother told me about her life before me, is that besides the fact they have nothing to do with me and are irrelevant to my life, they do go a long way to explaining her attitude towards me now. But even then, you can't blame others for what others did to you. I had nothing to do with how she was treated, or how she chooses to live now, but I'm a part of that life and it's one I never wanted to be a part of and I don't want to be until the day I die. More on that later.

More stories will come out in the carer section, as that's what I ended up being, but in this chapter I have stories about my father, grandfather, siblings, and several in-laws. There are so many stories I could write about as they come to mind, as one story recalls another, and that recalls another, and then five more pop into my head.

I'm going to explain our dynamic so it's not hard moving forward as I use no names. But, as two of them stalk me online, and as they'll read and/or buy this, they'll know who they are.

There are six of us alive. A boy was born in '58 but he died a week or so after birth. Those of us remaining are, in order, three girls, one boy, two girls, born in '59, '60 and '61, then '63 and '64. I was born in 1974 so they are ten to fifteen years older than me. By Australian standards, they are Boomers, and I am Gen X.

My siblings started having kids from an early age from 1981 to 1996. Six rambunctious boys I knew, and two girls I've never met. They're Gen Ys bordering with Gen Z for the last one.

Most of my nephews and nieces went on to have children

who are probably younger Zs to Alphas. That's right, I have great-nephews and nieces and I've never met them, except for one when she was a baby.

Moving forward, I shall number my sisters 1 through to 5 in order of birth, but my brother will be called brother.

But we'll start with my grandfather, as he's Mum's dad.

Growing up, I really only had one grandparent. My father's mother was alive, but I only saw her once, that I remember, when I was eighteen months old. My mother's father we saw a lot when I was little, and after coming back from living in Queensland after four years, we saw a lot of again. But they weren't great times, and the other grands were dead.

My grandfather probably had a lot of issues. Narcissism, hatred, anger. He was old, of an older generation that went through WWII and had to deal with a lot, like losing half of his arm in a car accident. But that's no real excuse, is it? The stories my mother has told me about her childhood and the things he would do and the abuse he inflicted would make your hair curl. He would also be pretty shitty to us as his grandchildren, but then, I don't know if it was just us or all of his grandchildren as I haven't met half of my cousins to know.

That abuse may have mellowed in later years, but it was still there, and I saw a lot of shit when we would go around to their place. After our holiday with him and his third wife and one of her daughters and her two children, we chose to never go around to their place again, and I chose to never see them or speak to them again.

Unfortunately, because we lived in the same suburb, we did see them up the shopping centre a lot. I chose to ignore them, but Mum chose to talk to him if she ran into them in the library which had moved into the shopping centre. It made going to the library so easy as we got our books at the same time as our food. I don't know why more aren't in local shopping centres.

I chose to not speak to them, due to the abuse and the bullshit. As I said above, he had mellowed, not changed. Just like my family. Must be something in the blood; the German English blood. I chose to not tolerate it. Mum chose to talk, but then she tolerated a lot of abuse from him throughout her life. It never changed. I don't know what was said, as she generally didn't tell me, although she has told me a lot about her life. She has said she wants to write a book about it. I told her to do it. She hasn't. Maybe she's waiting for me to say I'll do it.

As for my grandfather, on this holiday to Queensland and Sydney that basically ended what little relationship we had left, he just didn't stop. It was always obvious he spent his money on his wife's family. Never us. He grumbled the whole way there, and then ignored us for most of the two weeks.

He took her family to Pizza Hut and didn't invite us. He didn't sit with us anywhere for anything. When we got to Sydney things were worse. I met my uncle for the first time, along with his family, and one night we went out to McDonald's for tea. Mum told me to go and get a table, and I got one big enough for six or so people.

Can you guess what happened next?

They sat in the booth behind her family.

Halfway through the meal I heard Mum say, "where's Tiara?" and I finally turned around. I had been forgotten and ignored. They had to tell my step-cousin to come and sit with me, so I wasn't on my own.

How fucking sad is that? I was twenty, had realised, with

much shame and embarrassment, that my family did not give a flying fuck in that moment, and sucking up my embarrassment, had kept eating my meal on my own. I didn't move for them. There was no room for me in that booth anyway, but Jesus fucking Christ. It showed me that no one gave a fuck about me, not my grandfather, and certainly not my mother. Especially when other people were around.

It still resonates, but there's no pain, just sadness that adds to the life of me. The life that no one wanted. Wanted to love, wanted to be near. No one gave a fuck, and they still don't. Now *that* resonates.

As of 2025, my grandfather is long gone. He was run over by his wife as he was opening the gate for her to reverse out of the driveway.

She claimed she didn't see him in the rearview. She ran over something, didn't know what it was and drove forward, running over it again. When she didn't see anything, although she didn't get out to look, she reversed again, and then drove forward again.

Turns out, she was driving over him.

He was taken to the Royal Adelaide Hospital, and one of her daughters came around to tell us he was in there.

We didn't go to see him, as it was a hard place to get into and Mum had difficulty walking at that point, but Mum's brother came driving down from Sydney to see him and he went and got the story, so that's what we were told.

My grandfather died on September 3rd, 2011. Fifteen minutes to midnight, fifteen minutes to Father's Day.

There was a funeral, but we didn't go, and Mum said we weren't even invited. As for a will, I very much doubt he had one and his wife would've got what there was anyway.

At the time of the accident, the police came and towed her car away for forensic testing. I know, because the news crew was there, and we saw the car on the back of the police truck on the TV.

Nothing came of it, that we know of, as we didn't see them or speak to them, and we most certainly didn't speak after he died. I had kept on ignoring her when out and about, and I ended up in the dentist office while she was there. I ignored her then, too, and even if she had've said something, I would've blasted her.

But it didn't happen, and she left first, and I believe that was the last time I physically saw her. We've heard she's passed on, but that's not a loss either. If you knew what type of toxic people they were, you wouldn't have cried over them.

*****

I get the feeling my father and I were never close past me hitting puberty. I say that because I saw my parents fight, stopped liking him because of it, and didn't want to be near him. I got a weird vibe from him when I was eight, and things happened here and there and then my parents separated.

Religion was the main instigator in that, which is why I have such strong feelings about it and the damage it does to people, families, and countries. It wages wars and destroys everything in its path. Just like politics. But the one main factor was how it all came about and how it all ended.

We moved to Queensland at the end of 1981, and at the two schools I attended from 1982 to 1985, they had religious instruction. At first, in school #1 I was placed in the Catholic class even though we weren't religious.

I can't remember whether I stayed in that class for the remainder of my stay at the school which was only a few months, or whether I was moved, but once I moved to school #2 it was clear I wasn't going to be in any religious class, because, luckily, there was a small class for those of us who had no religion and we would sit and do homework, or computer work for an hour every Thursday morning. I never knew why it was on a Thursday; just the way the curriculum was created, I suppose.

Because of being placed into Catholic class at that first school, the obvious next question to ask my parents was, "are we religious?", and then, "why not?"

We just weren't. Unfortunately, I think that got my father's brain turning.

At some point, about halfway through our time there, my father broke his knee working on a construction site. He ended up in a full leg plaster cast, and the whole legal case started.

After another two years on the Sunshine Coast, we moved back to South Australia, but the compensation case continued until midway through 1986 when it finally came through.

Did we go as a family back to Queensland for a holiday to get it? No.

Did my parents argue about who was going and why he was taking the car and leaving us without one? Yes.

He drove all the way to Queensland, leaving Mum without a car to go shopping and pay the bills and me without a way of getting to and from school, unless I walked, or we borrowed sibling #3's car, as we also looked after my nephew so we could use it.

To say Mum wasn't happy is an understatement. She was so unhappy that two small red marks popped up above her eyebrows in the shape of horns.

Yep, Mum grew small red horns out of her eyebrows which we joked about.

She claimed she must've scratched herself; we knew better. Because once he came back, they disappeared.

And then more issues arose, as money and religion so often cause.

Mum didn't get half. From what I can gather, she got about a third. Me, I got nothing. She had to harass him to buy me a jacket when we went to Melbourne for a holiday in 1987, my first year of high school. She bought herself a car and a lounge suite, plus a few other things.

He bought himself a car, religious books, and gave away thousands to the new religious sect, otherwise known as a group, that he'd joined.

The bone of contention in my parents' relationship was that the church got more than we did. Their marriage was over within the year, and he moved out.

My relationship with him wasn't great. I hadn't wanted to be around him since I was about eight as I mentioned, and why would I after finding out he told Mum we were heathens and I shouldn't be wearing make-up or listening to music? I was fourteen, and he had moved out. He no longer had a say.

Mum waited until I was 19 or 20 before getting a divorce. We went into town to the registry office for them to sign the papers. It was just after my father had surgery to remove a massive tumour from behind his eye and he was wearing an eye patch and had to carry a bucket in case he vomited. But it was over. Their marriage was over, as they'd married when I was four or five.

We moved to a northern suburb of SA in 1994, and I

haven't seen him since. I vaguely remember him and Mum talking about him seeing me once we moved out here, but I think she told him I didn't want to see him, and it was pretty much over as I was an adult and could make up my own mind. There has been no contact since. I haven't heard from him, nor received any communications in the mail. I have no idea what he's doing, where he is, or whether he's still alive. Ancestry.com says he is, but I have no idea and don't want to know.

Family, and religion, ain't all that, believe me.

I originally wrote the above essay in January 2024. In November 2024, while putting this memoir together, I received a letter from a genealogy company looking for the daughter of a person believed to be my father.

Turns out, it was my father, and he died on May 21st, 2023 on my forty-ninth birthday.

Regardless, there is no emotion here. I hadn't seen him in thirty-one or thirty-two years, as I told the lady I spoke to.

I had my birth certificate in front of me so I could give her details, and she corroborated the fact I had two half-brothers by his first wife whom he married in 1969. I certainly didn't know about that wife.

Turns out, my mother was his second. She's never told me when they met, but with me being born in May 1974, there had to be sometime between the two and a divorce. My parents married in 1978 or '79 on my birthday. They disappeared to get KFC for dinner, and my sisters set the kitchen table with lollies and chips. They wouldn't let me have any, so I got grumpy, and by the time my parents came home with the chicken and were taking photos, I was even grumpier, and the birthday photos show that. I held up four fingers even though it could have been my fifth birthday. I don't remember which one it was, and Mum has no idea what the marriage date is. I didn't even know for years that was when they did it.

Then the year after we moved to my current location in 1994, he scored a third wife. The genealogist was also looking for her and gave me the names of the first and third wives and the sons. Not that any of that matters to me.

He never mentioned sons to me, and my mother only ever mentioned them twice; the first time was a rough five to ten years ago, and the second was after receiving this letter. I have no need for more brothers; the one I have is way too much with the garbage he's spewed and done, but more on him later.

I've often wondered what happened to my father; if he remarried and/or had more kids. It seems that after not seeing me anymore he went and married again. But then Mum had to make it all about her and get in that time he turned up to our house with a woman, and it was clearly someone from the religious cult he had become a part of as he didn't know anyone else. I didn't see them, I didn't know. We'll see what happens by the time this memoir is published.

See, life moves on, and death doesn't change one damn thing.

*****

In 1985, sibling #2 wanted to come up to Queensland with her then boyfriend. His mate then jumped on the bandwagon, and then sibling #1 with her firstborn, only two months old, jumped on the bandwagon.

They all came in the one car, bickered and bitched on the way, and kept it going at our place. #1 basically screamed at everyone who told her what to do with her baby and #2 rolled her eyes and scoffed at everything, then bitched about #1.

I had to give up my bedroom to #2 and the boyfriend, which I absolutely hated, while the mate and #1 and nephew slept in the lounge room. I slept on our foldup bed in my parents' room. It was a weird grouping; they didn't have the money to stay at a caravan park or motel. #1 didn't even have money to come up, which #2 occasionally goes on about today. But, as my siblings do, #1 only came because #2 was coming. You can't have one do something without another copying in this family.

I can't remember how long they stayed for, and I vaguely remember still going to school, but it was definitely May as I received birthday presents. That was the year I scored Peaches and Cream Barbie with her tulle peach ballgown, and I still have all of my Barbies, thank you very much. I also bought a few dozen many years later, some to turn into Nancy Drew dolls, but that's another story.

We took them to the usual touristy places, and Mum bought #2 a Spanish doll and fan for her upcoming birthday. #2 bought herself a black and white cardigan in Caloundra. Both caused issues and fights, and when they all finally went home, not only did I get my bedroom back, but we all sighed in relief that our life was back to normal.

I'd also lent #1 my baby sleeping bag and a blanket for my nephew. More on that later in this chapter.

*****

In 1994, #2 got married to her first husband. At their wedding, #1 decided to get drunk and start introducing me to people as her "baby" sister. Regardless of me being the youngest of seven, six of us living, as an adult it's incredibly patronising to be called a baby. And no, I don't want to hear how it's sweet and just a thing and not to worry about it. It's condescending, rude, and here's the absolute rub, it tells you exactly what and how they think of you. You will never be an adult; you will always be the baby. Beware of siblings calling their youngest the baby as an adult, it means they don't respect, nor care for the person's feelings, preferring to embarrass and humiliate instead. And we shouldn't have to put up with that.

Moving on four years, in 1998 Mum and I decided to go for a holiday to Queensland with #2 and her then husband. We talked about it for months, probably even a year beforehand, going over every detail, aspect, cost. But when the week came for it to happen, the shit started hitting the fan.

The day we left, we had to go to a car shop to get something done to their car as we were going in it. #2 decided to throw a massive shit fit about me going with her husband, even though he was my brother-in-law, and bitched to Mum about it while we were gone. Even though we had decided *all* of this the night before.

We got MacDonald's muffins before heading home and locking up the house. Well, #2 was in a shit of a mood and sat in the living room while I locked up the gate and padlocked it. I then locked up the house and had to get her off her backside to get out to the car, which was now out front, and then lock up the house.

All the first day she bitched and whinged, about utter bullshit, and we had to put up with it. It wasn't until we got to our first stop for the night that she realised she'd left one of her blankets at our house. Suck it up, buttercup, you were the one throwing a shit fit over everything and then forgot it.

Over the next couple of days as we travelled up to the Gold Coast, she caused all manner of issues. Bitched all the way, lied and complained. Claimed to not eat Hungry Jacks at Dubbo, though she had eaten it in the days before we left. She kept showing off her new mobile phone, and remember, this was 1998, it was just a small basic one then, but had to make herself look important because she was expecting a call from her boss. She was on holiday, mind you. Then she crapped on over a guinea pig that had gone missing and kept saying someone was going to eat it, (I hope they did) and that she had to go home and should be on the first plane home. By then, we were on the Gold Coast in our cabins and the first night was shit. As you can see, she didn't go home because she's all talk.

The next two weeks were up and down, and I won't go into each detail. I have kept a record of it as I love to write out what I do each day on a holiday. She and her husband argued, we shopped, and went to the theme parks, and then she did something I utterly hate. She involved me in her bullshit.

We were having Red Rooster for tea one night, and she told me what she wanted and to tell her husband. I did, in Red Rooster. #2 wants this.

He didn't buy it and I didn't even realise it, and then when she realised she wasn't getting a meal she came storming into our cabin and bitched about it. I kept saying, stop dragging me into this, but she went on, and on. Nope, bitch, not happening. It's not the first time she's done that, in fact, it's not the first time anyone's done that, and I hate it with a passion.

She also kept complaining about the few items I bought; a piece of material that folded up to the size of a book, a Nancy Drew book, some stickers, and a stuffed white tiger. We had been there in 1994 with Mum's family, which is a story that's been told, so I didn't need to buy much more. But she complained to Mum, not me, as usual, about me buying all of this stuff. Meanwhile, she was buying for every Tom, Dick and Harry. It wasn't me filling up the bloody car with shit.

So much went on I'd be here forever talking about it.

The rest of the holiday came and went, but let me tell you, on the three-day drive home, she just didn't stop. Mum and I sat quietly in the back seat, but it didn't stop us hearing the garbage spewing from her mouth, not to mention the arguments she caused with her husband. We were glad to get home. I unlocked the house and unpacked our stuff so fast it was a new world record. They finally left and we locked out the world and sighed in relief. We didn't see them again for almost two years, and the only reason they came by was to show off the husband's new car and brag about what they'd done. They only stayed about fifteen minutes, because apparently, that's all we were worth.

And you know, you'd think we'd learn. I did, but Mum didn't. Because we went on that merry-go-round again.

*****

Numbers 1, 2, 3, and our brother have the same father and he's buried in Mum's birthplace of Broken Hill. So is their first child who only survived a week or so.

In 2004, #1 and #2 had a headstone made for their father's grave and wanted to put it in place, so we all travelled there with #2's then boyfriend tagging along.

It was crap right from the start with him taking the wrong turn and getting shitty when we pulled him over. But we finally got there and booked into the caravan park and the week went to shit.

But when you're with family, what else is new.

When #1 and #2 get together, everyone else is forgotten. We've often been left behind when we've been out shopping and have often commented on it amongst ourselves. Mum says not to worry; just enjoy yourself. I say it's hard to when you're being ignored or forgotten by the people you're supposed to be shopping with.

One of the main issues on that holiday was #2 created a disturbance in the restaurant at the top of the hill. We had eaten, and it was time to pay for the bill. Instead of waiting for me to pay for our food, #2 ran off to the counter to pay for theirs. When I got there, she had left multiple coffees, cake, and a milkshake to be paid for by me. I said no, that's theirs, I'm paying for ours. Which I did. I then told #2 she had to pay for the rest of the food as we didn't order it, they had.

The arguments with the dude behind the counter blew up. #2 got riled up, her dickhead boyfriend got in on it, #1 and Mum got in on it. Meanwhile, I and my nephew were waiting outside in the hall joining the restaurant to the gift shop. I watched the argument happen and Jesus Christ did it go down to the point he kicked them out.

Once outside we were still talking about it, criticising #2 for creating the issue, and then the dickhead boyfriend, thinking he had the right to lean behind my sister's back, told me not to talk to her that way.

As if he had the fucking right. He didn't, but he did it and no one else noticed. I was shocked until I got in the car and told Mum about it. And because she didn't see it or hear it, she didn't believe it, which isn't unusual for her when it comes to me. She has an easy time blaming me for everything that happens in or around me even when it's not my fault.

I planned for the next time he said it and prepared to give him a mouthful. And before you say, yeah sure, it's true. When someone does something to me out of the blue and unexpected, I go into shock that they could even do it, or that it happened. Once I calm down and think it through, I prepare myself for round two. Most times, there's never a round two.

We ended the holiday by spending another day or two there as Mum had found an old friend and we stayed with her while they went home. When we did leave, we arrived home in the afternoon back to the peace and quiet and our own house and our own beds.

*****

The Scorpion Witch, #3, the Scorpio of the family, born on the 30th of October. I've often said she should've been born on the 31st as she's such a witch, but a scorpion is worse.

She's done the worst damage in this family. They have all done bad shit to me, and to each other, and haven't changed as they grew older, just mellowed. But #3 unleashed her tail and unleashed hell on multiple siblings over multiple years.

#3 came up to Queensland 1983. I can't remember what time of the year, but the weather was pretty decent. Because we lived in a two-bedroom flat, and #3 came with her two-year-old son, I had to give up my bed in my bedroom and sleep in my parents' room. My nephew got a bed in the lounge room.

But even though it was still technically my bedroom, and my clothes were in the wardrobe and my toys were in their bag, and she was sleeping in my bed, she had the gall to tell me to get out of my room. I vaguely remember a few other things happening, to which Mum pulled her up on her behaviour towards me and she sulked a bit. But she was the reason why #5 left. Their secretive conversations had clearly led to it, and while I'm typing this, I get that because she was a controlling bitch, that she probably wanted #5 to come back so she could control her. Because when she did, #5 stayed with her and was used as a babysitter until she was kicked out. So clearly #3 didn't care about #5, just wanted to use her as a free sitter.

She never was a nice person. Pretty bitchy, pretty butch, pretty damn mean. Which is why I mentioned she's a Scorpio.

We didn't talk to either of them after that, not until we got back to SA and both of them came crawling.

It must've been word of *my* father having compensation money, because my brother asked for $150. But, as Mum told them, there was no money as it hadn't come through yet. None believed her, and whinged to #1 that year that they couldn't get any money and Tiara had a brand new blue radio, not even caring about the fact that Tiara bought it herself for Christmas with the $80 she'd made from selling her stuff at garage sales in order to come back to SA.

Nope. They didn't care at all.

Three years later was probably the last Christmas we were all together.

She made a rice concoction for Christmas 1996. I scarfed most of it as it tasted great. Going down, that is. Not so much coming up in the middle of the night when I became sick and vomited it all up. I didn't eat rice for over twenty years after that, and that was probably the last time we saw her at home. We spotted her at trash and treasure, and a shopping centre, but that was it.

I do know she stalks me online, has set up fake name social media accounts in order to abuse me at different times, and has pretended to be other people. You can see right through it it's so pathetic, and she knows details, so yeah, it's her. She's checked out my websites and blogs to see what I'm doing and talking about, which means she'd see that I've released a memoir and is probably reading this right now to see if I'm writing about her. And yeah, bitch, I am.

*****

My brother has created a lot of issues in his life. He went through a windscreen at sixteen and ended up in the hospital. When we all went in to see him I nearly vomited and #3 had to take me out to the corridor and get me a drink. She didn't appreciate that, but tough.

His behaviour throughout my life has been a disgrace. So much so, that Mum had a restraining order against him and his previous thirty-plus-year-older girlfriend who started all of the problems. Oi, the stories I could tell.

He's taken money and items from #1 and #2, and created problems, fights, and arguments. #1 stopped seeing him decades ago due to them, but now speaks to him, and #2 does nothing but bitch and whinge while handing over stuff or giving them money. Yet she keeps doing it, even though I've told her she's keeping the issue snowballing by doing what she's whingeing about. She babies him, treats him like a child who can't live his life or make his own decisions, regardless of him being three years younger than her and a grown adult. She has an incredibly sick and unhealthy obsession with him. Not sure where it stemmed from, but it's there. She can't stop talking about or criticising him as if she's his mother, or owner, but she needs to let it go, and they all need to grow the goddamn fuck up. Whether his behaviour is down to him being the only boy, who knows. But all of it is very clearly a case of power and control.

At one point, when my nephew was about six months old, we didn't see them for three or so years. Then, they were in our life for a few more years and then gone again because of a piece of paper. More on that next.

His current long standing partner, two girlfriends on from the troublemaker, is also problematic. At first, like so many, you think, oh, she's nice and sweet and jovial, and then the lies start, and the insults against one's siblings start, and the games of one-upmanship start.

She never did anything bad to us; her behaviour was dubious at most, but #1 and #2 can't stand her. Neither could #3 according to what we've been told, whereas #5 loved her but has nothing to do with them, either. Interesting, that. They drove themselves so far away from the family by moving to the other end of the state, that only #2 bothered seeing them semi-regularly and yet she still complains about them. Fuck…this family.

With this girlfriend, he seemed to have changed.

I said *seemed*.

He threw a tantrum at the age of 34 when Mum wouldn't sign his piece of paper. We were already suspicious when he called and asked for her to sign it, but he never mentioned what it was.

When they arrived, my SIL ran to the door and said, "don't be angry at him".

We had no clue what she meant, but my brother came in and handed Mum the paper and asked her to sign it.

She said she needed her glasses and wanted to read it.

He said you don't need to read it; you just need to sign it.

When she insisted on reading it he threw his tantrum, snatched the paper up and stormed out. We didn't see them for fifteen years, missing out on my nephew growing up. And to this day, we still have no clue what that was about, or what he wanted Mum to sign. It's never been mentioned again, but there were clearly shady machinations going on.

Back in late 2014 early 2015, sibling #2 harassed Mum into calling my brother. She harassed her so much that mum ended up calling him. I told her it would be the biggest mistake she could make.

I was wrong. She made bigger.

She called him and he carried on as if fifteen years was nothing and they'd talked all this time.

And then she invited him to come.

Well, the fucking hoo-ha #2 created over this, acting as intermediary in Feb 2015, made me want to punch her in the face.

She came shopping with us and I was sick as a damn dog with a really bad ear, nose, throat infection and just wanted to get it done and get home. But she farted around, "oh no, he won't be here yet", "oh, let me just call him", "the little bastard isn't answering me". Which he wasn't because they'd been fighting for years, but it didn't stop him asking her for money, or her giving them stuff she didn't want and pretending to be the big kahuna.

"I want to go home," I said. "I've had enough."

Did anyone listen to me?

Of course not. No one ever did. And some still don't because I'm the youngest, and according to them the dumbest, yet I'm the one who gets shit done and looks after their mother without one fucking thing from them.

When we finally got home, they were already there and trying to burn the house down. They'd tidied up the yard for us, which actually created safety issues that I had to clean up after, and were burning the weeds, and then they left the hose out on the back footpath instead of putting it back around the tap that either of us could have tripped over it. All in all, they created more work by trying to help.

I wasn't happy. I was sick. I'd never wanted to see them again because of the problems he'd caused, #2 was farting around like a queen bee, I just wanted to get in and get the shopping done and put away and change and get back to what I was doing in my bedroom. Which I did. I kept the door shut most of the time, but I could hear them as they were loud. I just wasn't interested.

And then Mum gave him money for his birthday. She reasoned that because she had given me, #1 and #2 the same amount, he should get some too. The thing is, I don't actually remember getting money for my birthday the year before…

They left, and then #2 left, and I finally sighed in relief.

Not long after, they all came back and did it again. There was the repeated garbage of #2 being the queen bee and all bleating on.

I still wasn't interested. But the cracks started appearing.

And then they left, and not long after they came back, but #2 did not. By then lies had been told by my brother and #2 about each other, rumours had been spread, and bullshit was about to arise for me.

I had been selling a few things on eBay after about ten years of not doing so, and from that, my SIL decided to tell my mother that she was going to get me to sell some of her stuff on eBay.

Did she tell me that? Of course not. Mum did.

On another visit she walked into the house and declared she had borrowed some books from the library and solved my nose issue and had I heard of…something. I didn't quite hear what she said, but I think it had to do with nasal irrigation. I said I wasn't interested, and my furrowed brows must've exuded something as she later told Mum I'd shut her down when she'd told me.

I was in the office working and heard her as my door was now open. I nearly barged out there and said, "*What did you expect? You took it upon yourself to research my nose issue, something you know nothing about and which I've not mentioned, and you think you've solved it? You have no clue what my nose issues are and they're between me and my specialist.*"

How arrogant!

And it was. How dare anyone walk into a house a few times after not seeing someone for fifteen years, and declare you've researched their medical issue and have solved it. You haven't. Because you have no clue what it is.

And then there was another time when she told Mum she was going to take the jewellery I'd made for my label, Jewel Divas, back to where they lived to the markets to sell.

Did she tell me that, or even bother asking if she could?

Of course not.

People have a really bad habit of talking *about* me to Mum, but not talking *to me* to my face.

But, did Mum tell me the truth all these times? I have no idea. Maybe it's all lies; maybe it's all truth. My mother has a habit of lying to people.

They stopped seeing us for a while, except for the time my brother rang up and asked to borrow money. He came down and promised both of us he'd pay it back a hundred a fortnight until it was paid. That was 2015. He repaid some, but not all. And then throughout the year I found out Mum had given him several more lots. Not sure when she did that, but according to her she did. He didn't give her any more money until late 2023 when he won a legal case. At least he gave her more than he owed, I'll give him that. As I've said, mellowed but not changed.

Back to 2015, Mum became ill in December. For the first three weeks she was in and out of hospital three times and I had #2 in my ear every day bitching and whingeing with her bullshit. The weather was hitting 40 degrees Celsius plus and Mum had been sick. There was no need for me to go there every day. And #2 was whingeing about not being able to tell #1. I told her Mum said she'd call when she got out and to keep her mouth shut. All of that proved #2 can't keep her mouth shut and she loves to spout everyone's business to everyone else. Like she did with our first nephew when she saw him again after thirty plus years.

During this time, after Mum had been taken to hospital, my SIL called up at 8:10 Monday morning to see how we were. I'd barely had any sleep. I was dead. She went on for half an hour talking about her bloody mother who I was not interested in and had only met once, briefly, and then she said, "I want to write a book," and paused.

Paused for what, I wasn't sure. No doubt to give me time to reply or tell her what I was doing. By then, I'd released my first four stand-alone novels, five non-fictions, and my first kids' story at that time, but I wasn't about to tell her. She went on about how she didn't know how to start her computer that my nephew had bought her, and I told her to use the Word version that comes on it. I still have no idea if she's written a book or learned how to start the computer.

Back to Mum. Once she was out, she called all three and told them. And then what happened?

#2 said our brother had said and done this, and our brother said #2 had said and done this.

Yep, back to the old-school garbage from yesteryear of them each dobbing on the other to Mummy.

And could Christmas week have been better?

Of course, it could have, until #2 rang up on the 20th of December and dictated how things were going to be. Mind you, she'd called me every day Mum was in there and bitched in my ear about telling the rest of the family and had I been to see her yet. Not in 40 Celsius plus weather I bloody hadn't. And no, it wasn't your business to tell the rest of the family, so shut up.

"I'll take you shopping, and Mum can stay on her own and we'll do this, this and this," she said.

"I can't leave her alone. She's just out of hospital and someone needs to be with her,"I brusquely replied.

"She'll be fine on her own and she can call if she needs help."

Let me tell you now, don't ever dictate what happens in this household. Mum had been out of hospital two days and had already been sick. She needed care and looking after and you didn't even want to do that, look after your own bloody mother, expecting me to go shopping with you and leaving her alone. Dumb thing to say, and clearly you didn't remember a damn thing I'd told you on the phone in the previous weeks.

As it turns out, she was running late anyway and did her shopping first, then came around and watched Mum while I went shopping.

And then Christmas sucked even harder!

Thursday and Friday, Christmas Eve and Christmas Day, decided to be 38 degrees Celsius and stinking hot. It was uncomfortable and we couldn't really get into the Christmas spirit in that heat, so I was the one munching on all of the stuff I'd bought.

Around lunchtime my brother rang, and when Mum hung up, I said, "*Do not* tell me they're coming tomorrow."

"Well, grandson wants to see us."

I went ape shit. "You've told me for three weeks you didn't want anyone here for Christmas and now you don't say no to him."

"Well, I didn't say yes," she very weakly proclaimed.

Needless to say, I went off my face. I was so fucking exhausted from four weeks of scrubbing, cleaning, running around, back and forth, dealing with tradies not doing their jobs and phone calls, plus revolting heat, so I couldn't and didn't sleep, that I could barely keep my eyes open. And now we were arguing on Christmas Day.

I very loudly huffed and puffed while clearing out the lounge room as four weeks' worth of stuff that needed going through had piled up there. I had to move my pc and stuff back into the office as I'd been working in the dining room for a week. I threw or kicked everything into her bedroom and didn't care if I broke it. We argued and yelled, and I swore that all I wanted was a fucking holiday over Christmas.

She didn't even get what I meant.

I told her, "You said you didn't want anyone here; I've been scrubbing and cleaning and dealing with tradies and all I wanted was five days off over Christmas for a holiday before dealing with it all again."

And then she said something pretty dumb. "Well, you should have told me."

I was dumbfounded. "Why do I need to tell you? It's a weekend with two public holidays, what else were we going to do?"

She said, "Well, it's Christmas. They'll come tomorrow so you can still have two days off."

What the fuck sort of holiday was I going to have in two days!?

Either way, we were both so exhausted ended up in tears. Didn't stop my brother and his family coming, though.

By this point I'd done a lot of online shopping and just didn't care. You know how when you get so exhausted from not sleeping and working hard, your brain barely functions and you're just like, *I don't give a fuck, I need shoes and kaftans?*

On Saturday, they came after lunch, and I ended up sitting at the dining table before Mum forced me to go and get McDonald's for everyone. I kept saying I'm on holiday, but did she care? Nope! I should have said no because in my state I probably shouldn't've been driving, nor feeding a sick woman a cheeseburger and cheesy fries because the next day, Sunday, yep, she was sick again, and that was probably the second shittiest Christmas I've had in my life.

Meanwhile, we haven't seen my brother since. That's right, we haven't seen them since 2015. There has been the odd phone call for Mother's Day, her birthday, and Christmas. Nine times out of ten it's her who rings. And then in 2023, as I mentioned, he won some money in a court case and gave her a small four figure amount. Then in January 2024, he gave her another two lots. While he may have finally paid back what he owed nine years later, to me, it doesn't pay back for all of the hurt caused over the last fifty years. Whereas Mum, she'll pretty much forgive them anything, believing they've changed.

They haven't, because they still get up to the same old bullshit, and I most certainly *do not* forgive *or* forget.

Maybe I should tell you about the time my SIL blatantly lied on a Facebook page about my brother and what he is and does, and what she claimed my mother told her about his father when no such thing happened. And that was two years after we'd seen them again. Of course, #2, who'd told us about it, said she'd get on the page and set her straight, but she only made one comment and didn't pull her up or put her in her place about such blatant lies. Oi! #2 is such a blow-hard. Talks big, but never any follow through.

Or maybe I should tell you about the time my brother called his two younger half-sisters, #5 and myself, sluts, and said we weren't his sisters because we have different fathers to him and our three eldest sisters. Biology, dickshit, biology!

It's not hard to hate this family. They make it incredibly easy to, and incredibly easy to never want anything to do with them. Ever. Again.

But then, considering what an arsehole their father was,

it's not hard to understand why my brother turned out the way he did. And yeah, Mum has told *me* a lot about her first husband; she just doesn't bother telling the first four anything. I keep telling her, *I'm not the one you should be telling this to*, but for some reason, she doesn't want to tell them what an arsehole he was, and what he did before he walked across the road and shot himself in the head before my brother was even born.

*****

My sister, sibling #5, is ten years older than me and never wanted me around. That was pretty obvious once I was old enough to understand I had a pain in my chest every time she snapped at me.

As I grew up, I was told it was because I'd taken over her role as baby of the family. Well, that's the way the cookie crumbles, Mum had another kid!

We didn't get along, and even though the two of us always shared a room, shared a car back seat, I was treated badly. I only remember her being beaten once for something she did to me, otherwise, she was just told off.

We moved to Queensland when I was seven, and lived there from late 1981 to late 1985. We were only there for four years, but the gap grew larger. Most of my siblings came up for holidays; most were bitches. I've mentioned that #3 decided to take #5 back to SA with her. They sold most of her stuff and disappeared while I was at school. When I came home, we were all in shock and I cried. Even though she'd hurt me, I cried. And then, I moved on.

When we moved back to SA, we stayed with #2 and her

boyfriend and flatmate, celebrating Christmas 1985 with them. My brother was invited, but for some reason his thirty-plus-year-old girlfriend hated my guts and made the day uneasy. At some point through all of this, #3 decided to try and convince us that #5 really wanted to see us. They came around to #2's house and she looked completely different.

I had no idea what to say but was asked by #3 what I thought. It felt like pressure. I was put on the spot which I still hate to this day, since #3 was sitting right beside me and leaned into me when she asked. But what the hell did I know? I was 12, and my sister had dramatically changed, so I mumbled something along the lines of she looked as if she'd had plastic surgery. And it was in front of her.

Thinking back on that now, being put on the spot, I hated it. That shouldn't've happened, but then, my siblings are narcissistic cunts.

Years later, after a lot of weird shit happened, her being hurt by my comment came up, and not from her, but from another sibling. Well, sadly, other things had also happened with #5 and shit hit the fan. Mum and I both sent her a letter and I let rip. I said in mine that I knew exactly what she was going to do with that letter, send it around to the family. And she did just that. However, the problems that rose from that, yikes. She gave it to our brother who took it to #1 and #1 assumed it was for her. And because something had happened at her place that year, that made that shit even worse. But more on that in the Christmas section.

We haven't spoken to or seen #5 since.

I do know she stalks me online and has done for many years.

Very stupidly, #2 decided to start talking to her again, and because #2 has a big fat trap, she probably told her everything.

After all, she'd told our nephew everything, so why wouldn't she tell #5 everything. Because something happened for #5 to *not* know things.

The only way we found out was when #2 was talking to our ex-aunt and our ex-aunt said to #2, "how's your mum doing?"

#2 said something like, "what do you mean?" and our ex-aunt said that #5 had told her mum was sick.

#2 told us this when she was over one day, and we all sat around thinking about it. Then I realised it was because of the blog posts I had written in 2016 about Mum's time in hospital in late 2015.

There was only one way a sibling who I hadn't seen in over 30 years would know that, and that was if she'd read it, or been told by one of the others. Namely #2.

That's when we realised she stalked me.

I started making comments in blog posts about it, getting in little jabs, but eventually deleted those 2016 posts for privacy. I no longer talk about Mum's issues, and I rarely mention my own health, just so they have nothing to see. But I do hope they stew with envy at all I buy.

A few years on, she liked a two-year-old Instagram post about Christmas Eve lunch. She either did it accidentally, or on purpose. I pondered a snappy reply, but in the end, I just blocked her, along with a couple of others.

As to whether she still stalks me, probably. On most socials she wouldn't be able to see my page or profile, but she can still read my blogs, even though I no longer give details away, and certainly don't talk about Mum, so I'm not giving her anything.

Like #3, she'll probably read about me publishing a memoir on my website, and probably buy one to see what I talk about, and probably send it around the family as she did with the letter

I sent her many a decade ago. I told her in that letter that she would, and she did. But let's see what happens now and believe me, there are so many more stories I could tell about her.

*****

When I was sixteen a strange phenomenon occurred.

First, my brother-in law thought he could harass me about getting a job.

I remember it being a warm day. It may have been early in the year, but Mum and I were out with sibling #5 and her husband and son at the park near their home. Mum, my sister, and nephew went for a walk and he and I stayed at the table. Almost right away, when they were barely out of earshot, he started in on when was I going to get a job, what sort of job did I want, and so on. He pointed out that I was sixteen, had left school, so I really should get one.

I had no clue what to say because I wasn't expecting this line of questioning, and barely gave him the minimum of answers, shrugged a bit, and didn't really give him much to go on. I have wondered over the last decades, if my sister put him up to it, or whether it was off his own back. It could have been both.

Ironically, he didn't have a job, so what the hassle was, I have no clue. But he hassled me the moment Mum wasn't there. That was something my family constantly waited for.

Later that year, when Mum had to go into hospital for surgery, my father came and stayed at our house to watch me. One day, he took me to lunch at Pizza Hut who had their $5 pan pizza lunches which were free if not done in ten minutes. He took his chance while Mum wasn't there to harass me about getting a job…when was I going to get one, what did I want to do. Blah, blah, blah!

I saw a theme emerging.

I also knew he was a stingy bastard who didn't want to pay for child support, or anything else, or do anything else. He'd had so many jobs we'd lost count.

For another lunch, he was going to walk down to the local corner shop three houses down and buy our food. He asked me what I wanted, and I said a pasty. He asked if I wanted anything else and I said a donut. He said, "I meant something hot." I said no and didn't get a donut. If you're going to ask someone what they want, be specific the first time so you don't embarrass and humiliate them with your stupidity.

Of course, it wasn't the first time my father had been stingy. If you're going to tell someone they can order anything off the menu, and when they do turn around and tell them to order something cheaper, or that you meant something cheaper, you're a stingy bastard. Sadly, that probably set up my lifetime issue with people asking me what I wanted, as I no longer wanted to tell them in case they told me to pick something cheaper. I was saving myself from that embarrassment.

I find that to be so rude and a shitty thing to do to people. It's so embarrassing to be told that, or told they can't afford it, especially in front of others. Maybe you should've just handed over money or gift cards so I could get what I wanted.

Let's move on to sibling #2 at Christmas that same year, the year I was sixteen. We were at her house with her then boyfriend. #1 and her family and in-laws were there, and both siblings waited until Mum had gone inside at lunchtime to get something else, before starting in on me about getting a job. I had been out of school for a year, hadn't done much, and they thought they had the right to attack without Mum around. #2 was particularly bad, constantly comparing her crappy jobs with ones I should get, how I shouldn't be fussy, and telling me to get out and earn money.

I felt like screaming, but what would have been the point? I was always outnumbered in my family, whether they ganged up on me or not, treated me like shit or not. And even though I told Mum, as usual, and even now, she just doesn't believe me and what I say, and fobs it off, which pisses me off, because her first four can do no wrong.

And considering how bad #2 was at it, just two years later she gave the money she was giving me for my birthday to Mum to look after so I didn't "spend it all on rubbish".

It said a lot about her, not trusting an eighteen-year-old with twenty dollars. And birthday money is unconditional. You don't get to tell us what we buy with our money because it becomes our money once it's in our hands. But then, #2 would always give you things and then tell you if you didn't want it to give it back so she could give it to someone else.

You just don't do that.

*****

I hate people dropping by unannounced.

If I ever get my own house and have friends, there is no way in hell anyone will be dropping by unannounced. For anything. They'll need to make an appointment to see me, and only then it will be if I want to change my schedule in order to see them.

It's rude and arrogant to think the person you're dropping in on will drop everything to cater to you, waiting on you hand and foot. And I hate it. I did mention that, right?

It's not as though family haven't done it before. There are many decades of stories that Mum could rattle off for when her father or sister would drop by unannounced and then want to eat and drink and not bring anything to offer. Mum had to supply everything. Because narcissists are the worst.

The worst time that family dropped in on us unannounced, in my opinion and lifetime, besides the times #1 and 2, and then #3 came up, Mum let them stay. She didn't turn them away. Why, I don't know, as they weren't here that much during their time, but because she chose family, we missed out on an amazing weekend we had already planned.

When we were line dancing, and sibling #2 was married to husband #1, he was the drummer in a country band. They were playing at a long weekend up in the country that our line dancing club was going to. We had already planned to stay with my sister, had our outfits picked out, and we just needed to pack and go.

And then Mum's brother, wife, and youngest son turned up unannounced and asked to stay in our yard in their caravan.

Mum said okay. I told her no; we had the line dancing weekend planned. She said there would be another one.

There wasn't. Ever!

I hated her for that. I hated her for never putting our plans before other people's. I hated her for never putting my feelings or needs in time of need first over others. Not even once. It was always what others wanted.

Like the time when we first started line dancing and travelled to a town in the country, made friends with a male member, and would go back to his house for dinner. We stayed one night, even though I told Mum I didn't want to because it was that time of the month for me and I had pain, and no extra sanitary products. She overruled me. I was on his couch while he was on the floor in front of the wood heater. I didn't sleep. He did. Mum got his son's room.

Or there was the time when I was twenty, and we travelled to Sydney with her father and his other family and ended up staying at said brother's house in the car out the front. Again, I had my cycle, and it wasn't good for me. I just wanted a painkiller, a shower, and a bed. She didn't and put herself and others before my needs.

As an adult, I understand that sometimes we don't always get what we want. But when there are certain circumstances, you need to put those circumstances first, not other people's wants and needs.

But back to line dancing.

We missed out on an amazing weekend. And we know it was amazing because my sister told us it was, and that all of our line dancing friends asked her where we were. And then we found out from our line dancing friends when we saw them next that the weekend was amazing, and they asked where we were. I don't recall whingeing about not being there due to family lobbing in, but let me tell you this, the family who dropped in spent most of their time around Mum's old man's place and barely any time with us. They just used us for a free place to park their van and didn't care if we were doing anything that weekend.

For that matter, Mum didn't seem to care about ruining our weekend, but it's burned in me since, because that was a weekend I really wanted to go to. But once again, narcissists don't like others having their way, it must always be their way and they just don't care what you want.

*****

Christmases as a family have been difficult.

When we first moved back from Queensland in 1985, our first Christmas was with #2 and her flatmates. My brother and his partner came, giving me filthy glares. No one knew what it was about. She didn't know me, had no reason to hate me, but it made Christmas uneasy, and I was told to stay away from them even though none of us knew what the hell was going on.

Move onto Christmas 1986 and pretty much all six of us were in attendance at different times of the day.

I received a locket from #3 and #5 that year, and ate #3's rice concoction, which made me sick.

And it was the last Christmas we were all together. 1986. Jesus.

Each year after that, there were fewer, until, over the years, it's just been me and Mum for thirty plus years, with the exception of the odd visit from my uncle on Christmas Eve, #1 one year, and my brother one year on Boxing Day.

But the Christmases we had could be quite fiery.

1990 was spent at #2's house, and I mentioned that previously.

1991 to 1994 was spent at #1's house in the country and so many stories are about to come out.

In 1991 I was given money to go and buy a Caboodle; an American beauty case that was slowly coming to Australia. After Christmas, #2 came shopping with Mum and me and I bought it, with #2 scoffing and complaining about the money it cost and how could #1 afford it. For the record, it was $40AU, meanwhile #2 only ever gave me $20 for years for birthday and Christmas, so it's not as if her money present went up with inflation.

During the year, #1 finally got to see the Caboodle. She and #2 came down and we went out for the day, but upon arriving back at our house, she wanted to see it before she went home, so I told her to sit, and I'd get it.

I ran and got the magazine clippings I had and presented them as a show. "These are Caboodles, this is what they're all about," etc. I vaguely remember them hurrying me up and I ran and got the Caboodle and presented in on the kitchen table. I opened it up, slid the top layer back, "and it does this and it does that" and pow, #2's hand darted in and out between me and #1 touching everything, picking up everything, 'what's this, what's that, what's this do, what do you have that for".

That pisses me off. People touching your stuff without asking and not being careful with it.

I kept taking it all out of her hand and #1 did the same, but not to the same extent.

I was proud of it, and excited to show it off. When we were done, I packed it up and put it away.

Thirty-two years later, in 2023, my mother told me #1 was upset that I hadn't showed her my Caboodle.

What the fuck!

I questioned her, and reminded her, that I'd presented it on the table, so yes, #1 did see it, and Mum just shrugged and repeated what she'd said and then said, "I don't know".

Not good enough in my book. If you're going to state something, back it up and repeat it and don't cop out with "I don't know".

I have no idea what #1 was going on about. In all fairness, I have no idea if she even said it to Mum, or Mum made it up. But if #1 did, why? You saw my Caboodle the first chance you got when you came down. I presented it to you as a show. You saw it, so what do you have to be upset by? Especially considering what you've done to me. And as for Mum, if she made it up, why?

Moving on.

During one of these Christmases, #2 and #1 received handmade quilted carryall bags from #1s MIL. Mum and I did not. We were disappointed and wondered why. What was wrong with us that we didn't get one? I have no idea, but we didn't, and you just have to move on as it's not up to us what someone chooses to give us for a present.

At Christmas, #1's MIL would give us a small present every year, and one year she gave me mine and said she wasn't sure if I had wanted the treble clef decoration that came with it. She'd hung it on the tree, but because I was into music, I said absolutely. I should have grabbed it then, but I didn't. At some point during the day, I was going to take it, but bitchface #2 was on my heels, telling me I couldn't unless I asked for #1's permission as it was on her tree.

Stupidly, and because I was about 17, I did what she said and followed #1 around the house, with #2 hot on my heels, until I could get her to ask her. I never should have done that, but when you've got someone breathing down your neck, you want to tell them to fuck off. And back then, I didn't do that.

When it comes to Christmases at #1's house, #2 created a hell of a lot of issues.

But so did many others, to the point that we stopped going after 1994.

During one of these Christmases, #1 would run off and sit on her own where people couldn't find her. When we went looking, she'd get up and walk off. She did it a few times until her MIL asked us if we had BO. My sister had issues, no doubt, but in that case, don't have people over for Christmas.

Another Christmas, 1991, I think, #2 got a CD player, the kind that looked like a VCR, and they got there early and plugged it in to play some CDs. When we got there and saw it, she proudly announced having received it, thinking she was the first in the family to get one.

I told her I had one and the sour expression that slid over her face made me grin. She hated not being the first in the family to have one. The day only remotely got better.

The last Christmas we were there was 1994. It sucked massive shit balls of hell that lived on for years.

We arrived, unloaded, and greeted everyone. As we were all there, we opened presents. But the kids got to open their presents in a section of the lounge room, which, at that time, was an L-shape, and we were in the kitchen, just off it. #1 bundled the kids into the farthest corner to open their presents from their grandparents, so we didn't even get to see them and had no idea what they'd received.

And that was just the start of the shit that rained down that day.

The boys had received bikes for Christmas, and I very stupidly rode one when I hadn't done that in a good decade. Unfortunately, I had an accident where I ran into the in-laws' car. I slapped my hand on the car to push off, but the rubber handle made a very small dent.

The FIL grabbed the handle, hauled me and the bike about three feet over and went off his face at me.

I went into shock, got off the bike and nearly burst into tears. I rolled the bike back to the house where my mother, the MIL, and #2 and her husband were. All four them were in shock and on my side. The MIL, who was always so nice to us, apologised for her husband, and when Mum and #2 offered to pay for the damage, she said no. She was going to talk to him.

By now I was crying, and #1 came out, didn't bother finding out what had happened and ripped the absolute shit out of me.

He's got diabetes, he's on his death bed, he's this, he's that.

Mum, the MIL, #2 and her husband, all jumped to my defence and attacked back. Me, I was just crying my eyes out.

She finally stalked off and we hung around outside to all calm down.

A few hours later, the boys had jumped in the pool they had received for Christmas. Which one, I can't remember, but they had the old blow-up surf mat I'd given them as I didn't need it anymore. God, of all of the things I'd handed down to them there are some I wish I hadn't. No one else wanted to go in, so I did. I changed out of my clothes and joined them. The weather wasn't hot, but warm enough. Everyone else sat around talking. After an hour or so I got out and put my clothes back on. It was a dress I had bought on sale from a department store I had a six-week job at over the Christmas period. It was the only piece of clothing I'd bought all year.

I was quiet for the rest of the day, still unnerved from the morning, and tried to avoid #1. During lunch, I was playing with my nephew who had a big silver biker ring with an eye. I'd put it on and say, "I'm watching you", or "I can see you". He was young; he thought it was funny.

After lunch, Mum and I, plus #1 and #2, were sitting around the table while everyone else was out. #1 must've been drunk or smoked something, because she decided to go off her face at me again. A few months earlier, Mum had needed to have her ears done in hospital, and since I didn't drive yet, I wasn't able to drive home from the doctor's appointment. My sister decided that this was reason enough to sit there poking me in the leg in time with her words as she berated me for not having a driver's licence and driving Mum home and that if I stopped buying all of the clothing I did I'd have the money to pay for my licence.

Mum said nothing, and I just got up and walked into another room, once again being attacked, but not defended.

#1 had no clue about what I'd spent my money on that year. As I said; that dress was the only piece I'd bought all year that didn't have to do with working at the department store where I'd received $250 in vouchers to buy work clothes and I tried to buy pieces I could keep wearing once I left.

I felt even more like shit after that. It was the second attack, and I was more than distraught.

That afternoon, I stupidly rode one of the boy's bikes again, and came to a halt as everyone gathered outside ready to leave. As I didn't want it to cause damage, I kicked the stick down and stepped away.

It took about a minute to fall over, and everyone just stood there watching it. But, at least, this time #1 had a go at my nephew to pick it up after he complained to me about dropping his bike. I didn't drop it, it fell over.

As we packed up to leave, I asked one of my nephews if I could have the ring we'd been playing with. I thought it was a junk ring he'd scored at some point. Turned out it wasn't.

We finally got home, and Mum headed for the shower. While she was in there, the phone rang, and it was #1 but she was not interested in talking to me. She asked if Mum was there and wanted to speak to her. She was cold, and I noticed.

I told her to wait as she was in the shower and left the phone on the bedside table. I told Mum when she got out and she spoke to her. About half an hour later she finished the call and asked if I had my nephew's ring.

I said, "yeah, he said I could have it."

Apparently, he didn't tell *his mother* he'd let me have it, and she accused me, via Mum, of stealing it, which is why she didn't want to talk to me. Had she, then it would have been sorted out.

Turns out, the ring was from his grandparents and not the two-dollar toy we thought it was, as hey, remember we didn't actually get to see their presents because #1 hid them away in the corner while they unwrapped them.

I told Mum the story and she was upset that #1 had said what she did.

I was now even more upset than I had been all day. My sister, who couldn't even talk to me and ask me what the story was, told our mother I was a thief and had stolen the present.

We had a wretched few days after that, and I thought things through. I was going to send the ring back with a letter. Since she wanted the ring back, she could give my baby blanket and sleeping bag back that she had borrowed in 1985 for her first son when she'd visited us in Queensland. Mum had asked me if I could lend it to her, and I said yes. Two years later I asked for it back, and she'd asked to use it for son number two. I said yes, and she said she'd send it back when he was finished with it.

She didn't. In 1994 when #2 got married, I asked then for it, and she asked why?

Why do you need to ask why someone wants their property back? It's theirs, give it back.

She said it was behind her bedroom door. I waited. Then that Christmas I asked for it back in the letter I sent with the ring.

I didn't tell Mum I'd sent a letter. She chastised me, at twenty, and told me I should have shown her the letter. My mother always wants to chastise me and pander to them. It's happened all of my life and is nothing new. Even now.

The letter didn't go down well, and a new explosion was fast approaching.

When she received it she called and blasted the hell out of me, and said, and I quote, because I remember this, "does it have to do with the letter?"

"What letter?" I asked, confused as hell.

"The letter "brother" gave me."

Even more confused, I shook my head. "What are you talking about?"

She read a few lines and I said, "that was for #5, not you."

And she replied, "How was I supposed to know?"

You could fucking call and ask!

Turns out, the letter I had sent to #5 that year made it to #1 via our brother. And while I was surprised that #1 believed it was for her because I didn't put a name on the letter, why would I when it was sent to #5? I wasn't surprised that the letter had gone around the family as I'd predicted #5 would do it and wrote so in the letter. And that's what #5 did. She would whine to the rest of the family. In fact, that's what they all did when it came to me. #2 and our brother would whine to #1. #5 would whine to everyone. It was pathetic.

To cut a long story short, she more than likely had read the letter before Christmas, as our brother was staying with her. I didn't know at the time, but guessed it after she blew up at me, so that was more than likely why I was the target for the day, and then hell froze over.

I hung up on her as she attacked me and told mum what she'd said. Mum wasn't happy. I can't remember if #1 rang back, or if Mum rang her, but hell was definitely frozen for some time as 1994 was the year we'd moved to our still current location.

#1, you really should have bothered to find out and not just relied on what our brother had said or done, and #5, if you're reading this, I know you're going to be so happy you caused that shit pile, because that's the kind of cunt you are, and my letter proved it.

While nothing to do with Christmas, we didn't go back to #1's house until 1996, barely a year and a half later in March, for the town's street market and Mum's birthday. We spent most of the day in the main street looking at the stalls, buying stuff, and eating lots of pizza from the pub where #1 worked. We met my brother's partner. I was still wary, and our relationship was still strained, but we got along.

And then my brother and #1 got into it that night.

He got drunk in the pub and picked a fight in the main street with one of the drunk locals. Not the first time, I'd gather, but the publican asked Mum why didn't she control her son. He was an adult, dickshit; why should she?

He and his partner were staying in a caravan at the end of #1's driveway and at some point, they got into it in her kitchen, because she'd found out about the fight and didn't like it. They're both over six foot, and Mum, being an idiot at five eight, tried to get in the middle and stop it. Brother flung sister across her kitchen and surprised us all.

I hurriedly packed up Mum's birthday stuff while Mum

went to talk to my brother to calm things down. My sister went somewhere else, and I was done packing by the time she got back to the kitchen. She was in shock that he'd done it. I just wanted to get the hell home. She asked about Mum's presents; asked me to get them out of the car so she could have a look. I did, but I stayed on my toes while she looked at them. Mum finally came back in and sat down. We chatted for a while and Mum told me to go down to the caravan to see my brother. He apologised for his behaviour and not long after, we left. One more thing to be wary of when it comes to my brother.

We didn't go back until 2004 when we were meeting them to go on holiday to Broken Hill which is a story I've already written. We haven't been back since.

Things were not the same. They were icy and awkward. I was on edge when she was around, but I did eventually get my blanket and sleeping bag back, all nice and washed. Mum wasn't even sure if it was mine, and I had long forgotten what they looked like. But at least I finally got them back.

So Much to Come

Life lessons are not learned in school,
not taught or told or spoken of.
What we are taught has nothing to do with life.
The lessons coming will be hard to learn,
hard to hear, hard to discern.
What is life when you are so young?
So much to come, so much to come.

School of Hard Knocks

School is hard. Enrolling in multiple primary schools is even harder.

It's harder to make friends every time you start. Harder to find your way around. Harder to figure out what you're supposed to be doing.

I was a loner. Not hard to figure out once I hit primary school number three. I was at primary number one for two years. We were all starting at the same time and moved up to grade two as a class, which was a great idea. Then we moved to Queensland, and I was at primary number two for only a few months, if that, as we moved from Cotton Tree to Buderim. But those few months weren't great. They weren't bad, but they could have been better. Primary number three was probably the best. I went there for most of the four years, and while I had problems with other kids, was accused of kicking when I tapped my foot and had my headband broken for it, and then got into trouble for it, and dealt with stupid shit over a particular boy and got into trouble for that, those four years were fairly okay. And then we moved back to South Aus, and I started at primary number four. It was probably the second worst after number two. The kids all knew each other; had come up through the grades together. New kids never got off on the best foot well.

I would walk through the quad with my hands joined behind my back, head down, thinking about things that weighed heavily at the time. I can't remember what they were; being a loner and on my own most likely, but they were clearly heavy back in 1986. I'd sit on my own under the tree and watch other kids, or wander off and watch other kids. Thinking back, I have no clue what I was doing, but damn, I remember the feeling. Probably it would be known as fear, anxiety, or depression, now. I hated moving to a new school and, if I had kids, I would never do that to them because I know what it's like.

Finally, some girls took pity on me and asked me to hang out. I sort of made friends with other girls after that and hung out with a few of them through the year. But they had their friends. They only wanted me when they didn't have their other friends or needed an extra person.

One year at this primary was enough. Seven years of primary school is six too many. As for going to school during puberty. Don't put your child through it.

The fact that I had my cycle got around, all the way to the counsellor, who during one assembly, approached me and asked if I'd like a sanitary pad bin in the bathroom. The fact she knew still boggles my mind. It was either a guess, or she'd heard it, or some other kid in my class had told her. Because I sure as hell hadn't, and I don't remember my mother telling her. It was year seven. Yeah, I'd already had my monthly cycle for a year, having started it at age eleven in year six at Buderim. Some of us girls start early; it's just nature. But that doesn't give anyone the right to blab their big mouths about it, to not tell the counsellors. And it doesn't give the counsellors the right to approach us with the knowledge, without telling you how they know. Which she didn't. Again, it still boggles my mind how she knew.

I did so much stupid shit it would take the rest of the book to tell you. Did I learn anything from it? Probably not at the time, except that making the wrong choice got me into trouble and the karma police is still making me pay for some of the stupid shit I did.

God, school sucks!

*****

I started off my education at Mitchell Park Primary in South Australia. I spent the first two years of primary school there and believe me when I say; having five older siblings did not prepare me for it.

One of the things I remember from either grade one or grade two, were two boys, in a higher grade than me, who would follow me around at lunch, try to corner me, and then try to kiss me on the cheeks.

The girls I hung around with thought it was funny. I hated it and wanted it to stop.

Now, if grown men do that to women who aren't interested, it's called sexual harassment and assault. But if little boys do that to little girls, it's so cute and funny and oh my God they're dating. *Insert a massive fucking eye roll*

What. The. Actual. Fuck!

No, kids don't date. It's just your sick perverse mind that makes it so. Because that's what it is. Sick and perverse to push two children together and make them hug and kiss and hold hands. And parents wonder why their children end up with mental problems, or teen pregnancies. Goddamn that's the parents' fault.

Back to these two little shits. It went on for a while and I told my mother. She told me to kick them in the shins. Now, that was going to be the easiest thing to do, because my arms and hands were busy trying to cover my face to protect myself from these harassers and my head was naturally down in protection mode, so, all I saw were their legs. I made sure to wear hard shoes most days, either my cowboy boots or hard school shoes so I could kick them better. And I did. When I was cornered and trying to protect myself, all I saw were their legs. I kicked and kicked and kicked. And, as it happens, a few times of doing that made them stop for good.

I could finally breathe a sigh of relief and not worry about being physically assaulted and sexually harassed in the goddamn school ground at the age of six to seven.

A month or two after they stopped, I was walking to the canteen to collect the lunches. One of the boys was in the same area and he complained to me that his legs were covered in bruises. I can't remember what I told him. I have a vague feeling it was along the lines of it served him right for not leaving me alone, and I went on my merry way.

I wasn't harassed by them again. I don't even know who they were, their names, their grade, nothing. I just know that I was, in technical terms, sexually harassed and assaulted by two boys in my first or second year of primary school. And if adult men did that to me today, it could end up a whole lot worse.

For the love of God, people, *do not* make light of boys harassing girls, or vice versa. The attention is usually not wanted, not warranted, and illegal with the way things are going. Save your poor daughter the embarrassment of having to defend herself against something you think is cute. It's not. It's sick, perverse, and goddamn tiring.

*****

When we moved to Queensland, I started at the Maroochydore Primary School.

The first day I started school, I had no clue about how things worked. Who does when they move states?

All I know is, the bell rang, and I took my lunch box downstairs to the lunch area with everyone else in my classroom and started eating a Cruskit sandwich my mum had made. I then started on number two and at some point, realised that two boys were staring at me.

I stopped eating and put it back into my lunchbox.

And then lunch happened.

And all I had was a half a Cruskit sandwich to eat. My drink was gone and I had to use the water fountains. I was starving by the time the bell rang and Mum picked me up. Needless to say, I got more food for day two.

God the first day at school sucks!

*****

I was only at Maroochydore Primary for a few months, but so much happened.

There was a girl who ended up with the exact same school bag as me. That made it hard as I had to remember where I left it when we went to the library, or the school field.

One day, we were at said library, on the other side of the

school grounds from our classroom and the front gate, and we lined up outside. We had to leave our bags on the path where we stood in two rows, and just take our books and pencil cases in.

I was towards the end of the line and tried hard to remember my bag was there. But, after an hour, we rushed outside, and I grabbed the first bag I came to. Hers. I didn't even realise it wasn't mine.

I raced off across the grounds towards the front gate, not even bothering to put my stuff away, which is when I would have seen it wasn't my bag and had nearly made it when she grabbed me and told me the bag was hers.

I stopped short and we looked inside. I think I apologised and handed it over. But then I realised that she didn't even have my bag with her. She'd left it across the school grounds, and I had to go all the way back and get it, taking an extra five plus minutes to do so.

Of course, I was embarrassed. But I was also highly annoyed that she'd left mine there and hadn't bothered bringing it with her to exchange. All these years later, I'm still annoyed. I made a genuine mistake. She made a choice and made me deal with her choice. She wasn't considerate; she was just mean and uncaring, which I did not appreciate then and don't know why now. Funny how some things stay with you.

*****

Then there was a girl at Maroochydore who befriended me, and I did her wrong. I'm sorry, even now, that at eight years of age I didn't know better. We were near the canteen, and she was asking me what she should buy. When she made her decision, she asked me to watch the rest of her money. I have no idea why she didn't have a purse, or why it wasn't in her bag, or pocket, but she asked me to watch it while she went over. So, I did.

I was stacking it up on the bench when another girl in our class, one who had a pencil case I quite liked, came over and asked me to join her and her friends for a game. I said I couldn't leave as I was waiting for the girl and had her money, and she told me to leave it there; it would be safe.

In all fairness, I knew that was wrong. It felt wrong. It felt I was doing wrong and should have said for her to either wait, or given her a straight-out no. But I was new, eight years old, and highly uneducated about the world, other kids, and school. I stacked up the money on the bench and allowed myself to be dragged away before the girl came back.

I spent the rest of the lunch hour playing with the other girl and her friends, and then we headed back to our class afterwards. The girl who had befriended me ignored me. She was also angry, and I could see it very clearly. I don't know whether she was angry because I'd left, or that maybe her money had been stolen; which I don't know. I made a stupid choice as an eight-year-old, and if you read this one day, and your money was stolen, I'm sorry. I'm truly sorry.

School is not a great place to be, for any kid. It's hard enough to keep up with the rules and regulations set by the school, but we also have friendships to understand, and we're learning to manoeuvre through life as we grow, and it isn't fun.

*****

My third primary school was Buderim Mountain State School.

I was put into one of the grade three classes, and was then soon moved to the next one, simply because, after moving from one state to another, the schooling system was different, and I had yet to learn cursive writing or mathematics to that class's level. I ended up in what some called the stupid class and even had my parents come in to speak to the teacher because I had no freakin' clue what I had to do with times tables. What the hell were they? We hadn't learned them at Mitchell Park yet, but suddenly I had to know them in Queensland.

But still, I spent the most part of four grades there. I made friends there. Got mad crushes on boys there. And did very stupid shit there.

Sports days were not my best days. I have flat feet and didn't like running. I didn't like ball sports because I always thought I was going to be hit in the head by something, and apparently that's a very real phobia which I still have. I hate things flying around my head, balls, flies, or peoples' hands. But this one sports day in year three was the worst.

First, I'd been away the day or two before it and hadn't been reminded. I turned up on the day, left my school bag in the bag rack outside of class and wandered off to assembly, where it was announced that it was sports day and we'd all be going down to the oval and the classrooms had been locked.

I panicked. I wasn't dressed for sports day, and my bag was now locked in the classroom. I don't remember if I found my teacher to ask her to unlock the room. It was a part of the right wing on the upstairs floor, and once sports day had started that was it.

I tried to sit in the shade, became envious of my classmate's bag of goodies and asked for some. She said no, so I kept drinking out of the tap near the road as I had no food and no money to buy drinks, and the school sure as hell didn't supply any.

All day I went without food, water, and decent shoes. I had my dress shoes on, matched to my outfit. I wasn't dressed for sports day but I was still forced to participate in my clothes. I don't recall any teacher asking why I wasn't dressed for sports day, or why I had no bag, or no food, or no drink. Because, in reality, they didn't give a shit about the kids.

When the day was finally over, Mum picked me up and I told her about it. On Monday, I took another bag to school, cleaned out the one that had sat there all weekend and she took it home. The teacher didn't even ask why mum was there, because, again, they didn't give a shit and I remember that teacher would often zone out.

That day is probably why I hate sports so much. I hated sports before that day, but I definitely hated sports day more after it.

*****

I vomited at primary school. Not something I'd done before, and certainly didn't do again. It was grade three, the same grade as my sports day fiasco, and I have no idea why I decided to empty my guts on the carpet. But my guts had clearly had enough.

I cannot remember if it was a hot day or not, the usual reason why one vomits, other than food poisoning or by choice. But we would exercise every morning before classes started. Well, class started, and it was show and tell day, and while one kid was showing and telling, I was feeling crook as hell. I kept putting my hand up so I could ask to go for a drink, or something, but my teacher had phased out. My hand went up time and time again, and finally, because I hadn't received a response, I just leant over to the left and upchucked.

The kids went nuts, as they would, and finally the teacher came out her reverie of God knows what and flew into action. I was sent to clean myself up and have a drink, and she got to work cleaning it up. Or got a cleaner in to clean it up. I don't actually remember that bit. But once I got back, she let me lie down on the floor for the rest of show and tell until I felt better. It wasn't even an hour, from memory, until she told me to get back up and get to my desk. There was work to be done, and I had to do it.

I still have no idea why that happened. It's the only time I ever vomited at any of the schools I went to, and even though I've been sick, and had bad menstrual pains in high school which sent me to the nurses for painkillers, I only lost my guts once.

Weird!

*****

During that year, another thing happened. This teacher must have been cursed with everything that happened in one year, but at least she knew how to deal with gargantuan spiders that wanted to play indoors.

Yep, we have massive, hand and plate sized spiders in this country. Not all are poisonous. Huntsmen aren't, even though they can, and sometimes do, bite. But we have the grey wolf and other ones that I can't even Google to learn their names because spiders, *shudders*, blech.

But this was a massive mother of a spider, no idea which one, and it had decided to make its way into someone's chair bag. We had chair bags, still commonly used and known today for kids, google it, they do exist, and ours were grey and filled with our books. One day, a boy decided to start making some noise and suddenly we're all screaming from a massive mother crawling out of a chair bag.

The teacher carried the chair out of the class area, as it wasn't a traditional room with a door, and left it just outside in the cubicle area where we left our bags. Come morning tea time, the boys all raced out and one found it in his bag, and there was another outcry as boys will be boys about boy things, spiders, and spider things.

I mean, geez, people, as if we didn't know that was going to happen.

I can't remember what happened to it, I'm assuming it was taken out by the teacher, or another teacher, but still… *shudders*.

Ironically, even now, I still have to occasionally deal with a mother of a spider. Sometimes brown, sometimes grey, but I usually deal with them outside. A few years back I saw a massive black one with brown stripes on its legs just casually walk along the ground. I was so fascinated by the fact I'd never seen one like that before, that I just watched it, knowing it would be gone if I ran inside for my phone to take photos. I had no fear.

Nor did I have fear when a grey/brown massive mother dropped from the garbage bin onto my foot. I just looked down at it for all of about five seconds, and then kicked my foot. It scurried away, probably as surprised as I was. Again, no fear.

But we had a massive skinny grey in the bathroom two summers ago, and I just couldn't. I sprayed that mother with half a can of Raid. It upturned and died, and curled its legs in, as they do. I had to get it out the next morning as this was just after midnight and trying to get it out made me shudder. Because even dead and curled up, it was still freakin' huge. Double blech!

And then there's the massive, and very poisonous black ones...

*****

Of course, there are so many bonus stories to tell, but they're not overly interesting. I could talk about the time there was a blue tongue lizard living in the huge septic tank area we had behind one the classrooms, that we would all go and look at every lunchtime, or the time, over the Christmas holidays that tank was removed, and so was the lizard, and a nice new social hall was being built.

Or all the times we'd go through the lush tree area between the classrooms and the oval, or we'd climb the trees and end up with leeches in our socks and shoes. Or the time we were playing tee-ball, and I couldn't even hit the ball off the stand and fell knee first into the mud in front of the stand. I walked around with two muddy patches on my tracksuit pants all day. And that was my favourite tracksuit. Never mind the teachers not caring whether we could run, hit, or play, we had to do it, and none of them wanted to teach us how to swim, and they had helpers in who didn't help either. The expectation was that we should already know how, and many of us didn't.

Or the time I stayed late with my friend in the park across

the road from the shops her mother worked at, just down the road from the flat where we lived, and then lied about being held back by the teacher. Or the time I told a very stupid lie to a boy I liked and the shit that happened, oi. Or the time I ripped my skirt and had to wear my coat tied around my waist for the rest of the day.

Or the time I hounded Mum to wear my favourite Kermit necklace to school and lost it. But do you think I can even *remember* that necklace? Nope. Clearly I was incredibly traumatised by losing it.

Or the time I wore all of my favourite rings to school when I was told not to, and still regret losing them to this day. We'd done some activity outside and were washing up. I was the last one there and I took my rings off and left them on the top of the wash sink. I headed for my classroom before realising I wasn't wearing them and ran back for them, and they weren't there. I had barely walked fifteen metres away, in all open space, before doubling back and there was no one else around. How the hell did they disappear in those fifteen to twenty seconds? No one made a sound, no one was seen…there was no one when I turned around and started back, because I could see the wash sink when I turned around. There was absolutely no one there. And they weren't in or on the sink, or on the floor, or anywhere else. Where the hell did they go in twenty seconds?

One of them was a gorgeous purple crystal and silver Avon ring. Talk about one of life's mysteries.

I'll move on…

*****

When I attended my fourth primary school, Cowandilla Primary, for the final year, grade seven, it was once more a feeling of dread at having to make friends again. I wasn't great at it. I'd been at Buderim for most of four years. But we'd moved back to South Australia from Queensland (big mistake. Huge!) and I went on the merry go round again.

One girl, out of many, was a user. Plain and goddamn simple. Here's a couple of things she did.

1 - We used to do exercises in the mornings at assembly. Each person in year seven was asked to pick someone to do it with. We had to choreograph a routine to a song and get on a stage in the quad to lead everyone else from every other grade through it.

Embarrassing as hell and something I will never do again.

We practised a few times to different songs, and had an issue with another girl who wanted to use all of the songs we'd chosen. That was nigh on impossible since she had no idea what songs we'd chosen until we were in the rec room rehearsing at the same time. She complained to a teacher. The teacher sided with me and told her to pick something else. Suck that, bitch.

But my work out partner decided to start flaking on me. She stopped rehearsing, gave me the run around, and then turned up late. On the goddamn day! I was angry. Why wouldn't I be? I was feeling used and fobbed off, but I walked up on the stage, scared out of my brain I was about to make a fool of myself, and led the class through the routine. She barely kept up, but managed. We walked off the stage and I was done.

Now, I can't remember if this was before or after she used me again, but this girl screwed me over a few times that year.

2 - She was sitting next to me in class at this particular time, with our first teacher for the year as the regular was on maternity leave and she asked me to draw the cover of a book for her. It was a class thing; we'd all got a book from the library and had to replicate the cover. She asked, I did, purely because I was raised to be nice and friendly and help people out. What happened? All of the girls passed our table and told her how great her picture was. And what did she do? She THANKED THEM!

Not that SHE did it, oh HELL TO THE NO, she didn't do the cover herself and didn't say she hadn't, just accepted the credit for it. I don't know whether it was because she was Greek or the way she was raised, as a flake that flaked out of things and fobbed people off and let them down and yet kept on using them until they told her no more.

But she did it to me. Multiple times.

God knows what's she's been like since.

All of my life people have let me down, taken what they could take, and given nothing in return and it PISSES ME OFF.

I got so sick and tired of being used in primary school, that by the time I hit high school, year 10 especially, I refused everyone everything. I refused to lend my pencils and textas because I knew I wouldn't get them back (like my sunglasses I loaned a male classmate in our year 9 musical, and he gave them to someone else and gave me a shit pair in return) or I'd get them back broken. I was asked by a girl in my year ten class if I could draw the cover for her typing assignment. I said no, and she called me a bitch. Fuck you! Glad I didn't.

Because the other kids were unprepared, they believed they could borrow what was mine because I had stuff. I had *good* stuff. I had full sets of pencils and textas and erasers. All sorts of stuff. But no more. By year ten I knew how it worked and they could all go and fuck off; they weren't getting their paws on my stuff anymore. Not after the way they'd treated me and what they called me before and after I started saying no. Once they heard it a time or two, they stopped asking, and I sighed in relief.

*****

I was bullied a lot at Cowandilla. I'm not entirely sure why. I didn't know them; they all knew each other as they'd come up through the grades together, but when lies and innuendoes go around that the new girl has a crush, the boys get shitty.

I was hit, a lot. I was called names, a lot. And by some of the girls as well.

I was verbally abused, a lot. And by some of the girls as well.

Abuse came from both sexes, but mainly the boys.

I never understood why. Why boys thought they had the right to be physically abusive with girls they didn't know or like just because some girl told them lies.

Did I have crushes on some of the boys? Sure. Did they know? Not from me.

We were playing tee-ball one day during sport class with our teacher, and I hated it. I was in the outfield with my team and went after a ball. One of the boys ran after it as well and punched me in the arm before grabbing the ball from me.

The teacher didn't see. She didn't care. But I stood there rubbing my arm and frowning. Wondering why he'd needed to do that. Why he'd needed to be a physically abusive piece of shit towards me.

It doesn't make the person feel good. The one being abused. We all know it makes the abuser feel good; they get off on it, in many ways. They feel big and tough that they can beat up a girl, lord it over her, take from her. And they don't give a flying fuck what they leave behind.

A girl who's abused thinks less of herself, thinks less of boys, and then when she grows up, men. Even though she desperately wants to be loved and wanted by a good one. But where the good ones are, she does not know.

I wouldn't be surprised if many of the boys I went to school with ended up in jail for beating up women or just being abusive cunts in general. It seemed to be in their nature to take their anger out on one or two that weren't pretty enough, skinny enough, cute enough, popular enough, Greek or Italian enough. And some of us just weren't that.

*****

Don't trust your so-called friends.

I did. And she lied to me. Many did. In year seven, we tried out for choir. God knows how I got in, but I didn't last long.

I had a few practices, but then ended up being off school for two weeks. When I got back, my so-called friend told me the teacher had kicked me out of the choir so I couldn't come to practice, so I didn't go. Because I believed her.

Instead of finding out for myself, I believed my friend because she was supposed to be my friend.

I look back on this occasionally, and then the high school that I went to because she went there, and I didn't want to go to another school with people I didn't know. I chose to believe her. I didn't realise she was doing it to control me. That she was doing it so I'd not go, not be in the choir, not be better than her. Her insecurities made her control my narrative. And I hate that.

The choir ended up going to Sydney to sing with other kid choirs and my so-called friend went with them.

I should have just gone and talked to the teacher, but I didn't, and now I'll never know if I was actually kicked out or not. I'd say not. But then I also may not have been able to travel because of the cost.

My advice, even for adults, would be, don't trust your friends. Go straight to the person who supposedly said it and find out because more often than not, the bet would be your friend is lying and making shit up to control the narrative. Don't let others control your narrative, control it yourself. Believe in yourself. Find out for yourself.

A second story about this person…about fifteen years later, she turned up in my current suburb (2024 was our thirtieth year here), and almost recognised me in the post office. She walked up to me while I was talking to the man behind the counter and talked over both of us.

"Do I know you?" she asked. "You seem familiar."

I replied, "I know who you, are so-and-so and want nothing to do with you." And I went back to speaking to the man.

First, I hate people doing that, it's so goddamn rude. You do not interrupt a conversation that two people are having just to ask if you know them. You bloody wait.

Second, I found a message from her on Facebook *years* later, yeah, thanks for letting me know, Facebook. She had remembered who I was, and found me, and wanted to know what she had done to make me angry.

If you were referring to high school, a lot. If you were referring to that moment, you interrupted my conversation ever so rudely. All I said was I wanted nothing to do with you. Which I didn't and still don't.

I was bullied mercilessly at high school, and she, in part, added to it by jumping from me to other girls. When I left, I wanted nothing to do with any of those people, and I use that term loosely, and still don't all these years later.

Sometimes, you just have to get rid of the toxic people in your life. It's like when your bully wants to befriend you on Facebook. Why would you be friends with them now? And it has nothing to do with being the bigger person, because believe me, you'd be the bigger person by walking away and having nothing to do with them for the sake of your mental health, regardless of whether they're the same, or have changed and are apologetic.

I hadn't seen her since school, but I knew who she was the first time I saw her; and had seen her several times at the shopping centre. She'd popped out five kids, and was even taller than at school, but believe me, I recognised the face. I knew exactly who she was and knew that I didn't want to speak to her or have anything to do with her. And why should I? She treated me badly in primary school and used me in high school. I was long out of school and was over it. I don't need to talk to you just because you recognise me.

I remember years back when Taylor Swift had her squad and she'd made a statement about knowing who she wanted around her, and if you couldn't be her friend, and were just going to be a user or spread lies about her, then she wasn't interested.

Many women abused her for that. Yes, abused *her* for

that. Yet ironically, that was what Oprah and Dr Phil had talked about many a decade before. Getting rid of the toxic people and users out of your life. Well, that's all Taylor was doing, and she was slammed for it, seemingly, by females her age that were clearly a long way off learning that lesson that was already decades old. But then, many people, women especially, never seem to learn that lesson until into their 30s, 40s or 50s plus. Taylor learned it in her mid-20s like I did, and you can learn it now. Get rid of the toxic people out of your life. They are exhausting abusive users and you don't need them.

And remember this, just because you go to school with someone, doesn't mean you need to have anything to do with them when you leave.

*****

Music had been in my blood for years, if not since birth.

I loved listening, singing, dancing to it.

That is probably why I wanted to set up a singing group with some of my fellow classmates in year seven.

Aussie group, Pseudo Echo, had quite a few songs out across the '80s, and one of them in 1986 was Funky Town. I suggested calling ourselves the Pseudo Echoettes.

Original, I know.

We would act out our stage performance at recess and lunch, pretending we were appearing on music programs. We were twelve, so what did it matter? It didn't, we were having fun and daydreaming of being singers.

Of course, this little group didn't last for long, a week or two at most, but I think it did lead the way for me to not only want to be a singer, something that is very much not even remotely part of my life now thanks to no support ever, but which probably led the way to writing song lyrics, which I started doing a few years later.

Where does inspiration lead and when? You never know what, when, or how ideas will pan out, or where you'll end up after the idea has percolated for a few days, weeks, months or even years. And maybe for me, it started with this idea.

*****

Ah, high school…

High school didn't get off to a great start. I was originally going to Adelaide High. Not sure why, but that was the plan. In year seven we went on a day trip to the school to check it out and to see what we would be doing if we chose to go there, and I found it incredibly overwhelming, and was somewhat scared by it. Other girls in my class had sisters going there, and they were all excited. They already knew where everything was and how to use the canteen. It wasn't like the one we had at our primary school, so I was confused, on top of the being overwhelmed and out of my depth.

At the end of the year, I decided to go to Thebarton High. The reason, as mentioned, was that my so-called best friend was going there. She'd only been my best friend in my last year of primary. We'd been sitting next to each other for most of the year, and I stupidly chose to go because she was.

Big mistake. Huge!

She ditched me almost the moment the year started.

I'm not one to make friends quickly, if at all. I think other kids have always felt sorry for me as the new kid so asked me to tag along. As mentioned, I went to four different primary schools, and when you're on your own, it can suck shit balls.

High school was no better.

There were many bullies. One threw a rock at my head creating a massive lump. She was the older sister of a girl in my class and a right bitch. So much shit.

Anyway, my so-called best friend dumped me for two other girls in the class and we basically kept switching as friends all year. By year nine I knew how it went; you needed to survive. By year ten, I no longer gave a fuck.

One of my so-called new friends had an elder sister who also went there, and she was friends with the bitch of year ten. Teachers claimed this girl was so nice, yet that bitch bullied me like no tomorrow. There was also the older sister of another girl in my class, only a year up. I not only had a year nine bitch bullying me, but a year tenner.

Maybe the girls in my class were piss weak and needed to get their big sisters to do their dirty job. Maybe I was weak. Maybe I looked it; maybe they wanted a new victim, and I stupidly fell for it. I can shake my head about it now, knowing I should have done things differently, but one of these bitches organised for a mob of girls to beat me up after school one day.

And I know because the rumour got back to me. It also went around the school.

The original plan was to get me at lunch. I mentioned something to the ladies in the office and asked if I could eat lunch in there. They said yes, so I'd bypassed the smack down.

But, when the last bell of the day went off, I nearly shat myself. I knew what was coming, but so did others. The older brother of a girl in my class asked if I was walking or had a ride home. I told him Mum was picking me up and would be down the side street. He offered to walk me out of the car park and down the street, so I walked with him and his sister to their mum's car as she was parked in another side street. He told her what he was doing, and then walked me down the street where Mum was standing on the corner, listening to what was happening. We kept on going to the car and got in. We both thanked the brother, and he went back to his mum's car, and we took off, foiling their attempt at a beat down.

I have no idea who really planned that. I can only guesstimate it was one of my bullies. I have no clue what it was about, except another guess, some perceived crime that didn't actually happen or a vicious lie. I also have no clue why so many other girls were standing around wanting to get in on it. There would have been girls I didn't know from higher years, and probably girls from my year. Elevens and twelves didn't worry themselves with eights, nines and tens in 1987, so it wouldn't have been them. I can only put it down to one of the two reasons I just mentioned. If not both.

That didn't happen again. There was no other bitch fight waiting to go down. I did have some trouble from them both, but nothing like that. If any of the bitches from Thebarton High in 1987-89 read this, fuck you, you cunts.

I'm so sick and tired of bitches that don't know me, making up bullshit about me. Get a goddamn fucking life and fuck off.

*****

When I started high school we had a principal, a deputy principal, and a counsellor.

I don't even remember who the actual principal was, but the deputy head was an absolute tosser. So was the then counsellor who left at the end of the year. She believed everything was my fault and was just a cow.

In year nine, Mum and Dad separated and Dad moved out. I was having some issues with bullies and boys at school, and for some reason, the deputy head and counsellor loved to blame the victims. As did the teachers.

In maths class one day, I was doing my work and the girls behind me were talking. I turned around to tell them to shoosh, and who got into trouble from the teacher? Me!

He called me up to the front, and luckily there was only about five of us girls in the class at the time and berated my work.

Embarrassed and humiliated, I sat down after he gave me detention for talking. Even though I hadn't been.

I told Mum. She told me I wasn't doing detention, and we went home. At some point, letters went back and forth between Mum and the deputy head. He wasn't happy I hadn't done what I was told, and neither was the math teacher who was a bit of a dick. But Mum sent off a letter setting the deputy head straight.

Well, what did the deputy head do? He wrote a letter to my father, addressed to our house, and told my father to control his wife. I still have that letter, so yeah, I remember distinctly.

Since my father didn't live there, Mum opened it, got real pissed about it, and I have no clue what she did after. She may have sent another letter to him, or the actual principal, but those memories are gone.

The deputy head left and didn't come back for year ten. I was thankful. He was clearly an arsehole.

One time, when I was allowed out of class early, I realised I'd forgotten where we were having our next class, so I waited on the first-floor landing or the rest of my class. The second counsellor and deputy head came up the stairs and chastised me even though I told them I couldn't remember where our next class was and was waiting for my classmates, who turned up at that moment. I asked them where I should go. They told me upstairs and as I started moving, the deputy head and counsellor looked at each other and that bitch of a counsellor said, "it's on the liver."

Now, she clearly didn't think a fourteen-year-old was going to know the phrase "shit on the liver", but I'd heard it enough to know what she was saying. And once again, I told Mum, and she spat chips.

What is it with people in power? What is it with teachers, and counsellors and principals? Were their own childhoods fucked up? If so, why bother becoming anything to do with school and school kids?

Even today, the teachers, principals and counsellors are to blame for the majority of problems happening in schools with the kids when it comes to bullying. Your job is to keep us safe on ground and to educate us by the curriculum; not by your own dumb arse principles and bullshit values. You're all fucked up as adults, and yet you want to fuck the next generation up as well. Maybe it's time the whole system was overhauled, and we got rid of these people. Maybe we need to burn them to the ground and rebuild, because what we have now is far worse than what we had then.

*****

The year was 1989 and I was in my third year of high school. I was also the first to find Scrunchies. I found them at our local market that we went to on Friday nights. I'd get out of school, we'd go home and I'd shower and change, and then we'd go into town to the market. You could park upstairs and come down to street level and do the shopping at the supermarket, buy fruit and veg at the stalls; buy lollies, meats, and eat all kinds of food. It was a great place to go on a Friday afternoon; a very trendy and in place to hang out in the '80s.

And that's where I found them. A stall had silky strips of material in a sewed-up circle with elastic. They were called Scrunchies, and I bought a white one to go with our school colours. Of course, over the next few years I acquired many in every colour, but I digress.

I wore it to school on the Monday and all the girls in my year wanted to know what it was. I told them, *"It's a Scrunchie, but it looks like a bride's garter, doesn't it."*

Well, as school goes, and as bitched face molls called teenage girls go, the rumour soon circulated. I found out about it by the end of the week, in fact, probably after two days.

Tiara's so poor she has to wear a bride's garter in her hair.

God, fucking teenage bitches.

Of course, it wasn't the only rumour that ever went around about me. That's what happened to most of us. But there were those of us who were picked on and lied about more often. Usually we had more, wore more, and did more than them, so they spread the rumours. They had to feel good about themselves after all. And telling people that Tiara was so poor, when I wasn't actually the poorest in our class, that I had to wear a bride's garter was really fucking pathetic and showed the mentality of the bitches at school.

No wonder I hate being lied about today.

*****

Throughout my three years of high school, I was lucky enough to take part in two kids' TV shows.

Back in the late '80s there was a TV show called *Ridgey Didge*. It was a national kids' show where we could write in and see if one of the hosts could come to our home for segments.

I wrote in and thought nothing of it.

I didn't know my mother had received a phone call from Channel 10 and learned about it then as I hadn't told her. She then received a letter and kept it all a secret until the day of the shoot when she told me I was staying home from school, and we were going out.

She normally never told me to stay home so I was suspicious and wondered what was going on. It was unusual for her to even suggest it, even though I had a few days off each term. I got dressed, did my hair and make-up, and then there was a knock at the door. She told me to open it and I wondered what the fuss was about. Was it a family member? Were we going out with them? I had no clue. When I did open the door, there stood Chris Harriot and a camera man from *Ridgey Didge*.

I instantly knew who he was and was so embarrassed and overwhelmed it was ridiculous. To say I was shocked would be an understatement, but I invited them in and found out what was going on. He introduced himself and the crew and Mum introduced herself as well.

We filmed a segment with me and Chris playing my small keyboard on the dining table as I have no idea all these years later what I'd actually written in about. He asked some questions, and the camera was in my face, and I managed to mumble and bumble my way through the filming and then it was all over.

Mum took lots of pictures of us on the front lawn and I got autographs. I still have them to this day. Why wouldn't I? It was my first foray into TV.

The next day, I went back to school and handed my diary to my teacher. Mum had written my note in it, saying I had been absent because I was filming a segment for a kids' TV show, which *was* the truth. My teacher signed off on it, but still sent my diary to the head office. Not sure why, to get it signed I suppose, and I can't remember who by, but when I told Mum she thought it was ridiculous that the teacher had to send my note up to the front desk. My teacher clearly thought it was a ridiculous excuse and that the head needed to see it.

Either way, I got my diary back *and* had the photos for proof, if she needed them. But then again, how many kids use *filming a TV show* as an excuse for taking a day off?

Not that it mattered in the end. The show was unfortunately axed before my segment even aired. On one hand I'm glad, as looking back on it I was not looking my best that day with a pimple right on my top lip. On the other, it would have made all the bitches I went to school with jealous!

The second show came about a year later, in 1989, when I was a mere teenager all of 15 years old. I got to be an audience member of an Adelaide kids' show called *C'mon Kids*, with the infamous fluffy duck himself, Winky Dink.

Every Friday, the show would have a little quiz segment between the hosts, and school kids got to fill the seats in the audience. I can't remember the exact time. I vaguely remember it being August, yet the shows, yes, they spread them out across two, didn't air for a few months; October or November sometime.

All three year ten classes went along to Channel 9 in Adelaide and sat nervously in our chairs in the studio. The hosts came out, Winky Dink came out, and we were all introduced and told what to do, and the young female co-host ran up into the audience and egged us on. She was so sweet and nice with her short spiky blond hair and was very much a tomboy.

She loved my huge smiley face badge so much she asked to wear it for the show, and I willingly handed it over. She wore it front and centre and stood next to me and my friends who were essentially in the middle row of the whole audience. We all participated in the quiz show with the rambunctiousness of our teen years and called out and cheered with every question.

Once the first taping was over, the hosts went off to change clothes and clean up and we were all moved around so it didn't look like the same school class. We taped a second quiz segment and then got autographs and chatted with the show's stars. There were no phones back then so no pictures or selfies, and since none of us knew we were going, we didn't take cameras. But I'm not sure we would've been allowed to anyway. Then it was over. We were driven back to high school and that was that. All over in an afternoon.

It was my TV show debut but would've been my second if the segment for Ridgey Didge had've aired, and I was a TV star. Front and centre.

The host wore my badge with pride, and I got it back all

clean and tidy. This host went on to become one of Australia's biggest actresses, starring in many well-known, popular TV shows. Which means she's worked with probably all of Australia's TV stars. So instead of being 6 degrees of Kevin Bacon between me and Australia's acting community, I can very proudly say, it's only 1 degree of Tammy Macintosh! And to me, that's pretty cool.

*****

I was bullied a lot at high school, as many of these stories attest to and I've already stated. Looking back, I think boys have no freakin' clue as to who they like and who they don't. For some reason I was the one they hated, they didn't like, they hit and spat on. But something happened in high school that made me wonder.

Why do boys give girls they don't like more attention than those they like?

High school was not great when it came to being bullied, and boys in general, but at some point, and for some reason I can no longer remember, several of us in our maths class took baby photos along. Again, I cannot remember why the teacher suggested it, or why it happened. Because I didn't want to put my photo up, I asked my then friend to do it for me. There was only ten or so of us there that day, about half and half, and not everyone put a photo up. I stayed seated while my friend went up there, and those who didn't bring photos stayed seated as well. Once we were all seated, the teacher started talking about the photos and we all looked behind us at them. When he spoke to my friend and asked if my picture was hers, she said no, and it came out that it was mine. All of the boys in the class fled their seats as one and crowded around the back wall where the photos were.

It was surprising, considering how they insulted me with names most days, and left me confused as to what the hell was happening.

I was often called on to read books aloud in English, talked about behind my back in class and not just by the boys. I had one higher grade guy drop me on the ground, breaking my coccyx, and another day he spat on me. I'd had enough, so I decided to walk out and go home. I called Mum from the local shopping centre and she came and picked me up. I didn't go back to school that week.

Looking back in my fiftieth year, I really cannot figure boys out. I have no clue why they torment girls, unless certain people are right, and it really is because they like them. You know how the hair pulling, hitting, and whatnot, has been explained away to girls as the boys liking them. Maybe it actually is. Maybe the testosterone from puberty is making them crazy and they live in opposite world where they really like girls but treat them badly.

I can't blame a bad male role model on it, I went to school in the '80s when times were different, and many fathers were at home. I can only try and figure it out since I have no therapist to turn to. But if there is a therapist out there, tell me, why do boys torment girls, but seem so fascinated by a photo of them being a baby?

*****

It's not murder on the dance floor of a high school social, but murder nonetheless.

Have you ever looked back at your years of high school and thought about what happened to everyone?

I have. Absolutely. I've wondered who got married, who had kids, and who ended up with a high paying job or a powerful position. I went to five schools; there's a lot to think about.

In the years since I left I've seen about three of them with kids. The others, I have no idea about except for one.

The year before I started at my high school there was a stabbing.

Clearly it was not the right kind of area and looking back I would make the choice to NOT go to that school. But I made it for emotional reasons. Never again.

There was a guy in my class when I started who had been held back. He wasn't the best kind of kid to hang with, but he was okay for the most part.

I spent three years in high school, leaving at the end of year ten in 1989. He had left that year or the year before and a few years later I saw him working at the lawn mower place just across the road from me. A few years later he was arrested with a friend of his for the murder of a man.

It was a long time ago now, but occasionally I still think about those I went to five different schools with. He stands out. Because he's the one I know who did do something. He's the one who got himself in the news and became known. He's the one who beat the rest of us to fame and stardom.

For all the wrong reasons.

Going to school with someone who turns into a murderer is a very weird feeling.

*****

Life after school is a weird thing.

I've often had dreams of going back to high school, at the age I was, with the rest of my class, and finishing years eleven and twelve. I never got to do that thanks to my school turning into an adult campus; otherwise I would've stayed and finished. I would've had no problem doing that, but after converting, they catered to adults more than the remaining kids. I think a lot of us left then. It became too complicated to come to school for a class in the morning and then do nothing until the next class in the evening. It was ridiculous, and unnecessary.

I've also had dreams where we're back in the school yard and I'm running away from people who are after me, and I run and run and run and then jump up and fly up, fly around the buildings, zoom down to the quad on the other side and hit the ground running to get more energy for flying again. If anyone knows what flying means in a dream, there's a reason I wanted to be free.

I never understood why I had these dreams, until one day, I realised it may have to do with me writing books. I stopped, and asked myself the question, *"if I went back to high school to get my diploma and finish off the two years, what would I get out of it? What classes would I do?"*

In reality, I only needed English and accounting, and maybe art. I didn't need science, physics, sport, or anything else. I realised it would be a big waste of time to do it, take two years to find another school to complete subjects that have changed so much since the '80s. Hell, most parents who went to school in the '80s can't even help their kids with their homework now because they have no clue. I know I can take online English and accounting courses, but do I really need them all these years later?

And surprise, surprise, after asking myself those questions, and realising going back to school was unnecessary, I haven't had those dreams again. Once you figure out why, or at least come up with a reason, the dreams normally sort themselves out. And no, I don't need to go back and finish high school.

*****

Sometimes I wonder, if I'd gone to another high school, would everything have turned out the same.

The answer would categorically be no.

I would have finished, learned a few things, and gone and done what everyone else was doing. I have no doubt my life would be different if I'd gone to Adelaide High instead of Thebarton High. I feel it in my bones. And one can argue that everything that *has* happened in my life has made me the person I am and got me to where I am. And I can argue back that my life is shit, I've missed out on what most people experience in their lifetime, I have no money, no car, no house, no family, no kids. I *know* my life would have been different, as *I* would have been different, and I know Adelaide High would have given me opportunities that Thebarton refused to give.

If I had to write a letter to my twelve-year-old self in primary school, I would tell her to go to Adelaide High and to not be scared, and it wouldn't matter if she made friends or not because she was important, and they weren't going to last past high school. I'd tell her to take classes and courses and learn to sing and play, and make and create a world of music, songs, and books.

I would tell her to get her driver's licence and get a job

and get out of the house as soon as possible. To go to Marleston TAFE and do fashion for four years and learn the craft, as she was going to live around the corner from it and it would be so easy to walk to and from it. That fashion is where she'd end up dabbling and she could work her way up the ranks of some big fashion chain as she sang and wrote; and make the money to leave and live. To live her life her way and not by anyone else's standards so life doesn't turn out to be shitty and full of regrets.

Because that's what life has turned out to be. So yeah, when I say my life would have been different if I'd gone to Adelaide High, I know it would be, and that's exactly what I'd tell my twelve-year-old self.

*****

A lot of people tend to constantly look back on their schooling and blame it for the way they turned out. In all fairness, it's not just schooling, it's the way you were raised, what you learn in the school of hard knocks, and what you're taught, hear, see, that drives you to be the way you are. But as an adult, all of that is no longer relevant. You're an adult; you can learn and grow and change and be better. It's all a choice.

I've seen many online complain about the schools they went to. How it was a religious school, or an agricultural school. How they never learned to be creative, and they were taught art was not important compared to working.

Why did you cling to that? Why did you take that into your adulthood?

Just because a teacher writes on your report card that you need to concentrate more, or study more, or learn to be more productive, doesn't mean anything once you get to the real world.

Forget the report cards because here's a very valuable lesson to learn about them.

Your report cards are not for you.

I'll repeat that louder for the people in the back.

YOUR REPORT CARDS ARE NOT FOR YOU.

They're for your parents to help guide you through your education and to uncover any issues.

Most parents don't care, unless you're from a particular country that does value education, and then they will. But for the rest of us, what our vocation ends up being could turn out completely different to what we learned in school.

For me, art class was weekly. We were always doing something arty and crafty, whether doing tie-dye t-shirts in grades 1 and 2, or making books for the school library in grade 7, or a German school in grade 9, writing stories, doing projects, doing art class every week, or design class where we learned to design technical things like underwater subs and bionic diving suits.

We did basic artwork such as gluing twine to a piece of cardboard and then rolling paint over it to then press it to paper and make an Egyptian outline painting. Or we'd draw buffalo and colour the paper in ochres, reds, and browns to make it look like a cave painting.

We did so much in art, and I still have all of it in a folder.

I loved English. I loved music, so I guess it was no wonder that I wanted to be a singer when I left school. I didn't become one, but I did go on to write 639 songs from 1989 to 1996 and then one in 2002. I've written more since 2018, but that's because in my novels, I write about singers and songwriters and write my own lyrics, so I don't have to pay for anyone else's.

I ended up writing novels, novellas, non-fiction, short stories, essays, opinion pieces, poems and songs in my fifty years; all because I left school still creating as many did.

Now, if you left school creating and stopped doing it, that's on you. I kept on, making big black records to stick on my walls. I made album covers, music notes, a warning sign for my bedroom door to *beware* and keep out of my bedroom. I got into Andrew Loyd Webber musicals because the lead singer from my favourite band at the time left the band to be in Joseph and the Amazing Technicolor Dreamcoat here in Australia. I would then learn all of ALW's musicals by heart, get the cassettes from the library, draw the design on a page in an A4 notebook and then proceed to write out the entire set of lyrics from each one. I have two notebooks full of written out ALW musicals. I did the same with Indecent Obsession, Debbie Gibson, and more. All this was for the need to keep my brain going. To use it or lose it. To keep active and creative.

I didn't let my reports cards hold me back; I didn't let what my teachers said hold me back, and I personally think it's ridiculous to do so when you're an adult. Why are you living by 20, 30, 40, even 50, 60-year-old shit? Why are you living by your schooling, your church, your parents? Why aren't you living by your own narrative instead of everyone else's? And yes, I know it can be hard.

I really don't get why people constantly hold themselves back and make excuses by blaming everyone else from decades ago.

If you're an adult, get creative, get back to doing what you did in school, or uni. Get back to doing something you love that you had to stop due to life dictating survival. Or start something else. Make the plan to start something and actually start it. If your English isn't great, take free classes; if your writing isn't great, take online courses and classes, if you need to learn spelling, punctuation, and grammar, read books on the subject and visit YouTube for videos and teach yourself. There is no excuse anymore. No excuse to not learn when so much is free online, or in your local library, or in person at classes. Continue to educate yourself and stop blaming your teachers and your report cards.

There is nothing wrong with having left creativity behind to deal with the real world, kids, family, work, life, but if it's all settled down, then start it back up. No excuses. Get creative today.

Lessons

Little does one know the lessons coming one's way,
    when we are a child, a toddler, a baby,
        little do we know the lessons we will be taught.
I did not know when I was a child, a toddler, a baby,
    a teen, an adult, what fears and horrors abounded,
        little did I know how my life would go a different way.
Far from the one I'd always dreamt about, yearned for, cried for,
    demanded from the universe the lessons learned,
        little did I know they were demanding more.
Eager to crush me and break me and suffocate me,
    but even though I bend, I do not break, do not break,
        little did I know the lessons would push me to the brink.

Life is a Long Lesson

So much has happened in my life, from living in two states and travelling to two more, meeting celebrities, being used and abused by my family, to being a blogger and writer and then an author.

I've often felt the Universe doesn't want me to succeed. At anything. I'm yet to win the lottery, or an Art Union house, to have my books sell millions and make me millions. Nothing good has happened except the time I won $1200 in the lottery, and then had to hand half over to Mum, and the time a new checkout girl counted my money wrong when I was paying my credit card bill and said I was $60 out. I questioned that, another counted it, came to the same conclusion, and I forked over the $60. When I walked away, it felt wrong. Something said go back. I did and filed a report, and was told, "if we're ahead in the till at the end of the day we'll call you," and I walked away. The Universe then gave me $60 back in a scratchie and lotto winnings. The Universe knew.

But it also knows how shit my life is. How full of abuse and hell it is. But…the Universe doesn't want to help everyone. Just those who are touched by the golden hand. Those who make millions and squillions out of nothing, talent or not, and seem to have it all, while 99% of us have nothing.

And I've told the Universe on more than one occasion that it sucks.

And it does.

I know what I need to do to change my life, but how to get it is a completely different story. And how is damn hard. Especially when you have no support from anyone or anything.

*****

My physical health has never been great, and, like a lot of people, I've been one to suffer a lot of issues since being a teenager, and believe me, they were not growing pains.

Since I was sixteen I've suffered from ear, nose, and throat infections.

I used to have them twice yearly for years, then they dried out a little after we moved to our current 30-year location, and I had my tonsils out because I had six bouts of it in 1996. When I was due to have the operation in February 1998 I had to cancel because my tonsils decided to throw one last party before being removed and I ended up with a massive golf ball sized lump above my left ear. Because you aren't allowed to have operations when you're sick, I had to cancel, and they reorganised it for April.

These days, I can go two years without an infection, but then potentially have a second within six months.

I even got an infection in October of 2023, after going to an ENT (ear, nose, throat) specialist to see why I still can't breathe. He couldn't tell me why my nose blocks up, putting it down to allergies, which I am yet to be diagnosed with, or nerves issues as the nerves to my nose are the ones that cause migraines. I knew on the way out the door, when my left eye kept watering and my left sinus kept dripping, that the small camera he shoved up my nose to view my sinuses had irritated it and yep, up everything flared for the next four weeks. It burned, I lost my voice; it was hell, as always. And unlike Alanis Morrissette's song, this *was* ironic, and it was also Friday the 13th.

My nose blocks up at night, making it even harder to breathe. Sprays and pills don't work, and I've had two sinus operations to try and help. In 1996 I had my turbinates lasered, and in 2008 I had a septoplasty and my turbinates lasered for a second time. It lasts about five to seven years before my breathing starts to wane. They're unwilling to give me a third operation because there's not much else they can take.

I suffered from what used to be the four variants of migraines since I was eighteen or so. Now there seem to be eight to ten variants. I only found relief once I started at the chiropractor. My neck and back were so out of alignment that she said my head was bent left and forward. For several years after the first crack, the migraines diminished. But at certain times they would come back with a vengeance. These days, I only get the ones either side of the back of my skull which then invade my eye sockets, eyeballs, and the spots where my reading glass arms dig into my head. That's similar to what headbands used to do when I wore them. These migraines can last a few days, or be on and off over days or weeks, or I can go without them for some time, which is a great relief for a writer who handwrites all of her fiction. Having my head down for hours while I write can make migraines worse or help stiffen the muscles to bring them on.

And speaking of the chiropractor, I started seeing her at

the age of thirty-six. I'd had a curve in my upper thoracic spine since I was eighteen. Then, I was told I had scoliosis, and lived with it until I couldn't anymore. Over the years I had been told to see a physio, which didn't work, because nerves are pinched by bones, and in turn muscles and inner organs freak out, so physio doesn't work. I started at the chiropractor when they moved into my local shopping centre and within one year she cracked my back into alignment and much of my muscle pain stopped. I no longer had lower back pain when standing for longer than ten minutes, and the migraines stopped for a good chunk of time.

Over the years, due to being a carer and having to bend and lift, my back has slipped out of alignment periodically and other issues arise. Currently, my fifth lumbar is hitting my sacrum, pinching my nerve and creating issues. I was told thirty plus years ago my fifth lumbar *looked* as if it had arthritis, but she does now. I've had shoe inserts custom made to my feet which helps and have worn arch supports for my flat feet since I was twenty. But they only fit in enclosed shoes, not sandals, so I wear sneakers with my new innersoles around the house in winter, and wear Scholl orthopaedic sandals around the house in summer so I have the support. It's helped cut down the calf and leg cramps caused by my lower back.

I found out at 43 that I have arthritic hands which isn't great for a jewellery designer and writer and found out years later I have arthritis in my back, knees and feet. I have osteoarthritis and take a medication my dermatologist first put me on for my nail psoriasis. It cut down the pain in my finger joints by eighty to ninety percent. My knuckles are still thickening, I can't stop that, and have the odd bolt of electricity shooting through them which can hurt like hell and makes me drop what I'm holding.

I have multiple skin conditions. Keratosis Pilaris on my arms and thighs which Urea cream helps soften. Psoriasis in my nails and on my scalp, and small bouts of eczema on my wrists and fingers. Advantan cream works well for both. I have spider and varicose veins suffocating my legs and ankles, pigment issues on my face. I have moles all over my body, and scars from mole removal. Normal moles, basal cell carcinomas, and melanomas. Since I was seventeen. Yep, I had my first melanoma removed at seventeen.

I have a fibroid *on* my uterus and have had the most monstrous menstrual pain throughout my life, thanks to starting at age eleven. I had an orthoscope to figure out why I was suffering from pain in my right side abdomen, but they didn't find anything. And, at this point I'm not even menopausal.

Then there's weight. Being a woman does not make it easy to lose weight. As each decade passes we need to try other ways of dropping the pounds and kilos. I did the gym for two hours a day, three days a week, for five months and lost nothing. I did the low carb diet in my twenties and that helped, but the loss from that diet slowed down into my thirties and forties. Low calorie works now, but only to get so much off and then I plateau. It's easy to gain and easy to maintain, just damn hard to lose and that's an ongoing battle which is why I took the medication my doctor prescribed.

My rheumatologist had told me to lose weight years earlier, and my doctor and I had tried different things. So, in my fiftieth year, I bit the price bullet and started buying injectable pens once I could find a chemist that sold it.

Semaglutide by name; Wegovy and Ozempic by nature. I started injecting on May 1st, 2024. I lost an average of two kilos a month by starting on .25 for a month and then staying on .5 for the rest of the year, losing 3 stone, known as 20 kilos, or 42 pounds by the end of the year. I had chosen to do it slowly, so my body gradually became used to it. In January 2025, I amped it up to .75 to get it moving, but in March, I went up to .1 to lose more before the first anniversary of taking it was up. As of this printing, in total, I've lost 4 stone, or 25 kilos, or 55 pounds.

So that's arthritis in almost half of my body, skin conditions over half of my body, other issues killing off my insides, and sinus issues that mean I can't fully breathe.

At the rate I'm going, I'm going to be a crippled, shrivelled corpse who suffocated to death.

I suffered panic attacks in my teens and twenties, but then, few probably didn't. I grew out of them towards my thirties and after losing weight. Weirdly, there was a study to corroborate that losing weight helped panic attacks. I haven't had them since my thirties.

And then there was the time, in the early days of line dancing, that other dancers and teachers kept saying I must be anaemic because I was so white.

No, I wasn't, because I'd had many blood tests. I just happened to be whiter than you.

And then there was the other time, as a teenager, I had all four wisdom teeth out and turned them into earrings. Because I'm weird like that.

The bottom ones came through first, followed six months later by my top ones. I was seventeen, and the tops were so sharp, they dug into the gum still partially covering my bottoms. I had the tops out first, at seventeen and a half. It was one week before my eighteenth birthday when I had the bottoms out, and I had to mash bananas and hot chips with a fork and suck them down, and sip soup through a straw because I couldn't move my jaw. They were the worst, killed me with pain, and gave me fat lips. I don't do well looking like Mick Jagger. Ten Panadol didn't work but two anti-inflammatories did.

It sucked!

I had told the nurse when having my tops out, that I was into making jewellery and asked to keep them so I could take them home and turn them into earrings. I soaked them for a week in bleach, then wrapped cotton around them and stuck a jump ring and hook into it. Two weeks later, when I went back for a check-up, I was wearing them.

The dickhead dentist demanded, "You did clean them didn't you?"

Well... DUH.

These days I only wear them when I go to the dentist, and they can't believe they're actually my teeth.

As I said, I'm weird like that.

As for my mental health…that's a whole other story and being an unappreciated carer shits on your mental health. Not being able to have a life, career, family, shits on your mental health. There are people out there who have only looked after a parent for a few months, or couple of years, and still don't believe that this life can be so bad because they either took time off from work or looked after them before they went into a home. Great, good for you, you did the job for a few months or years, not decades, like many of us.

The mental and physical health of carers is shunted to the

bottom of the pile and trodden on. People don't care about us. It's the job, just suck it up and do it. Why the hell should we? We deserve a life, a family, a job, careers, kids. We deserve to be able to jump in the car when we want to go somewhere. Why do we have to suck up a life we didn't want, or don't want any longer?

Hell, at eighteen I figured I'd have kids at twenty-eight. And then along came thirty-eight, and forty-eight. And all I can ask is why the fuck didn't my life turn out the way I wanted it to? Why the fuck is the Universe sacrificing my life for someone else's? I have no clue, but I'm not the only one, and fuck the Universe for giving power to a few, while ripping it from so many others.

*****

Back in the olden days, when I was young, I had insecurities like so many others. And I'm sure some people will probably poo-poo this, but I watched Oprah in the '90s and '00s and I learned a hell of a lot of lessons about life from all the experts who were on.

Two were from Dr John Gray.

It was a two or three day show he did and each day was a valuable lesson.

One lesson was, *if you don't like the family you've got go and get yourself another one. Whether it's your partner's, your best friend's, your local church or community group.*

Now, I get it, you're probably thinking how "blood is thicker than water", "we don't pick our family", yada, yada.

According to the law of karma we do pick our family for a variety of reasons, but I'm not getting into that.

What John explained was, that if your own family is treating you badly, go and make other people your family. Your partner's family, your best friend's family, your church group, your choir group, your whatever group. If you know a group of people that treat each other with respect and dignity, and you're already a part of that, make them your family. In most cases, unofficial family, but family nonetheless.

It was a lesson I still remember, and believe me, if I could get the hell away from my family I would.

But back to insecurities.

Another lesson I learned, and I can't remember who taught it, was *the day you stop caring about what other people think of you will be the most freeing day of your life.*

I changed it to, *the day you stop giving a fuck about what other people think of you, will be the most freeing day of your life.* You gotta add a strong word in there to make a point.

Many people, my mother included, constantly worry about people they don't know; people judging them, worrying about them, watching them, listening to them.

It's arrogant to think people you don't know are wasting their time and energy thinking about you, so why are you wasting your time and energy worrying about them?

Seriously.

All of those lessons seemed to make my insecurities ebb and flow away. Was I still a little anxious when meeting people for the first time? Sure. Was I still a little anxious about joining groups for a period of time? Sure. But those anxieties stemmed from being young and inexperienced, still needing time to understand how to "play" with others, even in my twenties. We're not yet real adults; we're still mentally teenagers. We need to learn how to be in society, and it takes time.

I never really cared if people liked what I wore or how I wore it. I grew up in the '80s. The fashion was amazing. I loved it, so I kept wearing it into the '90s and '00s, my twenties and thirties, and I still wear what I want now and still don't care if you don't like it because me liking it is the only relevant opinion from the only relevant person. I never had insecurities about my fashion sense. In my twenties I still had a few about my looks, my weight, and dealing with my family and parents. The anxiety was real. Having to deal with life was real.

By the time I was through my thirties and hitting forty I had no insecurities concerning anything else in my life. I don't have insecurities about my writing and jewellery designing, so no imposter syndrome for me. I don't have insecurities about who I am or what I do. The only one I have left after the last two decades, is my many skin and health conditions that I can't actually get rid of. I can treat them, but I will always have them. It makes me self-conscious about my looks.

I know there are women out there who bang on the drum about women needing to accept themselves and love themselves, but I call bullshit on that.

I actually don't have to like the way I look. I actually don't have to like the way I feel in my body, in my skin, in my bones. I actually don't have to accept the way I am or how my body works or looks. I have health issues that make my body work harder. I have skin conditions that will never go away. I have breathing issues that will never be fixed. I have a body that doesn't work properly, and I don't bloody have to accept it because I'm told I need to.

I will do what I want when I want in order to try and change or fix my issues and will continue to do so for as long as I need. I don't need to be told by a person I don't know that

I need to accept my body because you had issues accepting yours. I don't need to, and neither does anyone else. There is always something we can do, try, and practise in order to make ourselves more mentally and physically sound, and you have no say in that.

So when I turned fifty, the only insecurity left was about my looks, because I got rid of the rest of them with all of the lessons I learned in my teens and twenties.

Learn some life lessons, people, and stop giving a fuck what other people think of you. It's worth it, believe me.

*****

Many a decade ago, when I was a wee lass in my early to mid-twenties, I had to see a therapist in order to qualify for some medical thing. I won't mention what it was; it's no one's business. But he asked me a series of yes or no questions.

This was after my time at Myer, where we were taught to not ask yes or no questions because it meant the conversation would be shut down and we had to keep the customer talking. I remembered it clearly.

The therapist was asking questions and one was, "do you have any brothers or sisters?" I answered yes. Because it was a yes or no question, I gave him the right answer.

Well, he got pissed. Because I didn't supply him with enough information, he cracked a shit and demanded I say more. I told him, all the while thinking, *but I don't need to say any more, it was a yes or no question, and I gave a yes answer.*

Ugh, some people.

I don't know whether he did it on purpose, or whether he thought getting answers out of me was like pulling teeth, which it probably was. But then, I definitely would not have been the first person he'd seen who had withdrawn into their shell out of nervousness.

I mentioned my cousin passing away, and a few other health issues I had. And in the paperwork he sent to the company, he deemed me depressed.

I don't believe I was; I was just incredibly nervous and a wee bit scared, and if he couldn't tell the difference, then what sort of quack was he?

*****

When I was a child, I was a member of multiple fan clubs and would write into TV shows and newspapers. I even got my letter read out of TV.

When I was young, and we were living in Queensland, I watched a show called Wombat which included a puppet called Agro. After that ended, he went on to have his own show, Cartoon Connection.

Kids could write in to Agro and send him a bag of gravel which he loved to "eat", and in return the letters would be read out on TV.

Guess whose letter got read out on TV!

I nearly missed it, too. The TV was on, and I was walking from one room to another when I heard my name called out and my letter was being shown. I was so excited I ran into Mum's bedroom and got her out of bed. I was about 8 or 9 at the time and received the following letter from the bathmat (what he jokes about being made out of) himself.

He said he would keep my letter forever!

Well, I certainly kept his and still have it to this day. I've posted it on my website. I also have an Agro stuffed doll and a mug, they're around somewhere.

I love you Agro! *teeny bopper scream*

The Cocky's Circle Club was run by the Australian Family Circle magazine. I received a certificate with my secret club name of Kingfisher 335 (not so secret now), and I had to use that name in all correspondence. Club members would meet in the Junior Circle where I was entitled to claim prizes for any comps I entered and won.

Club members also solemnly promised to be kind to all animals, to care for trees, and to encourage others to do the same.

I became a member of the *Swamp* by Gary Clarke, fan club back on the 13th of June 1984, according to my certificate. I did a blog post about it in 2013 and posted it to socials, as one does, and posted the story on the Swamp Facebook page. Gary Clark couldn't believe I still had my paperwork, and as a faithful fan after so long, he asked for my address so he could send me some goodies. He not only sent four books, but he autographed them as well, and yes, I'll be keeping those for another 40 years.

Back in 1985 my mother signed me up to the Barbie fan club. I can't remember if it was just for here in Australia, but I didn't care. I still have the letters, the certificates, and eleven fan club news brochures.

I loved Barbie and have Barbie dolls and have bought several others over the years. What I'm after are the ones from every ten years of my birth, 1974, 1984, 1994, 2004, 2014, and 2024, and have managed to acquire a couple.

Just like millions of others I became a part of the Cabbage Patch Kid craze. I had resisted at first mind you, as the first ones were ugly redheads, or not very nice-looking blondes. I went without for a year or two until I found the one.

We found her in a toy store in Toombul in Queensland, as we'd travelled there especially to look for one. Mum bought her for me, and I received her papers via mail. Her name was Abigail Fiona. Yuck! And she was born on July 1, 1985.

But I soon renamed her Misty Blue King and received a new certificate for the trouble, and on her first birthday she received her very own birthday card from the hospital!

Since then, the kids have done so much stuff. They were all over the place, even doing an Aim toothpaste "Toothies" ad of which I have the poster.

And then there were the people who claimed theft, that thieves were stealing their babies in The Star Enquirer on February 1st, 1984. There had to be one somewhere.

Either way, Misty Blue has been my baby for way too long and I am feeling way too old! At least I got her out of her dummy, and her nappy, finally, when she was about 28…

In 1992, when I was eighteen, I joined the Indecent Obsession fan club. I'd been a fan of theirs since 1989 and had collected so much. I won a gift pack from a radio station which contained a CD, t-shirt, photos, and so much more. It also had a list of other things you could buy, so I sent off my money to the address and received the extras. I had managed to find another t-shirt at a market stall in the Central Market and cut the front off both t-shirts as I was going to make a cushion cover out of them, and I don't wear white. I still have everything from that pack, and most of my Indecent Obsession collection. The CDs, records, 7 and 12 inches, cassingles, cassettes, and folders full of clippings. I used to have the Spoken Words cardboard cutout, but that eventually went in the bin.

The last fan club I joined was in the '90s or '00s. It was the Nancy Drew and Hardy Boys fan club in the UK from the UK Pocket printed Case Files series. Both sets had colourful images on the covers. Nancy's had a flower with an image in the middle, and two petals were actually fingerprints and falling off. The Hardy Boys had a fingerprint with an image. They're incredible covers. In fact, they're one of my favourite versions out of all the printings. I received newsletters, two Nancy, four Hardys, one postcard, two door hangers, and two decoder wheels.

I also have the '70s fan club packs but was never a member because I was born in the seventies and knew nothing of these world-wide phenomenon teenage sleuths.

Times are a changing of course. Fan clubs in their original form are long gone. For many years, website forums have provided the information, the websites of bands, singers, actors, and also do the job where you can buy goods and support your favourite artist. In a roundabout way, they still exist, just in the electronic form not the physical.

And could I tell you about the CSI New York forum I was in for a couple of years. Yikes! When I asked whether or not a particular actor had a fan club that we could join the ridicule from one member almost made me leave within minutes of joining. Jesus, the younger generations have no clue how things used to be so shit all over it. Meanwhile, the bullshit that happened made a lot of people leave, even though the mods asked what the reason was that would make people leave, and then they never lived up to their changes.

The garbage spewed at me when I started calling Carmine Giovinazzo, who inspired characters in two of my books, Carmie, was an absolute disgrace and I was attacked and told to stop doing it. We Aussies give you nicknames; you don't get to tell us we can't because you don't, and it had nothing to do with disrespect, it was an endearment. Get over it.

Time to leave, peeps.

I also joined a forum to talk about Henry Cavill and then left within a year…

You'd think I'd learn.

*****

The year was 1988, I was in year 9 at high school and somehow, I ended up in a modelling class on Saturday mornings for one and a half hours each week.

We received a folder full of information about what we'd be doing every week, and every week I went. Since I was very arty and crafty, then and now, I decided to make a project book on my experiences and filled it in with brightly coloured pictures as I wrote all about what I did week after week.

When the course was over, we did a wine and dine runway show for the families of the students. It was at the Festival Arts Centre, and we models were backstage getting ready, our families were at their table watching with their wine, and I was first on stage.

It was embarrassing being the first to go out in front of everyone, more so when the host told me to imagine everyone naked. Not exactly the thing you tell a fourteen-year-old girl, mate.

I knew why I was there. It was because a girl in my class had done it the year before and I'm somewhat competitive, still am, but my two eldest sisters had also done one back in the '70s.

According to Mum, sister #1 complained to her about me

doing it, but then, she doesn't get the right to say anything when she did one herself. I have no idea what her issue was, but it doesn't matter at this point, as it didn't matter then.

As for my fellow student, something weird happened to her during the Christmas holidays between 1988 and 1989. When she turned up at school on the first day of year ten, she was completely different. Her hair was a straight bob cut on an edgy angle from one ear around to her chin on the other side, she smoked, and wore far different clothes than she used to.

Unless her divorcing parents were suddenly spending a shit tonne of money on her, or she had hooked up with a rich guy at the ripe old age of 14/15, I have no idea, and never found out, but it certainly got her a lot of attention for a few months. Maybe it was the aftermath of the modelling course. Maybe it was something else.

*****

Let me tell you a couple of stories about men.

When I was fourteen, I was standing in Target reading a book in the book section when an elderly man, possibly 50s or 60s, started chatting me up.

Yes, he chatted me up. Asked if I had a boyfriend, and many other things I cannot remember thirty-six years later. But I remember thinking, I need to be polite, that's the way I was raised. But don't tell him too much, just enough and hope he goes away.

What a weird bloody conversation to have with yourself. Even at fourteen. I don't really remember whether he left first, or if I put the book down and walked away. It doesn't matter in the grand scheme of things all these years later. But having to be polite at fourteen because that's the way I was raised, really didn't teach me how to deal with old pervert men.

Then there was the guy when I was sixteen.

We were having a garage sale, and towards the end of the day a guy turned up and bought our old TV and something else. Mum pushed me into helping him carry the stuff, something I hated with a vengeance when I was young. My mother always pushing me to do stuff I shouldn't have done. I carried it down the driveway to the path where his car was parked, and as he was packing the items away, he asked me out on a date.

Yep, he asked me out on a date.

It was awkward, it was weird, he said something else, and I stumbled and stuttered and managed a no, quickly walking away and feeling creeped out.

I was sixteen, uneducated when it came to boys, and certainly when it came to men. I had no idea how old he was, I'd gander a guess at early to mid-twenties. But even then, I wasn't interested, and even now it's like what the!

And then there was the so-called business mentor I saw in 2013…

But I discuss him in the jewellery section as it was in conjunction with my business.

*****

We first discovered line dancing in our state in early 1996, when my ex-brother-in-law was in a country band in the town where he and my sister #2 lived. So much more on that at the bottom of this story.

I saw a friend of the singer dancing in front of the stage

late into Australia day, the 26th of January, when most people had gone, and there were only a few of us left.

We learned about it over the coming months, learned some dances from the singer's friend, and would do them at the gigs.

We then discovered a line dancing club not far from us, after they ran a social night that the band was playing at, and the next thing I knew, we were heading to a couple of country towns to take classes.

A lot happened from that time, and I won't get into the personal side of things, so I'll just get into the dancing side of things.

We went from one small town to the next, met other members along the way, and found that they were jealous cunts who wanted to tear people down. And there were many.

We were lied about to others, not just by other members, but the mother of our line dancing instructor, with whom we'd become close. She spread rumours and lies because she was clearly jealous, and I'm not saying that frivolously. She made snide remarks and comments to us, and behind our backs. One day, in class, our instructor told her mother to move aside and asked me to stand at the back of the class to help with the instructions when the group turned around. The mother hated it. I loved it!

Our instructor gave us work books, jackets, and a few other things. We bought the rest. She travelled to a town in another state with us for a line dancing weekend, held many performances for the club team, and seemed sweet and nice. But she was having issues with the owner, and we got shoved into the middle of it.

Because we're loyal, when she said she was setting up her

own club, we went with her. So did a few others from her classes. But the night she started her new classes, there were issues, and we left, going back to the normal class we'd been learning in. The owner, who had taken her class, welcomed us back. And the irony is, he knew full well what she was like, as he had warned us not long before, telling us that we were sheep. We didn't get it then, but we got it after, and we didn't see her again, as an instructor.

We realised we'd been treated badly and made the decision to not keep following her. We stayed with the original club, but problems kept arising there, too.

I was treated rather badly by many members and instructors. They thought they could use me to teach them dances in the breaks at socials, and hate my guts behind my back, make them mixed tapes, write up dances, or help them with things. And I did it, because I was raised to be nice and polite and to help people. I was raised to not ask questions like, "where did you get that?", "how much was that?", and "who gave you that?" because the question is rude and the answer was none of my goddamn business. I was raised to stand in line and wait my turn instead of jumping the queue, like some of them did. I was raised to wait to be invited to sit at someone's table and not just sit down unasked, as many of them did. I was raised to not interrupt people's conversations and stand and wait for them to finish or turn to you and speak, because it was rude, as many, many of them did.

They would pretend to be interested in me, ask questions yet turn away when I started answering. They would pretend they were going to help me with something, like getting into the competition group, and then do jack shit because they knew I was better than them, but more than likely, because I was young and wouldn't be able to cover costs and travel, not that they knew that. This is understandable and a reason I have only just realised as I write this 26 years later. They treated me like some insignificant immature twaddle they could use and abuse, but when they did so, I turned my back and did no more for them.

The thing was; they hated me because I knew dances they didn't. They hated me because I was better than them. They hated me because I was younger with younger legs and a younger mind to remember ALL of the dances. And the instructors couldn't stand the fact that I corrected their mistakes when we were in class.

So fucking what!

I paid my hard-earned five bucks and I wanted to learn the damn things properly so I could dance them at socials. That's what we were all there for. That's why I was so damn good and could stay on the floor all night doing every dance that was put on.

Because I was that fucking good!

I was that good that people hated me. I was that good that women old enough to be my mother told me what to do, how to have my nails (which were long and painted all the time), how to wear my clothes, how to dance in line-ups. They wanted to know where I got my shirts from, my country and western accessories from, my jewellery from.

I was that fucking good that people hated me, my clothes, my accessories, my guts, and my dancing feet. And yet they all wanted what I had and tried their damndest to replicate our clothing when we very stupidly told them who made them. Before we knew it, many were turning up with similar style shirts.

The bitches couldn't help themselves; they had to attack while trying to be me. And it just didn't work because I was better than all of them.

We went to the Tamworth Country Music Festival in 1998 to line dance. It was an amazing ten days, once we were there, and stinking hot, but we'd saved for months for it. We bought clothes, got into clubs to dance, and shopped up a storm when we weren't dancing. I saw '80s singers Paul Norton with his wife Wendy Stapleton in a Chinese restaurant, and Channel 10 stalwart, entertainment reporter, Angela Bishop, in a pub at lunchtime. And we went to a Lee Kernaghan concert.

But some people just had to make the experience unpleasant.

First off, the owner. As he was going early, he offered to take some of us, and Mum and I scored two seats, as did two of our friends, and a fifth woman we didn't know.

He'd outfitted his line dancing van to accommodate us and our luggage and had booked hotel rooms in a town halfway for us. With our money, that is, and that's important to this part of the story.

We took off a few days before everyone else, and made a few stops along the way. It was fun and exciting, but I soon learned he loved to make a mockery of what you said or did, and he mocked me a couple of times. But what pissed me off was this. When we stayed overnight in our hotel at the halfway mark, I didn't order breakfast because I didn't want anything on the menu. I was trying to keep to my diet at the time because I knew we'd be eating a lot once we got there. Well, he dared to criticise me over not having breakfast because "he'd paid for it".

I didn't realise for quite some time, years, probably, that *he* didn't actually pay for it. *I* did. He used *my* money to book my room, and breakfast came with it. If you're going to rub people the wrong way, lie to their face about what you did with their money.

Then there was the woman we didn't know. I don't even remember her name, but she was a pain on the way and created issues once we got there. Luckily, we only saw her for a couple of days before everyone else turned up.

And when that happened, then there were issues with an instructor. I'd had dealings with her before. She'd raised her hand to me to quieten me when we were waiting for a demonstration, and she'd asked a question. She had asked the owner, but you know how it goes when you're nearby, you answer. And she threw her hand up and didn't even look my way.

But I looked at another dancer next to me who we knew and was performing with me, and we both had an incredulous look on our faces. As for the bitch, she was a bitch and had become known as one. She tried some fancy footwork during the demonstration and fucked up royally, all because she was showing off and trying to look good. She didn't. She was also next to me and I made no mistakes because I did my damndest to not let her shit ruin my performance. Suck that, bitch!

But in Tamworth, she complained about us. How we'd turned on the light in the boys' college dorm room we were staying in, when we got back late one night. How we were rowdy and noisy and left the lights on when we went for a shower.

I know she complained to the owner, because she was complaining to him as I passed her, and he glanced at me.

During all of this, I had to deal with a woman who was forcing her son on me. We would go to a monthly social in a particular area and meet up with friends. She would come over, say hello, and make small talk. As time went on, she would linger longer and longer and talk about her son. He was twenty-six, had depression, but owned a house, and had $40,000 in the bank. Like…he was a catch!

I was early twenties then, single, not interested, and just wanted to dance. She was often times rude to me, like the time I was dancing, and she was on the sideline at our table and called out hello. I nodded my acknowledgment and kept on dancing. She then complained to Mum that I didn't speak to her. No, I didn't, because I was on the floor dancing and wasn't going to stop to talk to her so I nodded my acknowledgment of her. Jesus, some people.

Then came the time things came to a head. After months of being hounded and joked about concerning me and her son, which we all brushed off, we went to the club for our social and had dinner there beforehand. Once we were finished, we walked into the room where we'd be dancing and settled at our table, had drinks, and was waiting on the instructor to turn up to get the party started. But who arrived first? Yep, with her son in tow.

Jesus fucking Christ. She dragged her son along to our line dancing social to introduce to me and walked up to our table and bold faced said, "why don't the two of you go for a walk and get to know each other?"

What the actual!

I didn't know him from a bar of soap and barely knew her, was pissed off that she had been doing this and never taken the hint that I wasn't interested, and now I was embarrassed to the core and in such an awkward situation. I very politely declined, made some mumbled excuses, as we women do, and she finally got a clue and walked off with the son running along behind.

Bloody hell!

The instructor arrived and the dance got underway, but during the night, I was headed for the bar to get some drinks and she followed me again. I can't remember if the son was with her as I wasn't really looking. But I managed to tell her she'd put me in an awkward situation and I didn't appreciate it.

She told me, *"Oh, he got the vibe."* I don't recall much else of what she said, but she walked off soon after and I stood there thinking, if only you'd got the bloody vibe earlier that I wasn't bloody interested.

We danced from 1996 through to 1999. It was a great time, excluding all of the arseholes who wanted to make our life hell. We line danced a bit after that when the band had gigs and we went along. Some of the line dancing crew would be there, or sometimes not.

We had Christmas socials. I invited Aussie quartet, Human Nature to one, but they turned me down. We had demonstrations in schools, pubs, clubs, shopping centres, pretty much everywhere. We travelled and danced and learnt dances with other instructors from other states. We stayed in Mildura and Tamworth, we bought lots of western wear and music, and had a ball. And damn if I don't miss it all, all these years on.

If I could turn back time, I'd head back to the '80s, and the late '90s and relive those years over and over. Because that's what music and dancing does to you. It fills you, lifts your soul, and sets you free.

Now, onto sister #2…

When we first started following the band around, she became partners in crime with the partner of the guitarist.

They would bitch about the singer's friend who also followed them around and they'd say nasty things. But that wasn't unusual for my sister, she'd said nasty things about me for years. Although I wasn't the only sibling she spoke ill of.

She and the other WAG (wife and girlfriend), as I'll call them, ganged up and thought they were the bee's knees. They weren't. They were just nasty and rude and tried to drag us into it. And it didn't stop.

When we went to one of our first shows, it was with Craig Giles, and was for a line dancing company who had a social at the same time. It was the first time we'd seen it as a group, and it was the one we ended up joining and the one I speak about above. But the wag just couldn't help herself, she had to get in an attack, and I put her straight back in her place. My sister bitched a bit that night too, so Mum and I ignored her and had a good time despite both of those bitches.

We got into classes and socials after that and continued for three years.

A couple of years into it, 1998 to be specific, when we had a line dancing Christmas social, I had lost weight in the months leading up to it, so I was speaking to the wife of the bassist about it and #2 waltzed up. She interrupted by making a snide remark. I put her in her place and kept on talking to the wife. #2 realised she was being ignored and walked away.

At some point, either the band broke up, or stopped touring, and we didn't see any of them again. Then Queensland happened so we didn't see #2 for a couple of years either. But that meant we didn't have to put up with the rubbish from the partner of the guitarist, and we all went our separate ways. In one respect this was sad, because dancing, line and country, and listening to bands and going to country dos on weekends was actually a great time. It's a pity it didn't last long because I still love music and would still hit up a line dance class or social if they were around.

*****

Of course, Tamworth isn't the only place I've been to, especially when travelling for line dancing. Mildura was another place, and we had been there many times.

If I name every town and city it would be a long list.

When I was young, we went to Queensland for our first holiday, and a year later we moved there for four years. We travelled to many places while there; Gympie and Bundaberg to name two, and we lived in a few more. First we lived at Bli Bli in a caravan park just down the road from the Fairytale Castle, renamed years later as Sunshine Castle. We then moved to Cotton Tree opposite the beach, then Maroochydore, Buderim, Alexander Headland, and Maroochydore again before moving back to South Australia.

In South Aus, we've also been to many places.

We went on holiday to Melbourne in 1987 and saw many towns in Victoria. We travelled to Queensland in 1994 with my grandfather, and then down to Sydney, New South Wales to meet Mum's brother's family. We saw many places, including Luna Park, Wollongong, and Campbelltown where they lived, and even more towns on the way up and back.

We went back to Queensland in 1998 with sister #2 and her then husband—I've mentioned those stories in the family section—and saw many more towns. We've then travelled to Broken Hill, Mum's birthplace, and all towns on the way and back, with sister #2 and her then boyfriend, sister #1 and her youngest son, in 2014, and Jesus Christ the stories I could write about that.

And I have, in the family section as you would have read already.

*****

Back when I was 18, in 1992, I did a retail sales course for about four or five weeks, and at the end of it we had to do a week's worth of unpaid work at a store of our choice. I chose Target, but that's not the point of this.

A lot of things happened in that course that I still remember so clearly because it had an effect on an 18-year old's brain. There was a clique due to members knowing each other, so they would huddle together, and bring stuff and then exclude the rest of us from what they were doing. I wasn't the only member who noticed; an older lady certainly did, and we had a conversation about it.

There was snobbishness from one member, not that much older than me, because she didn't like me cracking jokes during a session, even though the instructor laughed and didn't mind. The course wasn't serious, so we could have a joke and a laugh, but I think she was just too serious about herself and her life as she appeared that way through the whole four weeks.

We did a test to see which one of us would qualify as an accountant. There were two of us; me and a male member. That completely surprised me because I failed maths at school, but the test clearly said I'd make a good one.

Nothing came of that, and looking back, accounting was probably something I should have tried out, or studied, as it would definitely come in handy now.

Then there was the game we played where we had to stand around the table and answer the questions the instructor gave us. If we said yes, we moved to one side of the room, and if we answered no, we moved to the other.

We were given one particular question and I answered no, so I moved to that side of the room. I was the only one. And instead of it being a peaceful, "hey why did you say no", I was shouted and yelled at by the rest of the group who were trying to convince me to change my mind.

I didn't because I believed in my answer. And still do to this day.

Did the instructor do anything to ease the tension? Of course not.

Could I have turned my back or walked out and taken a breath? Sure, but I didn't, even though I was being attacked.

To this day, I don't understand why people need to yell at others to change their minds. I fully understand that families do, and mine have done that, but people you barely know? Why would you do that? Another person's opinion is theirs to have, not yours to destroy.

Oi, people!

Life is weird.

You meet many people, pass them by, chat to them in the street, live next door to them.

But not once do you think someone you've spent four weeks with will end up dead.

There was a girl, although I should say woman, 24 or 26, in my course. She was one who knew others in the class and so they got along. Yet for me, one day she just rubbed me the wrong way.

I've always hated being told what to do, and one day,

when we were having a make-up expert in to tell us how to do our make-up for work, we had to come with none on.

I did, along with the other girls.

Once the woman explained how to apply shadow and mascara, foundation and blush, we were allowed to put our make-up back on.

I started applying it the same way I did every morning. It may not have been an expert job, but I still pretty much do it the same way today and it was not a problem.

Yet this girl in my course seemed to think it was, and she told me so.

She proceeded to tell me exactly how I should put my make-up on and that I was doing it the wrong way and I should try something different.

Of course, I bristled at that. Who the hell was she to tell me when lo and behold she wasn't taking her own advice?

I said something, can't remember what now, but it didn't go down well in the room, because the expert proceeded to place her hand on my shoulder, yes, *my shoulder*, and told me to calm down.

That didn't go down well either, and since her hand was at my eye level, I gave it a dirty look and then my attention moved up to her face and she removed her hand but continued telling me, *me*, to calm down when I started nothing. And did nothing wrong except defend myself.

I hate that. Placing a hand on one's shoulder is patronising and an invasion of space. I hated the expert and her patronising hand.

I also hated this girl in my class for telling *me* what to do and yet she didn't even take her own advice, but simply put her own make-up back on the way she did it every single freakin' day.

Hypocrite.

Some years later there's a story in the news about a young woman that had been murdered. I heard her name. It sounded familiar. I saw a picture of her and knew exactly who she was.

That feeling, the one inside that makes you mildly freak out at having known someone who was murdered is weird. Weird and strange and not normal.

A while later, we saw sister #1 and she commented on how nice and polite she looked. I sat there thinking, "yeah, bullshit she is", but didn't say anything and let it go.

It's funny how you can form an opinion of people based on a photo, or someone's testimony about them, but that's not to say that's how they are with everyone. We all rub people the wrong way, just as people rub us the wrong way, and you never know who's going to disappear because of it.

*****

Following the job search course, I ended up with a six-week Christmas job at a huge department store. It's an institution and has been around for over a century, but that didn't stop staff being rude to newcomers.

I had been trained for two weeks; that was it, training for two weeks. For the first week, we sat in a room and talked about the business and different aspects. In week two, we did more of that but moved into the adjoining room to learn how to use cash registers.

During this week, I got into trouble for turning up late from lunch. In my defence, I didn't know we only had half an hour, I had been told at twelve to be back at one.

I had been in our normal room when the instructor

started telling us about lunch and deciding on a time to be back. I stuck my head out the door and asked another member who was walking towards me what he'd said. She told me that he'd said to be back at one.

But she either lied to me or got it wrong herself, because she was in the room when I got back, so it was only me turning up half an hour late and going bright red but trying not to let it affect me.

The instructor called me back at the next break and asked why I was late. I could have stuck her in it, but all I said was I was caught up in the other department store in the shopping centre, and they didn't do the job we'd just trained to do.

I was eighteen. Maybe I should have just told the truth. I didn't speak to her for the rest of the week, and she didn't bother speaking to me, so, maybe she was in the wrong and didn't want to admit it because she was embarrassed. But then again, maybe not.

On the cash registers we learned to take cash, give change, charge credit cards, and give refunds. The basics. What we weren't told to do was to ring up stores and price check items we had without saying we were from the store, or to ask another register to change out a large note for change.

Both of these things I got into trouble for with a particular staff member, and she did it in front of customers, leaving me embarrassed.

I don't know how long she had worked there, but her attitude was not friendly. She didn't know me from a bar of soap, nor I her, but as I'd been raised to be polite, I was to her and the rest I worked with. But I think the expectations on a new young staff member were ridiculous. To tell them to do something without telling them how, and then telling them off, seems stupid and counter-productive to me.

How was I to know how to do those things? I barely had decent training.

And don't get me started on the time the manager grabbed me right on the dot of five as I was leaving to tell me I needed to stay and work until nine when on the paperwork I'd filled out I'd explicitly said I wanted a twenty-four-hour warning.

They didn't care. They didn't care how they treated me. They didn't care how one manager disagreed with the other and left me confused. One had an issue with my festive nail polish for Christmas; my manager didn't. What the fuck was I supposed to do?

For some reason, so many businesses seem to have the most basic screwed up issues concerning how things are done, when it would be so easy to figure them out and change them. Instead, you treat staff like shit and then wonder why you lose money, lose staff, and go out of business. It's because of you and how you treat people.

*****

In 2012 the playground one house behind us was being bombed and blown up.

I dialled 000 and after about five minutes, the police and fire brigade arrived and put out what was still a burning fire.

The next morning, I went to the park and expected some of the play equipment to be on its side after being blown up, but all I found was a black mark in the dirt.

Unfortunately, this wasn't the first and it won't be the last thing that happens in my area...

Every New Year's Eve we get fireworks going off, and one

New Year's, the ex-neighbours across the road thought it would be funny to let off fireworks in the intersection of my street and theirs. *Three times* they did it. How stupid.

Christmas Eve and New Year's Eve 2004 saw the old neighbours behind us get one of their two palm trees in their front yard burnt down, and their fence borders my house at the back, so I was out hosing down my roof and lawn. There were two other fires in the neighbourhood that night!

And then there are the accidents, murders, and deaths.

- A car sped down the main road, spun out of control, and slammed into the corner of a house.
- Another car sped down the road and smashed into a tree. The tree died; he didn't.
- There have been shootings and murders around the corner at the soccer centre.
- A guy across the road tried gassing his family to death and attempted to blow up his house with all the cops, ambos and fireys outside, and all the neighbours watching, of course.
- A man down the road tried to kayak across the strait between South Australia and Kangaroo Island with a mate and they both drowned.
- A woman had just returned home from a stint in hospital, to be left alone in the house bedridden while a cigarette set the spare room on fire, and she ended up back in hospital and died.

I found that quite suspicious as she didn't smoke, was in her bedroom, and there was no one else in the house, and yet a cigarette was smouldering in a waste bin in the spare room. Highly suspicious.

- There have been rapes, murders, break-ins.
- In the early years I had kids bang on my window late at

night or ride their skateboard down my path and along my porch.

- I've had an attempted house bombing from someone leaving a parcel of barbeque heat beads smouldering on my porch.
- The flat across the road was broken into by kids, and when I called the police and they came and took statements, and then took the kids, who had the guts to come back for more stuff, they told me nothing was going to happen.
- I've had my outside light globe stolen and a garden frog statue put on the porch as some sort of offering instead.
- Our first next-door neighbour painted cars and had a lot of paints, acrylics and solvents in his yard and then one day his backyard started smouldering and he wasn't home. His wife also got drunk one night and banged on their door yelling and screaming down the neighbourhood. They also claimed their van was stolen and torched, but I have my suspicions.
- And then there was the morning I found a dog in our backyard, walked around the house to see if it had dug its way in, and since it hadn't, called the RSPCA. He came and took the dog, and the woman from next door drove past at the time he was loading the dog into his van.

Her husband later asked Mum about the dog that had been chucked over the fence.

How did he know it was chucked over the fence? Said his wife had told him. But since she didn't know the story, it was clear he did. And the only way he could have known is if he knew who threw the dog over or did it himself.

- We've had three neighbours to our right, three to our back, and multiple across the road. The current across the road neighbours not only have a massive rat infestation and no, that wasn't inspiration for my T.K. Wrathbone story, *Infestation*, but they keep dumping their trolleys on our corner against our fence.

In fact, he has dumped so much over his fence and against ours that we can't be bothered reporting him. He dumped a piece of sectional sofa over the fence right as the NAWMA recycling truck came around the corner. He then dumped that into a trolley, filled up a second trolley with weeds, and dumped them both beside our fence. Another time he strolled out of his driveway wheeling a trolley with an old TV in it, and then dumped it beside our fence. His visitors also dump their trolleys beside our fence. Not sure why our corner is so great when he's on one himself. It's as if we have an invisible trolley bay there or something. Just into New Year's 2023, I counted ten trolleys on the corner as if some kind of weird nesting ritual was going on and they were breeding in multiples.

It was weird. Strangely weird.

- And then, on Christmas Day, 2024, someone set fire to the paddock attached to the cadet barracks just down my very road and behind the shopping centre I live behind. It was one o'clock and I was standing in the kitchen opening up the slab of ham we were having for lunch, when I saw white smoke in the air down the road. And then I heard a low flying plane which looked like an acrobatic plane. And the fire helicopters turned up, and cops sped down the road and blocked it off, and fire trucks went in and out of the streets down the road to do something, and the plane bombed retardant on the houses and the paddock. Yeah, Christmas Day 2024 was a hoot.

- When we first moved here, the neighbour across the road came along and introduced herself. She was the local Avon lady and shoved her way into everything. She shoved her way in and invited herself to our food. She shoved her way in and heavily hinted at wearing my earrings for New Year's one year. She even told us that her friend down our street thought we were lesbians when we moved in.

I'm sure this imaginary friend didn't, as it's fairly obvious where the lies and rumours came from.

When we had new people move in behind us, she barged her way over there and pushed in.

We were all invited to lunch one day, and the four of us ladies were in the dining room chatting, while the two menfolk were outside, and I'm speaking to the owner of the house when the bitch from across the street loudly tells me to shut up. I turned from the homeowner and we both stared at her and then each other, shocked that someone had said that out loud.

My mother said nothing either, and I said to the homeowner something along the lines of, "clearly, I can't talk to you in your own house". The shock didn't wear off.

*****

Following on from the intro of this chapter, there was a time I did almost win the lottery and it pisses me off that I didn't listen and follow through. Every time I tell this story people are shocked by it, so here it is.

One month after my 27th birthday, in June 2001, I came down with the chickenpox.

Yeah, I know.

And because I was so ill with fever, spots, and pain, we

stayed home as you should. During this time, I didn't shower for days due to those millions of spots and pain but gave myself a sponge bath in the bathroom. In my feverish state as I slept, a voice kept telling me to buy a System 6 ticket in the big Thursday night lottery.

I wondered why I'd be thinking about this. I was sick. I certainly wasn't thinking about the lottery at this time, but the voice persisted over several nights.

Because we stayed home that meant everything was delayed. The shopping, buying of lottery tickets, and other things, but finally, I was healthy enough to go out and we went to a small local shopping centre in the next suburb over.

We did some shopping, and I got my lotto tickets there, not even remembering the voice. We also had car issues, so that took up our brain space. It wouldn't start, and we had to call the road service, but then it did start, and I cancelled the road service. It was an old shit car; it had regular issues.

When we finally got to go to our shopping centre that we live behind, we walked in what is known as the Kmart end, and as we headed for the entrance of a supermarket called Foodland, we passed the newsagent that was to my right, and that voice popped up and said, "go and buy a System 6 in Thursday night's lotto".

And what did I do? The same thing millions of women do. Made excuses and didn't do it.

I've already bought my lotto; I don't need to buy more. I don't know how much a System 6 costs; I can't afford it.

And I kept on walking into Foodland.

Well, do you know what I'm going to write next?

That Thursday night, when the big lotto went off, 23 million dollars went to a couple in my very suburb with a system-freaking-6 ticket!

Why I didn't listen to that voice I don't know. All I can say is that I was sick and not even in my own mind. Why my muse, guide, helper, the Universe, waited until I was sick and not in control of my brain, I don't know, but that was a life lesson that was damn hard to learn.

I was twenty-seven, and looking back on it in my forties, I realised that many things would have happened, and I would have stupidly gone along with it. Whereas now, I wouldn't. I don't believe, regardless of knowing what I would do with it at twenty-seven, that I would have fully been in control of it. There would have been a particular parent dictating that I hand over half, and stupidly, at that time and age, I probably would have. Whereas I won't now because I know full well it would end up in the hands of my siblings, as it would have then, so why would I give any away. We're not that type of family. Regardless of all the sucking up my siblings have done to Mum over the years by giving her small sums of money, there's no way my lotto money will end up in the hands of my family. I have plans for it. Big, huge!

I once heard a person on TV say something along the lines of, *if the Universe really wants you to win the lottery it will do everything it can until it happens. Even if you don't listen the first time.*

Well, I'm still waiting on that. Come on, Universe, where's my money!

*****

We've had a lot of things happen over the years, as most neighbourhoods do. We've had dead birds, a bird play dead, and he did it very well, academy award winning well, and lots of baby birds born. We had a brown snake slither across our front yard. We even had a massive black rat with black beady eyes get himself caught between the metal mesh and the metal pattern overlay of the front screen door.

And I saw a UFO.

And yes, I mean, by definition, an unidentified flying object, which, by the way, has nothing to do with aliens or a spaceship. It's just an object that was flying that I could not identify.

It was cylinder-shaped, and I thought it was a zeppelin. I saw it out my window in the distance, slowly moving in the sky to the left. It went behind some trees but didn't come out the other side. It didn't go back the way it came, it didn't go up, but it sure as hell didn't keep going past the trees. It simply disappeared. So yeah, a UFO! And not the first time, either. But that was in another neighbourhood.

This area has had so much stuff happen I declared a long time ago that it had bad karma. The whole area just has bad karma. Too much shit happens, and while I know other suburbs and states do have stuff happen, and Queensland is one of them, it's a place I desperately want to move to, because I know that shit won't stop happening in this neighbourhood, but at least I can leave it.

What is Okay?

What *is* okay?
Mediocre, Average
Above or below
Middle of the road
Don't feel this way or that
Not good not bad
Not recognisable or sad
Bottomless pit I'm falling into
But not climbing out of, Just stuck
Hovering in the middle with nowhere to go
Going nowhere
Middle of the road
Average
Not okay.

Caring

In 2013, I wrote a book called *Carers Need Help and Support Too: One Woman's Personal Journey Through the Sacrifice of Caring*. I published it in 2014.

I decided to unpublish it about six years later, for two main reasons. The first was that a review had been right. The reviewer had called it a rant. And it was. Of course it was, it was my journey as a carer and what happened to me and how it came about. There's anger and hatred in it and how life doesn't always go the way you want it to. The other reason was because it didn't suit any of my names moving forward and I had grown and moved past it and there was no need to have it out there anymore. The time for ranting was over, I was moving on and setting up a publishing house. In 2023 I saved it in my essay folder instead. But when I came up with the idea of putting together a memoir, I pulled it back out and went through it to see how much I could add. Because it's still relevant all these years on.

I've given it an edit, and narrowed it into focus, removing some small sections that I made into bigger stories in other chapters. It's funny how some things come back around. But even eleven years later, it's still relevant to how I feel and how my life is, because while not much has changed, and a lot has grown worse.

*****

I am so bloody tired.

So tired of not only doing all of *my* things, but all of *her* things, the *household* things and *everything* else like dealing with all the tradesmen that keep on coming.

So tired of sitting in hospital and doctors' waiting rooms since I was ten. That's thirty years of my life and ongoing, as of this writing. The only one wasting time doing shit I don't want to do, never *wanted* to do *and hate* with a passion. Because with her visits it's *her* pain and *her* issues, hence *her* anger, resentment and hatred. Those three things have slowly wound their way into my heart, body and soul like evil black tendrils of poison slowly eating their way into me, my blood, my veins, my arteries, to clog and congeal like death.

I used to be happy. I really did. Before my parents became angry. Before I realised my siblings hated me. Before my parents split up and my mother transferred her hatred for my father onto me with digs such as, "you're just like your bloody father", "someone else used to do that to me too", and "you definitely take after him". Thirty or so years I've heard that. Thirty or so years I've heard anger, felt resentment and grew hatred for the way I was treated like shit. As if *I* didn't matter. As if *I* only existed to look after her.

Unfortunately, your environment is not always good for you. Not good for your body, your health, your mind. Good for nothing really, except turning your life into shit.

What was once a happy place has turned into anger. I feel

as if I'm living in the evil Queen's castle. Pick a fairy tale, Cinderella, Snow White, Sleeping Beauty, any one that has an evil stepmother dressed in black and staring into mirrors or smothering themselves in creams from the fountain of youth. I am living in a black, ugly, horrible world, life, existence. The evil has enveloped me. Your environment definitely depicts how you will turn out.

The people in your life, in one way or another, be it neighbours, family, colleagues, will rub off on you. It's all got to do with you being happy and they are not. They shit all over you to make themselves feel better and you end up wondering what the hell is wrong with them and why are they being so bloody rude. Regardless of what you say, or do they don't change, so you get angry that these people cannot see how badly they are treating you and really, they simply don't care that they're treating you like shit. *They.just.don't.care!*

They just want to do it to make themselves look and feel big, important, and better than you while making you feel small and belittled and like scum.

You grow angry, resentful and eventually as bad as them, sniping and whining about all the things they did. And you *know* it's not you, the *real* you, deep down you know you're quite nice away from them and relate well with people who are happy and upbeat because that rubs off on you too. Positivity does rub off on you in the right place.

You get to be yourself with others and not a controlled doormat because you can't control your life with these people. That's why you become two personalities. An angry one with them and a happy one away from them. *Or maybe that's just me!*

You *want* to be happy. You *know* it's in you. You *know*

it's in there somewhere. Other people think you're fantastic but the person you have to look after thinks you're nothing but a piece of shit, a doormat for them to walk all over and dump their crap over. You're their personal toilet to shit in when they feel like it and they feel like it often.

And regardless of how much you stand up for yourself, regardless of how much you know what *really* happens and how things *really* go, they will *always* blame you if things go wrong. They will *always* blame you no matter what. Ridicule it as if they know better. Call you a liar if they believe they know the truth and that you're not telling it. Accuse you of all and everything, deny *they* are wrong, deny they *did* wrong, and deny they are *ever* wrong.

They are right, *they* are pure, *they* are almighty. It's delusional. *They* are delusional and believe their own bullshit because they believe their bullshit is one thousand percent right and all powerful. It's tiring. It's exhausting. It's bloody mind numbing.

I didn't *want* to do this. I didn't *choose* to do this. I *don't* get paid, I have *no bloody* qualifications, I have *no* life, *no* partner, *no* kids because all of this was dumped on me as the last in the family. They don't help. Why would they? They left home as soon as they could in the seventies. I was left as the only one at home because I was very young, and as I got older I didn't know what I wanted to do but it sure as hell wasn't to be a carer.

I had hopes and dreams that were thrown by the wayside.

At fifteen, I wanted to be Australia's answer to Debbie Gibson. I had the denim jackets with funky brooches, I wrote songs, and had a high ponytail. I had her tapes and memorised the lyrics to her songs and used hers as inspiration for my own.

I wanted to take singing lessons to further my ambition of being the Australian Debbie Gibson, but she wasn't interested and told me so.

I should have realised then and probably did, that she was simply not interested in helping me achieve anything that I ever wanted to do or to be in my young years.

The years went by, and I wished I had gone to the Marleston TAFE which was just around the corner. It had clothing and accessory design, but high school had been bloody tough, and I really wanted to get away from the whole stupid schooling concept.

More years went by, and we moved north so we were close to my grandfather. But that didn't stop her being unsupportive.

We started line dancing, did trips and tonnes of socials and lessons, and in the middle of it all, about 1997, she started having joint problems. That's when it kicked into high gear.

Even though I had spent fifteen-plus years of my life trailing around to doctors, now we had even more surgeries, more doctors, specialists, pain, anger, hatred, resentment.

After her knee replacement in 1999 we did end up going to Queensland with sister #2 and her then husband. Mum needed to be wheeled around the theme parks and shopping centres. My sister was such a bitch and needed to be punched in the head, but instead of saying anything my mother shooshed me because we had all come in the same car and needed to get back in one piece and not on our own.

One more year came and went, and I was not allowed to say anything.

She also got worse. More pain, more doctors, more anger, hatred and resentment.

And then there's me. My problems became worse as the

doormat of that anger, hatred and resentment. Going without, being told to stop being selfish, stop being a bitch and think about someone else besides myself. That's *all* I got.

That became my life as I ended up looking after her, going to doctors with her. But the anger *had* started years before, so why would it be different now?

It started when I was a teen, most likely when my parents split; I always copped the negative, the anger. Every time I was excited about something I'd done she'd pick out the mistakes, if I'd made any, or tell me I should have done it differently. That hasn't stopped. There is a big difference between being a supportive parent and a negative bitch who believes in pointing out all the things you did wrong as some kind of parental need to do.

Over the years I've tried doing stuff, and *have* done a lot of stuff for myself, but I simply stopped telling her about them or what I was doing at the time.

What would be the point?

I knew what she was like, what she would say. It would all be negative. "Why'd you do that?" "You should have done it that way." "I don't like it."

Parents are supposed to be the champions of their children, the ones who support, coach and lead. But they aren't. Many aren't. And mine sure as hell isn't.

When I started writing I never told her I had written a novel. *Why would I?*

Back when I was eighteen I figured I'd have two kids by the time I was twenty-eight, and be on my third or fourth, *at most*, relationship. When I reached twenty-eight there was nothing. No partner, no kids, no life. No nothing!

I had decided (rather stupidly at the time, because so

many are still stupid at twenty-eight) that I would consider drastic measures at thirty-two if I didn't have kids, or more specifically, a partner, but when I turned thirty-two I couldn't be bothered and had no money, and no partner. It was a very stupid thing to think and looking back now I have no real idea what I *was* thinking, let alone *why* I was thinking it. *Stupid, idiotic, naïve me!*

I was now thirty-two and still living with and caring for her and still dealing with all of her shit that got dumped on me, and I had no idea what the hell to do. But I still had time. Didn't I? It was 2006, and my life was shit and disappearing before my eyes.

As for my writing career, my first novel was something I had wanted to write after reading a Jackie Collins novel and the idea for a villain stuck in my head. Eventually I wrote it in July/August of 2006. I didn't tell her. I just joined writing sites for advice, sent it off to publishers and did a whole load of stuff where it was concerned.

In 2008 I wrote my second novel, sent it off to publishers and competitions, and it was only then that she found out because I had to rush off to the library to finish photocopying three copies of it for a publishing comp because I had run out of ink.

She never read it. I never wanted her to.

In 2010 I wrote my third novel, and in 2011 learned about self-publishing. I did it all myself, stressing myself out by getting two books edited, assessed, formatted and then put up for sale which took six months from go to whoa, looked at getting number one redone, found out things I needed to know and do, edited and released my first in 2012. I did it all myself and she still hasn't read them. I don't want her to.

I know what she'll say so what's the point? Nothing positive, nothing decent, she'll just whinge and whine about the swearing and sex and say I should be ashamed of myself for writing it or tell me she would have done/written it this way.

For the same reasons I don't want her reading my author blog, even today.

I knew as an author I needed a website from before my books were published, so I set it all up on Blogger, all by myself, and went live on January 1st 2009.

She didn't know about it and still hasn't read it.

While I was doing all of that I was also setting up a jewellery business. As the lady with the amazing clothes and jewellery, it was probably expected that I was going to make and/or sell jewellery at some point in my life.

I had a psychic reading done via mail early 2008, and while she was completely wrong about everything else, I did follow her advice and decided to do some WEA courses. My mother complained but drove me as she didn't want me "going on my own".

I started buying goods on eBay and from wholesalers here in Aus and she complained about the money I was spending but certainly didn't mind taking stuff from the bulk lots I bought and having me make earrings and necklaces for her.

I had someone take photos and do the original website. She complained about that but then so did I. My time and energy were wasted, and I was pissed off at the people wasting it.

The woman who did my original site pissed me around, took my money for doing nothing, told me everything I "should" be doing because she'd "also done it on Myspace and had parties". But she wasn't in it for the money; she just wanted something to do.

I *was* in it for the money and with the determination to start an actual business and grow it into something big. Besides which, I'd had nose surgery and was still in the recovery phase while making the jewellery, getting the photos done *and* getting business cards sorted. She pissed me around. I haven't seen or talked to her since. I don't like people who piss me around and want nothing to do with them. They are time wasters and money spenders. *Your* money, not theirs, so they don't care about wasting time because it means more money for them. She couldn't even tell me how much to pay her. She rang up, spoke to Mum, didn't want to speak to me, complained that I owed her and needed to make a payment, but couldn't tell me how much to pay her. How idiotic is that? I had to push to get a price out of her. As I said, "I can't pay you if I don't know how much to send."

2008 was not a good year for me.

I'd also had *bad* pain in my lower right abdomen and knew it *might* be from stress. With having written a second novel, sending it off to publishers, starting a jewellery business, and setting up blogs, in January of 2009 I asked my doctor for a referral to a specialist to see if I could reduce the stress. By specialist I mean psychiatrist.

While the woman setting up my website was wasting my money and my time, my mother was criticising my business name choice. The first thing out of her mouth when I proudly showed her my business name certificate with *Jewel Divas* on it was, "shouldn't it have been around the other way?" My heart sank. You'd think I would have learned by then.

She had also come up with a list of names before even bothering to ask me if I'd come up with any and was then disappointed when I said I had one, as though *I'd* wasted *her* time.

I saw that psychiatrist for six visits across six weeks while all of this went on and I talked her ear off about everything going on at that time. And it did help. In the short term.

Talking always does. Getting it out of your head is helpful. My mother was suspicious the whole time and I could just tell she wanted to ask things and say something. She also questioned everything I did about the business, trying to come off as more business minded and more of an expert in the field when she knows stuff all. I had nowhere to vent, but while venting in the short term helped, it didn't change the long-term problem.

My pain stopped for the meantime, but the stress continued. Part of it was the normal stress of trying to run two businesses, make enough jewellery, blogging, writing, getting books good enough for publishing, getting a website up and going, dealing with hosting companies, you know, the usual. My author blog was the place to vent. It was the only outlet I could come up with. I vented my frustrations, anger, hatred and resentments; *everything that had been building and unfortunately, five years later, it's worse.*

I try not to vent as much as it's now an official author blog and not just a place to bitch about my problems. But life is worse and more stressful. And I still need a place to vent.

After the hassle with the original jewellery website designer, I had to hire an actual company and have them redo everything. That *too* was not only a waste of time and money, but the way they ran their business and dealt with customers was ridiculous.

I also started a jewellery blog from July 2009, along with

multiple social media sites I'd figured out how to use and decorate myself. And that's quite a strenuous task in itself.

So that was one website, two blogs, two sets of social media, making jewellery, taking pictures, getting it up for sale on the website, plus pain, plus being treated like a doormat, seeing a shrink and having a laparoscopy to find out the source of my abdominal pain on Dec 1st leaving me flat on my back for three weeks and making me gain one stone. That's fourteen pounds or six and a half kilos for those who use other terms.

It was one hell of a busy year!

Back in 2010 my second book was wanted by a publisher, but after thinking long and hard I had to say no. She knew about that too as she'd answered the phone one day after they surprised me with a call. She didn't say too much and didn't ask to read them.

I didn't want her to.

She has brought it up on the odd occasion, like some sort of accusation, *oh woe is me, my daughter doesn't let me read her books.* One time was in March 2014 when I had to go and see an accountant to sort out some tax business and I mentioned that money was coming in dribs and drabs from sales of my books.

She said, "Books, you mean there's more than one? I thought you only did one."

I said, "Yeah, so, I did more than one." Not that it's any of her freakin' business.

Why do I need to tell her my business? She sure as hell doesn't tell me everything she does, and I don't want or need her reading my books and doing nothing but criticising me. I don't want or need that shit in my life.

The worst years ever, thus far, was 2012-2013.

I published my first-written book, turned thirty-eight, didn't win my *Scenic Tours* holiday on *The Today Show*, and knew I had to do something two years out from my fortieth to change my entire life, but didn't know what. Come August, everything changed again.

At this stage, I'd been going to a chiro for two years due to severe back issues and chronic sciatica, and in August she finally got to go to the Royal Adelaide Hospital's Spinal Clinic (after our doctor piss farted around for two years putting the forms in, just one more person who pisses me off by wasting my time and energy) and besides being told there was nothing wrong with her even though a cat scan said she had bulging discs and sciatica (yep, the so-called specialists did a MRI and after pissing her around for another month because he was on holiday told her there was nothing wrong with her), she herniated her back.

We're not sure what exactly happened, but she couldn't walk or move and couldn't sleep in her bed, so she slept in the lounge room in her recliner for a couple of months.

That first day it happened was a bad day. A bad, bad day!

We got a call from the Housing Trust about a visit, I got a migraine and my menstrual cycle, and *she* stuffed her back. I was in full on pain for four days straight. Migraine pain, menstrual pain, back pain, because my back went out bending over to help her, and no sleep pain because I didn't sleep. *At all!*

It was non-stop 24/7 looking after her.

I became angrier, more hateful, more resentful, not only at her, but at God, the Universe, my guides, my helpers, my angels, life in general, to the point I was so physically, emotionally, and mentally exhausted I knew I'd never experienced exhaustion like that before in the previous fifteen plus years, or *in my life time*!

I also wished she would die. It wasn't the first time and I know it sounds bad. But that's what hatred, anger and resentment does. So does pain. Pain was *never-bloody-ending.*

It was all about *her*, even when I kept telling her I couldn't bend over to pick her legs up because my back was stuffed, and I was in pain. *She* didn't care. It was all about *her* and me looking after *her*. It didn't matter if *I* was in pain or how bad that pain was, I was there to look after her in *her* time of need and that's all there was to it. I was only there to *serve her. Nothing* more. And she's still like that now. My pain does not exist to her, it's only her pain in her delusional world and I and my pain do not matter. *At all!*

I kept telling her we needed to get help in. We needed someone to come in and do the vacuuming and help with the dusting and cleaning the curtains as I couldn't bend over or reach up. It was the worst time. I couldn't do anything without pain searing through my lower back. But she didn't want anyone. No matter how much I harped on about it, no matter how much I kept telling her, she just didn't want anyone in to help and I had to do it all.

During that time, she made several stupid comments over the way I helped her into bed, once she was *able* to get into bed that is. First, she claimed I wasn't a good enough nurse, that I didn't know how to treat her, and nurses would do better. I've never been, never will be, and *am not* a bloody nurse. I *was not* getting paid to look after her. I *didn't want* the bloody job, *never* asked for it, wanted it, and couldn't wait to get away from it.

The other stupid comment was something like, "just as well you don't have kids, I'd like to see how you treat them!" It was stupid because *when the hell was I supposed to have bloody had kids?* With my life being taken up looking after her, when the hell was I supposed to have found a partner to have kids with? I haven't had the opportunities or time because she's needed looking after. She's been a control freak who has worn me down. Besides, there is absolutely *nothing* here in my area for singles to do anything and it's not as if I could go out for hours on end or have a night to myself without an argument or bullshit.

Back in 1999, when she had her knee replacement, she didn't mind me walking to the library, doctor, or the shops to carry home food, drink, a new microwave, or get her prescriptions filled. I didn't have a licence at the time and walked everywhere.

She had no problem with that. *No, no freakin' problem at all.*

But as the years went on and her body stuffed up, I had to go shopping. Every time I suggested going somewhere on my own she'd use the same excuses. "The car has problems." "I don't want you going on your own, it's not safe." And if I needed to go somewhere she would complain that she was in pain and didn't want to go.

That's what she does. She uses her pain as the excuse to get out of doing things. *Doing anything.* And I have to suck it up and deal with it by getting angry or silently crying.

I got so bloody sick of the arguments and missed out on so much. Functions, friends, concerts, markets, dos. *All because she's a bloody control freak.* I accused her of that one day and she denied it. *Of course!* I told her I was sick and tired of her excuses for me not going anywhere on my own and missing out on so much. I know it's most likely my fault for not forcing the issues, but that's what happens. Arguments ensue and you really don't want to deal with them because *it's bloody exhausting.* And when you're exhausted you don't feel like doing anything, let alone arguing. Let alone fighting for your own rights and freedoms to do what you want and be the person you want because you just can't do that.

Since her back pain in the early noughties, it's been going downhill. The troubles in 2012 that went through to 2013 escalated a million fold.

I was a book behind and needed business advice. I couldn't find it, and got a mentor who was an arsehole. I decided to transfer my jewellery blog, which had been a style site for two years, over to WordPress, so I needed a new hosting company. The old one was screwing me around and I needed to keep blog posts going, plus set up the new blog for migration. I also closed down my old jewellery website and set up shop on MadeIt instead to ease some of the emotional and mental burden it was all becoming.

I got blocked by incredibly stupid people on Facebook for incredibly stupid reasons. Why block someone because they write something you have no comprehension of? If it's one thing I learned about certain types of bloggers and businesses it's that they are nothing but two-faced hypocritical bullshit artists who will jump at the chance to preach all about positivity and not wanting any negativity on their page, and yet they are the ones rushing to judgement and acting negatively towards *you* by blocking *you*. *Bloody morons!* Nothing but control bloody freaks who just want to ruin everyone else's lives and I already have one of those living in my house, thanks very much!

I had to get a new novel written. I decided to write a jewellery book and take the photos, plus this book, plus a guide to self-publishing and one about why positivity can be a bad thing. I had to get a new jewellery collection made and *still* had to look after her. And also, I had to fit in my chiro who noticed the changes in my back.

I also saw a counsellor late 2012-13 for ten weeks. The initial reason was to find a way to get to Queensland, find a way up there and a place to stay, but I ended up seeing a different person and she was of no help at all because hello, *I'm still fucking here.*

That's the problem with being a 24/7 carer. That's the problem with being the family member that gets *stuck* with the job. We have no life, no partner, no friends, no kids, no opportunities to have them, find them, or make a life with them.

We have nothing. We have fucking nothing! We get left behind, stuck behind, ditched, dumped and thrown out with the bath water and the rubbish bag.

It's different for older people. They get the chance to go off, have jobs, lives, partners, families and then they get stuck caring for an old parent. But the stress of looking after a parent *and* kids plus running a household and holding down a job is too much and eventually either a nurse is hired, or the parent goes into a nursing home. I wish she would.

For young people, we never get the chance for all of that. That's why, at my age, I feel so sorry for kids who are dumped with the adult responsibility of looking after a parent or sibling. And there are many; I've seen them on TV and in articles. They're applauded and congratulated on being a wonderful child looking after Mummy when she needs help most.

But do they *ever, once,* stop to think that these children, which is *what* they are, should *never* have this adult responsibility dumped on their poor little shoulders?

Of bloody course not. Adults don't give a shit as long as they don't have to do it.

I've seen kids as young as six and eleven, charged with the care of a parent. *What the bloody hell!* They can't look after themselves, tie their laces, get their own food, or get their homework done without having to make sure the parent gets all of their medications, gets their food, and possibly feed them— and what about getting them to the toilet or shower?

Where are all the bloody adults that should be doing this job? Where are the bloody carers? The helpers? I feel so bloody sorry for kids that get dumped with the job of caring for a parent or sibling. They are sacrificed like the little lambs they are.

Does *anyone* care about them? Does *anyone* help them? Does *anyone* think about *their* life, *their* future, and *their* possibilities?

What do they have? What do those poor kids and teens have if their life is now taken over and taken up with caring for a person 24/7? It's not as if *they chose* the job. It's not as if *they* get paid for the job. And what happens to their own learning, their education, their relationships, children of their own, partners, family, life, future?

Some think it's great. They're caring for a parent who loves them, and they would do anything for, yet…that's *now.* What about in ten, twenty, thirty, forty years when they grow up and resent that parent? Their life is gone, and they have nothing because it was taken away from them the day they started caring for that parent or sibling.

And partners? I guess it all depends on your partner's disability and whether or not you *want* to care for them. Some people leave their partner if they become disabled in an accident or from illness. They realise they cannot cope with the stress and strain of caring for a disabled person and walk out. I seriously don't blame them. They have the choice of whether they want to care for a partner or not. For those who stick around they stand by them, for better or worse, maybe not realising the enormous amount of work it will be and how bad "worse" will actually be, the stress, the strain, the exhausting nature of it all. Exhausting, mentally, emotionally, physically. No wonder people walk away. I wish I bloody well could! And I really believe that if I do end up with a life and a partner, I will not be able to care for them either. I have done this for too long and hate it too much to essentially transfer to caring for another person I did not choose to care for. We either hire someone or I leave. It will all depend on my mental stability at the time. If that even happens, of course.

What's out there for carers, as in the partners, parents, children of the person they're caring for? *Nothing!* It's not as though we're being paid a wage. It's not as though we get to leave and go home to our own place at night. It's not as though we have a life and get to go home to our own partner or family. It's not as though we get holidays and annual leave. This job is 24 freakin' 7. It's painful, exhausting, and it can leave you angry, hate-filled and resentful.

I remember back in 2007 when Jackie Collins came out to

Australia. She was on a show called *9AM with David and Kim*, and it was either Carer's Day or week and they asked her about being the carer for her husband and fiancé. She said something I vaguely remember; it was along the lines of, "everyone is so busy caring for the person who's sick, making sure they have everything they need and are not in pain that the carers are forgotten about. The carers are the ones bearing the brunt of the anger, hatred and resentment of the person who is sick or dying as they vent their frustrations with what's happening to them."

No one cares for the carers. No one cares that the carers are the ones bearing the brunt of the sick person's frustrations. And what about the carers? What about those of us having to put up with the hell we have to live in?

They don't care. They're angry, hate filled and resentful of what they are going through. They don't care that they are dumping their shit all over us. They don't care if we get upset at their treatment. They don't care if we want to do something with our life or future or do something to take our minds off it. No, they don't care because it means our attention is taken *off them*. They don't care how *we* feel, what *we* want, what *we* want to do. To them we *have* no life. *They* are our life. Outside of them we should *have nothing*. We should *be* nothing. Nothing but doormats for them to walk all over. Toilets for them to shit in. They don't give a bloody fuck about the parent, child, or partner looking after them.

Don't get me wrong, I'm not saying it's *all* people. There are many who understand their carer partner/child/parent needs a life or hobby, and there are many carers who do have that. Unfortunately, I'd say there are far more angry resentful arseholes being looked after by helpless, hopeless people, be it parent, child or partner who feels they will die where they are because they can't see a way out.

We know *what* we would love to do. *Have* our own home, our own life, our own job or hobbies. Go *where* we want, when we want, how we want. We know *how* we want to live our life. We know *what* we dream about. What we *think* about. What we *wish* for. We just don't know *how* to go about getting it. *How* do we move if there's no physical or financial support? If we have no family or friends to rely on as a place to stay, if we have no money to move to and live where we want to live, if we have no idea how we'll get there, where we'll stay, how long it will take to find a place? Will we have the money? What about moving our stuff; what about transport? *So many questions we just don't know how to answer.*

We know *what* we will do, we don't know *how* to make it happen, unless we win money, a house or we apply for and get a job that's interstate and provides a house or apartment to live in or find a way out of where we currently live. Without money or physical support, we cannot change our life. We certainly can't rely on other family for help. They are busy living their own lives to the point they don't give a shit, especially if *you're* caring for a parent. All they want is what they'll leave behind when they die. Yep, experienced that one.

They don't see or care for, they don't ring or write. They know you are there so you will do everything. They'll just rock up when the parent dies to get what they think they are owed or deserve. *Selfish bastards!*

The shit I've had to deal with because they cannot be bothered giving a shit about their mother! But she doesn't get that. She doesn't get that they don't give a shit about her, that they don't care about her in any way, shape or form. Oh no, to her they are off having and living their own life because apparently, I'm not entitled to or deserving of one.

Oh no. I don't have a life. My life is to serve and slave away looking after her. I realised in 2012 when she herniated her back that that was the expectation. That I was only born, or there, to look after and serve her. That's what my life was for, for looking after her.

To her, I am nothing. *To her,* I will be looking after her for the rest of *her* life. *HER* LIFE! Never mind having one of my own. Oh no, I *cannot* have a life of my own.

An acquaintance jokingly said she was going to set me up with her brother who was forty and in I.T., but then realised he still lives at home with their mother.

I said, "But I'm nearly forty and so do I."

Mum said, "Or maybe that should be the mother still lives at home with her daughter."

Which makes no sense in any way, shape or form since the house is in her name, the bills are in her name and she wasted *my* money on our clapped-out car.

I told our friend, "Well, hey if he can help me with my computer problems…"

Mum then said something really stupid, like always, that's really telling of her thoughts and what she thinks of me. It was something like, "you're not looking for a bloke."

Later at home she said something like, "I don't like the idea of her trying to set you up."

Yeah, as if it had anything to do with her. That comes back to my mother being a control freak. She said to me one day, many a year ago, "I know you better than you know yourself." *BULL.FUCKING.SHIT!*

No one ever knows you better than you know yourself.

You are the only one in your head. *You* are the only one thinking what you're thinking, dreaming what you're dreaming, wishing and hoping and wanting what you're wishing and hoping and wanting. There is *no way in absolute hell* that *anyone* will *ever* know you better than you know yourself.

She didn't know I wrote novels. *She* doesn't know I've written this and three other books because it's none of her damn business. *She* doesn't know what I do online except when my sister "reports" back to her. She'll tell me she saw what I posted or wrote about and will then tell Mum all about it. I've no idea why she's so childish but I'm over the bullshit.

On Christmas Eve 2013, we had no phone or internet due to a technical fault and I Instagrammed about it. Sister #2 saw it on FB and then tried ringing Mum's mobile phone. We didn't hear it, so we didn't answer. We were sitting watching the Christmas carols when the cell phone rang again and I answered. My sister was so pissed off that we hadn't been answering her calls she was angry the moment I answered. *Fucking seriously!* Sister, you need to get over that bullshit because you've been shittin' it for ten years. Yep, every time we didn't answer the mobile phone in ten years she got shitty. Never mind the fact that when she does ring, and we don't answer she doesn't even bother leaving a message. She's an idiot like our mother. In fact, she and Mum are so similar in the backward way they think these days that it's bizarre. She then "reported" to Mum what I had written.

I asked Mum after she hung up if she'd "reported" what I had put on my FB wall and that it was stupid and why did she feel the need to repeat everything I put online.

Mum said she hadn't done that and didn't see it that way.

I said, "that's exactly what it was", and Mum said, "why, don't you want me knowing?" and I said, "what I put online is my business, it's not hers to run to you and tell you about it, and you know I do Instagram and stuff and I'm not going to explain it to you every time because you don't understand it anyway." Talk about freakin' control freak!

She needs to stop. My sister the dibber dobber needs to keep her nose out of other people's business when she can't even sort her own shit out. In fact, she once claimed that "she had been chosen to deal with the family's issues" and we pissed ourselves laughing.

We had another of our million fights because she sees her "other" children differently to how *I* see them, even though their father treated her worse than mine did. Of course it's clear. *They* can do *no* wrong, *ever*, regardless of what they actually do. Though that's all they've ever done, and I do nothing *but* wrong, apparently.

I'm the stupid bitch that's here wasting her life away cleaning up after a hateful angry woman, getting her meals and snacks, helping her in and out of bed, her lounge chair, the car, and every door around the house. Do the full vacuum, change the beds, do the dishes, carry the shopping, move the furniture, make all the phone calls because she can't even be bothered doing that, and getting yelled at because I get angry at having to jump up and down to be at her beck and fucking call while trying to watch one of my favourite shows while she gets to sit on her arse watching hers. And then she has a go *at me!*

I fix the TVs, the VCR when we used one, the DVDs, put her CDs in the player because she can't be bothered doing that, help her put her clothes on, run around the house like a bloody chook with its head cut off because she wants something, and on top of all that, go to the doctors, get her walker in and out of the car, make sure she's got food and water, help her in, help her out, and run her prescriptions into the chemist almost every bloody week and *still* try and run two businesses, and get my own health and dental done.

Like all the years she didn't want to travel ten kilometres to the closest Skin Cancer Clinic because it was in a town she didn't want to travel to and whined about "why isn't there one in this area". Fucking hell, if it ain't in "our" area she ain't interested in going.

For five years I kept getting on her to get to the cancer clinic so we could get checked out, but she just didn't want to go until I finally cracked a shit and told her that it was all well and good for her to tell her other children to go and get checked out, but she can't even be bothered getting us to a clinic and I should be checked out even if she didn't want to be because she'd already had a melanoma and I was at risk of getting one.

She relented and I called, and then found out they had moved to a suburb on the other side of us that's twenty-five kilometres away, so it's even further than the suburb she first bitched about. And because of all that waiting, I found out I had two cancers and had them removed; a basal cell carcinoma from my left arm and a melanoma from my left hip.

Yep, because of all of her piss farting around I ended up with skin cancer because she used her pain as an excuse to not travel; to put off what was so enormously important. Yet she certainly goes for her breast screens when she gets the papers, so why she put off going to the Skin Cancer Clinic, when she had a melanoma herself cut off in 1984, I don't know. All I can put it down to is she just doesn't give a fuck about me, just herself. *Thanks a fucking lot!* Fortunately, they removed it all and I'm okay, but that's not the point now, is it?

I'll be going back the day before my 40th birthday, and will probably have more cut off, all because she couldn't be bothered going because it was not in the area we live in.

I also have to make the phone calls for tradies to get stuff fixed around the house, make calls to fix all of her shit, like her phone, plus do *my* countless tasks, make jewellery, write, blog, keep across online stuff which is a bloody fulltime job in itself and when I do she whinges, "I don't know what you do online/on that computer all day, but it makes you angry."

What makes me angry is I'm trying to do *my* job and get *my* stuff done and all I want to do is sit and do it without interruptions or the hassles of looking after someone, but you keep yelling out for something, making me jump up and run around the house a million times instead of asking for it all when I'm actually up and helping you.

Seriously, she waits until I leave the lounge room and am just sitting down in my office before calling out for something else. *Bloody seriously!* I've explained to her what I do, *a million bloody times*, so she knows full well. She just refuses to understand or acknowledge it so she can use it against me in arguments to throw back in my face. And she did that in 2013 when we had a big blow up and once again she threw it back in my face and I told her, *"You know full well what I do because I've told you, but you don't give a shit you just want to attack me with it."*

She disagreed, of course. Because *she's always right*. I'm always wrong. She does attack me with it and went even further. "It's not a business; you haven't made any money."

Ouch! That hurt. *Of course* it did because it's true. It's not from lack of trying though and she pulled that card again in March 2014 when she said it again, about having not earned money from my jewellery so I can't call it a business if I'm not making money. However, I make money from my books, and since I am releasing more books there is more chances of making more money, so yes, *I do have a bloody business!*

The point is, she *never* supported me in anything I did with my jewellery business. She just whinged and whined and complained about the money I was spending on the goods to make the jewellery in the first place. And she still whinges and whines about me not having enough money to move to Queensland whenever we get a credit card bill and I have explained it all to her time and bloody time again it costs money to run blogs, pay for domains, hosting, my chiro, goods, etc. She still doesn't understand about internet stuff and I'm over telling her every time she asks because she doesn't give a shit anyway.

But she still says it. "So, *you* won't be moving to Queensland then." *Not. One. Ounce. Of. Support.* That's why I don't tell her about my books or what I blog or post online through my author blog and social pages. It's mine. It's for me. It's the place for me to be free.

Although I have mentioned the hatred I've got and *some* things I've blogged about and the idiots I encounter and she said something like, "I hope you're not doing anything bad like swearing." Hell, my sister will tell her what I post, but Jesus Christ, no support means failure. And I've failed in part. I know that. I don't need someone who has no bloody business acumen *at all* to tell me that. It's like knowing you're fat. There will always be someone who will keep telling you

you're fat and need to lose weight, because they don't believe that you know it or get it. Let me tell you, dickheads, *we fucking get it!*

I know there was probably more I could have done to sell my jewellery and myself as a jewellery designer and business but there are no markets out this way and no stores that take on designers wholesale, so it's been a bloody hard slog to get myself known.

In 2012, I decided I needed to see a business expert and rang my local business centre as I'd dealt with them years before. However, due to lack of government funds they were unable to help me and directed me to my local council and someone who *could* help.

I rang and found out there was going to be sessions for small businesses coming in the next few months. After phone calls and arrangements, I made an appointment.

She didn't like that either because it meant she had to sit in the car, *not* that she actually *had* to. I made the appointments to be before my counsellor appointments so they would be the same day to make it easier. I told her in the beginning to stay home so she didn't have to sit in the car, but control freak her *had* to come, to keep an eye on me and so she didn't miss out on anything. *Regardless* of how much pain she was in.

I saw the business expert a few times and in 2013 he sent me a link for a social media conference, and we could get four hours of free mentoring if we went. It was a hassle to get her to agree but we decided to go shopping afterwards so it was a full day out.

Well, about a week and a half before it was the Easter long weekend, and she decided to fall out of bed at seven-thirty a.m. I spent two hours trying to get her up, stuffing up my back within seconds, and finally had to knock on the neighbour's door for help. They called the ambulance, but got Mum up themselves as I had at least got her on her knees.

Well, a week and a half later, on the day of the business meeting, she tripped over a rug, fell into her chair, spilt her breakfast and the first thing out of her mouth was… "This wouldn't have happened if you'd carried my breakfast in." That's right, blame me, *again.*

I told her breakfast was not the problem, her inability to get rid of rugs was. She had been told that several times by other people, paramedics included, to get rid of them because they were a safety issue as she's been on a walker since stuffing her back. We rang the ambulance again and managed to make it to my meeting. *Barely!*

Four months later she fell out of bed again at one-thirty a.m. I was fed up after the first time and a week and half later, as if right on cue, she tripped on another mat. This time she ended up on the floor and she said if my door had been shut she wouldn't have fallen. Mind you, she was always bleating on at me to keep them open for air. *For bloody God's sake woman, make up your fucking mind!*

I told her that she really was not listening to what the Universe was trying to tell her.

She said, "What?"

I said that she needs to make it easier for herself, as in new bed, new chair (she's got both, but bitches about the bed) so she could manage better. She seemed to think about it, but she is a very slow learner and would rather argue about doing everything her way and how she wants it done than listen to someone that she needs to cull and clean out to make life easier for herself. I had to harp on for years about getting a new bed. And even now she just will not throw things out to make it all easier.

Her adult comprehension is incredibly seriously lacking. It's as though the older she's got the younger her brain has become, reverting back to a child that cannot understand the simplest of things. She cannot understand how simple things work, how to do things, or how to put them together. Comprehension is sometimes beyond her. It's backwards because that's seriously how she comes across with the way she thinks things through.

She likes to blame the pain in her shoulder for not lifting her arms, the pain in her back for not getting up, the pain everywhere else for not doing things. She likes to blame her pain for everything and it's the only excuse she really uses. I'm not sure if that makes her lazy, stupid, or useless. *Or all three.*

If there was ever an emergency or fire, she would not be able to go out the window. She could only go out a door *and* on her walking frame so she wouldn't be able to move with haste and would probably die in the fire. Hell, I'd either leave her there or die trying to get her out. And what's the bet she would *still* blame me. Blame me for the fire, for not getting her out *and* for dying in it. Yep, she'd blame me because it would *not* be her fault!

And if we had a break in, she would not be able to fight or move to get out or away. If she fell over, she certainly couldn't get herself up and I've clearly proved I can't get her up either due to her weight, lack of ability and my stuffed back.

This place is a freakin' death trap in more ways than one. At least throw shit out and cull regularly, but she has great hoards of stuff and junk that she doesn't wear, need or use. But apparently it will "come in handy one day," or, "I might wear it again one day." BULL.FUCKING.SHIT! The place is bloody packed to the rafters.

It's a bloody hard slog trying to make things easier by cleaning stuff out, but she fights bloody tooth and nail every step of the way and tells me to deal with my own shit and don't worry about hers. Yet *I'm* the one who's cleaning out her shit and moving it and dealing with it because she sure as hell doesn't and can't, and *then* she wonders where something is because she can't find it. She can't find a lot of things and would rather accuse people of stealing it over her putting it somewhere she can't remember. Jesus Bloody Christ!

She also seems to think "we" are still moving to Queensland. We lived there when I was a kid and I've wanted to move back since 1989, but I realised a long time ago that she's not interested in moving again.

Why 1989?

Well…let's just say a Queensland band called Indecent Obsession made me want to move back there. I was fifteen when they came bouncing onto the music scene in their ripped jeans, funky jackets, catchy tunes, and one hunk of spunk keyboardist!

When I was eighteen, I was sitting in a doctors' office somewhere in Adelaide and leafing through a magazine while she was in getting an exam. I came across the live music page where there was a snippet about I.O., as they were affectionately called, and the gigs they were playing in Brisbane. Even now I remember that tug on my heartstrings, if I had still been living in Queensland and not come back to shithouse Adelaide then I could have gone to their gigs. I remember that twinge. I remember that article. I remember that hallway where I was sitting. It was narrow, slightly tropical, and made me ache for Queensland. *And* Indecent Obsession. *That* is why I've wanted to move back since 1989.

For her it's "one day". Well, one day has been happening since 1989 and will *never bloody happen* because she does nothing about making plans or actually going.

If one of us won lotto or an Art Union house, although that would be me since I'm the only one buying tickets, she expects "we'll" be up there in weeks. Never mind the fact she has so much crap she refuses to chuck out *now*, but apparently thinks she'll get rid of it if "we" win lotto or a house.

I've often told her "One day will never come", and, "if you can chuck it out if we win lotto then you can bloody well chuck it out now." Hell, even Dr. Phil says something like, *one day never comes unless you make a plan and set a date.*

She doesn't get it. She has to hang on to everything and it's tiring. She thinks, and this gets back to before, that I'll still be living with her forever. That "we" will move to Queensland. That "we" will have a nice flat or apartment. That "we" will have a life up there.

I know there is absolutely no way in hell she'll move, unless she wins lotto, or I win lotto and give her half. Yeah, like *that's* going to happen. And I know there is absolutely no way in hell I'll be moving with her. I *do not* want to waste the next twenty years of my life looking after her and wasting away into an even emptier shell of the person I already am.

I *do not* want to be sixty, single and childless because she consumed my life, sucked the living soul out of me, emptied me of all goodness and happiness and replaced it with her own angry venomous hatred. If I won lotto or a house I'd be up there within two weeks on my own and that's just all there is to it.

She has enough to move up there. She should have; she's taken thousands of my money and saved her own while I went broke trying to make something of myself. It would be easy for her to move up there. She expected me to pay for half a new car. I barely drove the old one, why should I pay for a new one? I told her to spend her own money and buy it herself, I had no money. She didn't like that. In fact, she greatly criticised and tried to guilt trip me. *Well, tough! You made me bloody broke!*

Twenty years of my life wasted. And let me tell you, if I knew then what I know now, I would change *so much*. I'd go to a different school, finish school, go to Marleston TAFE and learn dress design and accessory making. I'd get a job and save for my own car and move to Queensland. I'd do things *so* differently.

My parents are the ones to blame for us leaving the Sunshine Coast. When we lived there I was seven to eleven years of age, and when we left I had no say in the matter because I was too young and didn't make the decisions, so I hate them for it. If we'd stayed, my life may full well have been *very* different. *Better*, even. As for now, I know it comes down to *my* choices. I'm an adult. I *choose* to not live here, this place, this life with this person. But I don't have the money or the support to do anything about it, and that bloody sucks! I have the choice to choose happiness, yet I have no happiness within me. That left a long time ago along with compassion, forgiveness and understanding. They all fucked off out the door and up to Queensland and never came back. I have *nothing* to be happy about.

You can only understand someone's anger and frustration for so long. You can only have compassion for them and their situation for so long before you have been treated like shit one too many times and it all fucks off out the door for a better life, leaving you behind, the shell that you now are, to deal with the shit that's left over, the shit that's still to come.

I watched *The Secret* many a year ago and Oprah suggested a mood board or folder. Well, I did all of that. I made a red folder (good feng shui) of coloured scrapbook paper, made double page spreads and looked at it every day. *"Dreaming is ninety percent there,"* they said. *"The hard work's done,"* they said. *"You can have anything you want,"* they said.

BULL.SHIT!

If that was the case my books would be mega best sellers, my jewellery business would be a bricks and mortar store, I'd be living in Los Angeles, married to Michael Weatherly and living the life *I* wanted to live.

Yep, I would be! *No, I'm not kidding, I really would be!*

What they don't tell you is that you have to work bloody damn hard at what you want to do. It doesn't matter how hard or how much you dream, that bloody dream is *nothing* unless you slave your guts out making it happen. *And if it doesn't actually happen, what then?* What do you do when the one thing you've slaved your guts out over never comes true?

We're all here to learn life lessons. Love, forgiveness, compassion, understanding. I understood that a long time ago. I stopped having compassion a long time ago. There is only so much you can give before you realise it doesn't work and you're now an empty shell.

Some people being cared for *claim* they want compassion, forgiveness, understanding and help but really don't. They just want someone to shit all over and do their bidding.

Well, I'm over it. I've been over it ever since I was a teen. Since her anger and hatred for my father got directed at me. Since her control freak nature has told me, but not in actual words, *"you cannot leave me, you do not get to have a partner or a family, or a life or a career. You do not get to do anything on your own or without me. You have nothing, you are nothing, you will be nothing."*

She once said, in the heat of an argument when I was about twenty-three and she'd taken my TV away as "punishment", *"who do you think you are? You're nobody special."* Hard words to come back from and she never remembers what she actually *does* say to me, which she proves all the time. She just makes all the shit up, like when she tells people I said this, or did that. It makes *me* look and feel bad and people look at *me* as if *I'm* a bitch because they don't know any better and automatically assume that everything out of her lying mouth is true. I said something to her about that one day and she said, "So, who cares, it's not hurting anyone." Apparently she didn't consider that lying about me and what I don't say and do as not hurting me and thus she's saying she doesn't care about my feelings or me in any way, shape or form. She just doesn't get it.

She also loves to disagree with everything I say, and I'm constantly accused of being rude and impolite, of yelling or screaming when I'm actually not. She doesn't want other people "hearing" what I'm saying so tells me to be quiet or shut up, and says, "what will they think". *Like I give a bloody shit if they do hear.* It's *none* of their business anyway and unlike her, I'm not arrogant in thinking they *actually are* listening and *actually do* give a shit. I'm constantly told I'm rude and any discussion is vehemently disagreed with, shit all over within seconds and is rude and obnoxious. I'm not entitled to think an opinion, feel an opinion, or speak an opinion, and I apparently have no idea about anything unless she's the one putting it in my head because the way she was raised to do it is the only way apparently. Never mind me actually doing things my way because I'm my own person with my own way of thinking and doing things that are easiest for me and my back issues.

Experts reckon what parents say to a kid in the first seven years of their life lives with them forever. Well, it doesn't matter what age, harsh words always hurt, especially from the people who are supposed to be your biggest supporters.

And after twenty-five years of Oprah and Dr. Phil, I want to get rid of all the toxic people in my life and yet I have no idea how to get the hell away from them. Sure, they're dying off and I don't see most of them, but there's one I *really* want to get away from and just don't know how. I know *what* to do; I don't know *how* to do it. And it's bloody hard!

It sucks the energy, compassion, health, life, soul out of you until you are left a resentful, angry, hate-filled shell that is a reflection of the person you're caring for. *Except they don't see themselves that way.* Think Scrooge at Christmas, people hate him, but he has to see it through three ghosts to realise what an arsehole he's been.

I have analysed myself for the last twenty years. I've had the time. Oprah, Dr. Phil, books, blogs, websites, I have read and watched and listened. I know *why* I'm angry. I know *why* I cried myself to sleep many times over the last twenty years. I know there is no one out there to help me and really do wonder if any of my guides, angels, or helpers are doing anything to help me. I have cried and wailed, albeit silently, into my pillow, begging who and whatever was listening to help change my life, to bring money or a person into my life, or to let me win enough money or a house so I could move and start living the life *I* want, the *way* I want, and *how* I want. I seriously need saving because I don't know how to save myself.

No one really understands or gets what carers go through. They think we're fabulous people who choose this path but a lot of us didn't. We didn't *choose* it; it got dumped on us because we had a disabled child or parent. We didn't *choose*. We had *no choice*. We were not *asked* if it was what we wanted to do with the rest of our God damn life.

We didn't and *don't* have the support from family, partners, parents or children. We have *no* support from the government. We have *no* support from our country. We have *no freakin' support* from our state or community. I don't want respite. I don't want a two-week vacation. I want a life and that's what people don't understand.

I don't know how old people think I am, or if they even consider whether I have my own family, but they don't question it when finding out I care for my mother, and so probably don't understand I live at home unless I tell them. They don't care. They tell me how wonderful I am, not even understanding what an overwhelming, soul-destroying thing caring actually is and that it means I don't actually have a life outside of it.

I don't want respite; I want a fucking life. I want to live where I want to live. I want to do what I want to do and *when* I want to do it. I want to say and think and feel what I want to say and think and feel without being told to shut up, say nothing, be quiet, stop talking, don't tell me that, don't say that, don't feel that. Basically, it's just shut up, sit in the corner, and die.

The person we care for is not grateful. Mine certainly isn't. She didn't even want a woman here who could have told her about all the things that could have helped her. She wasn't interested except to get the garden done. And I *still* had to go out and finish it off because *she* certainly wasn't going to. She did offer to give me fifty dollars as well as fifty for other things, but I had to give it back because I owed her for the hundred I'd borrowed from her to get my teeth done. Her thanks are few and far between. *Very, very* far between!

She craps on about how no one will help her and yet when I try to get help she shits all over me, tells me to stop running her life and she doesn't want anyone here, even if having people here will help her *and* me in the long run. But she doesn't give a fuck about that. She's a stubborn old mule just like her bloody father. Whines about no one helping but refuses when they do, doesn't want to be told what to do but she sure as hell doesn't mind telling her carer what to do. *Angry, hateful hypocrite.* Do as I say not do as I do. In other words, shut up and do what I tell you because you're worthless and mean nothing.

I have read countless stories, fictional and real life, of people killing their parents. A lot of times it's for the family inheritance (money does so much to people), but mostly it's because they are sick of the ridicule, sarcasm, criticism, abuse, insults, rudeness, disrespect, anger, hatred, hostility or they couldn't find a way out of the situation. I could go on.

It can wear you down to the point you just want them to shut up. *Just shut up.* Shut the fuck up and die. Get out of my life and drop dead. *You* dropping dead will save me a load of hassle. Just drop dead and leave me alone. Leave me in peace. I will finally be free. Free to *do* what I want, *be* who I want, *say and do and think* what I want, and you won't be around to criticise and demean, to insult and shit all over. Because right now I am *not* free so just die and make it easier. I can *really* understand and sympathise with people who kill their parents. Cause all we want is for you to shut up, so we are free to be ourselves.

These days society is sending us mixed messages. One week we are good enough and should love who we are, the next we're being told we need to lose ten kilos, get rid of our cellulite, get a fake tan and bathe in the fountain of youth. Plus, deal with the two-faced hypocrites online who block you because they don't want their followers expressing thoughts and opinions on anything other than what they believe in their rush to be "positive" and non-judgemental against you. What a way to piss people off, by controlling them in the one place they actually thought they were free to express how they feel and what they think. Not to mention the businesses and companies you deal with that can't even be bothered ringing you back or doing what they tell you they'll do when they're supposed to do it. And I don't appreciate being accused of doing things I know I don't do. I get enough of that shit at home and online, I don't need it from companies I do business with.

I am so sick to fucking death of being controlled. It does not matter what I say or how I say it, it's shit all over, by her, by people online, by two-faced fucking hypocrites. I just want to be me. The person *I know* is screaming away inside to be let out. The person *I know* is good. The person *I know* is happy. The person *I know* gets along with the world when she's not being controlled and shit all over! It's bloody hard to do that when you're surrounded by, living with, or caring for, a negative person. Negativity 24/7. *Bloody hard!*

Carers are people, with thoughts, feelings and emotions. We're not doormats, and we sure as hell ain't toilets to be shit in. We want our own lives, our own family, our own homes. We want to be free to be ourselves and not get ridiculed or insulted for it.

She picks fights. *Over anything*, and I *mean* anything. Over me *doing* the dishes, *how* I do the dishes, *why* I do the dishes. How I *wash* the clothes, how I *hang* the clothes. *How* I vacuum, *when* I vacuum. *How* I buy things, *why* I buy things, *why do I spend so much money*. Why I don't put food or bottles or things away. Even if I'm about to use them she doesn't care. She creates the mess in the house by dumping her crap everywhere and then complains about how the house is in a mess and needs tidying or a vacuum and how she has to do it all because once again I do *nothing* around the house to help *her*. I do nothing to keep the house going and get the things done and sorted out. *No, nothing!*

She picks fights over all matter of things big, small or so minute you'd be scratching your head in disbelief at the stupidity. She picks fights over pretty much nothing. *NOTHING!*

She would absolutely fall apart without me here as she would have no freakin' idea how to fix appliances or deal with her phone, make calls or anything else. She would know nothing and do nothing except get meals and wash clothes. She just would not be able to cope without me as her slave. And she says she doesn't care if the house falls down on her, which it is at the moment, but she *would* care if it actually did because she'd be stuffed.

The people we care for just don't care how they treat us, what they say to us or what we think of it. It's all about *them*. What *they* want, what *they* feel, what *they* want to say. It doesn't matter how much you try and defend yourself they will walk all over you and make everything your fault anyway. Because that's the way it is. *Everything is your fault.* Like the father who blames the child for being born for the rest of his life because his wife died giving birth. You killed his wife, nothing else matters. Not even you.

These arseholes don't care if you have feelings, they don't care if their words hurt you. They don't see that what they are saying is hurtful. Or they pull out the old chestnut to back up their words. *"The truth hurts, doesn't it?"* The truth generally doesn't hurt because we already know it, so what you're saying isn't the reason we hurt. It's the fact you use the truth as a weapon to hurt, destroy, and insult that's the problem. It's the utter lack of respect or compassion coming from *you* that hurts. You show just how little you give a shit about us. Besides, you wouldn't know the truth if it smacked you in the bloody head.

She's often asked me what's wrong *with me.* "What went wrong *with you*?" "I didn't raise you this way." "It isn't my fault you've turned out this way." "Why are you such a bitch?" Meanwhile, she's saying these things in the middle of me being absolutely sick and tired of defending myself, in the middle of an argument that *she* started because *she* picked the bloody fight. *Over the stupidest of things.* Even the moment she gets out of bed she says stupid things to which the answers should be automatically known. Everything I do around the house or for her is *absolutely* unappreciated. The last year there has been the odd, "I really do appreciate everything you do". But then her attitude towards me the rest of the time belies the truth. What she says is bloody bullshit. She doesn't appreciate *anything!*

Just like the hours I spent trying to get her mobile phone sorted out by making calls to the company and our phone provider. My sister kept ringing and I heard the call waiting beep. The guy I was talking to mentioned it and I told him this was more important and the person calling could wait. He was quite surprised, as clearly other people had hung up on him to answer. I told him it was rude to do that, and I was dealing with something important, and it would be disrespectful to answer another call while talking to him.

Once I was off my sister rang again and when I told Mum afterwards that fixing her phone was more important than my sister's stupid mole that she was having cut off (which turned out to be nothing), she disagreed and told me not to call my sister stupid, *which I hadn't,* but it goes to show where her loyalties lie, where her priorities are, *and* what she does and does not hear. SHE DOES NOT BLOODY LISTEN TO *ANYTHING* I SAY!

And I'm sick and tired of being the stupid idiot trying to figure out or fix every bloody thing in this house. Like I don't have enough of my own shit to sort out and fix let alone trying to figure everything else out. The TVs, the remotes, her phone, which she can't even be bothered learning how to freakin' use for God's sake. She'd rather blame the object instead of her choice of not learning. It comes back to that inability to comprehend and not understand the simplest of things unless it's a *choice* to not bother comprehending because it uses too many brain cells and too much energy having to think about things.

Mind you, she'll often tell me she has too much to think about to do things. Yet she sits on her arse all day watching TV or reading magazines making her *so* busy that she can't even make a phone call to sort out the rent or even her own bloody phone. She knows she doesn't understand the internet, but criticises *me* for it anyway.

It always takes someone who knows fuck all to criticise and insult those who do know.

I break my bloody back in this household. My lazy arse siblings don't give a fuck, society doesn't give a fuck, so that means I'm the only stupid person giving a fuck enough to stay and do something. *But only because I don't have a way out.* I know *what* I want for my future but slogging my guts out trying to make and find that future just isn't happening.

For all the books I've read and TV shows I've seen, I've been wondering if anyone even gives a fuck about *me*. My guides, helpers, angels, the Universe. They seem non-existent. *Help* is non-existent. At least the help I *actually* need. There's no saviour, no rescuer, no knight in shining armour to ride up on his jet-black steed and sweep me off my feet to whisk me away to his palace for a life filled with love. And I desperately need saving because I just can't see a way to save myself and get myself out of this situation.

There is no one. There is *no* thing. There is just a bleak anger and hate-filled future. That is the only thing you end up seeing. A bleak angry, resentful, hateful future and life. Doing the same thing day in day out for the rest of your natural life.

It may as well be a prison sentence. *It may as well be a death sentence.*

I've heard the stories of young people taking on the

responsibility of siblings when parents die. Sometimes, if they're lucky, they have the street, the extended family, the community, to rally together and help them. That's different to what I'm going through.

Parents having children that need caring for is different. That is the job. You had the child, so you need to take care of it. Looking after a parent or sibling is *not our* responsibility.

I don't go to school, so I can't ask a teacher or counsellor for help. I have no one to ask. I'm at a dead end. Literally. The street, the suburb, the community has nothing and no one to ask or go to for help. The state has nothing and no one. There is no proper support; there is no support for our *actual* problem or needs.

As I've said, I don't need or want respite, I need a life. I need to break free and go my own way to live my own life and stop having it sucked away from me by someone who's so mean and narcissistic that she'll start a fight over nothing. Blame me for everything that happens even if she did it and make me give up things just because she's in pain and I have to go without because there's no way to get it or do it.

Well, I'm in bloody pain too! I'm in physical pain, emotional pain, and mental pain. But she doesn't give a fuck. *No one* gives a fuck! I'm in pain and know that even if I left her it would take a hell of a long time to get over all the years of shit I've had to deal with.

Am I emotionally scarred? I don't know. I *do* know I'm angry and resentful. I *do* know there is almost nothing that makes me happy except for music, sparkle, jewellery, and pink and blue. I *do* know I don't laugh like I used to. I don't *feel* like I used to. I *do* know that getting away from her or her dying is the only way I'll be free. That's the problem.

There is no way I can leave without support or money and I have neither. There are the lotto, scratchie, and house tickets, plus TV show money competitions I enter, all in the futile vague hope of winning enough or a house to finally have the opportunity to leave and start a new life. All in the vague hope that the Universe has made me suffer enough in this lifetime and has finally deemed me worthy of a better life from now on. *That makes me cry, that does.*

It implies that I *did not* choose this life, *in* this life, but my soul may have before I was born. And what I think of as punishment may just be a part of the plan my soul chose, and I know nothing about. *That sucks, that does.* Trying my damndest to change things but realising with every closed door that maybe this was the life I was meant to have.

That's not good enough for me. I want more. I want better. I want bigger and I damn well deserve it because I sure as hell don't deserve to be verbally and emotionally abused on a daily, weekly, monthly, yearly basis. I deserve more and I'm working to make it happen. Unless a psychic comes along and tells me there *is* more and more *will* happen, I've got the sickening, sinking feeling that this is my life *for the rest* of my life. *And that fucking sucks.* BIG.TIME!

That means I get to go without everything that I really want. A life, a partner, kids, a family, a home to call my own in the place I want to live.

Many nights are spent crying, many days are spent crying; crying that my life has come to this and that the most productive twenty years of my life have been taken away from me, never to be captured again. I don't want the next twenty years of my life to be sucked out of me, but considering her father lived to his nineties, she's got at least twenty years and that will make me sixty.

No life, no kids, no partner, no family, no friends, no future, no fucking life. *Nothing!* I'll have nothing but the stuff I've bought in the vain hope it will fill my heart with some small vein of hope and happiness because that's all I had. That's all I *have*. All I'll *ever* have. *I don't want that.* I don't want to live with nothing but stuff for the rest of my life. I don't want *this*. I don't want this life anymore and haven't for many, many, many years.

When I was twenty-eight I read a letter in the psychic column of the *Woman's Day* magazine. It was from a forty-two-year-old woman, and she asked questions that left me drop dead cold. Freezing cold fear fled through my body and the first thing I thought was that I had come back from the future to warn myself that that is what my life would end up like if it didn't change. I've tried. I've clearly failed. It's 2014. I'm forty. Two years off that letter (as of this writing) and clearly that was future me warning the *then* me. A warning I did not heed. A warning I clearly could not do anything about.

I do want to change. Although I cannot ever see myself being happy here with her in this situation, I know it would all change if my living arrangements changed, and I don't mean moving up to Queensland with her. While I might be where I wanted to be the situation would still be the same. But then maybe I'm looking at it all wrong and should make the most of moving, if it ever happened with her, and then find some opportunity up there to change everything else. At least something would be happening. As much as it would be the same situation, it would be a different place, it would be a step in the right direction, albeit a *side step* in the right direction, wouldn't it?

I am *so* sick and bloody tired of being told I said something I didn't. Of being told I have no idea what I'm talking about. Of being told I'm lying and need to tell the truth. Of being told what to do in general, all day, every day, every fucking week, month and year. And not just by my mother but by companies I do business with and people online in general. I'm over people believing in their arrogant bullshit and shitting on me.

I'm fucking over it all. Over being treated like fucking shit. Of being told what to do, what to say, what *not* to say or to shut up.

I am fucking sick and tired of starting a conversation and then having her go off on a tangent about something completely unrelated to what I had said, or something I was not even talking about because she cannot even grasp the actual point I was trying to make.

I am *so* fucking sick and tired of being verbally kicked and stomped all over. I am *so* fucking sick and tired of being treated like I *do not* matter. Like I *do not* warrant an adult response. Like I *do not* need an adult conversation.

I am over being accused and treated like shit. I am over the arguments that ensue. I am over the bullshit that comes with them. I am over living with an ungrateful cow who doesn't give a flying fuck about anyone but herself. Oh, except her *other* children!

I am over living this life, this existence, this bullshit. I am over living in this house, this neighbourhood, this state. I am over being talked all over. *I am over being treated like shit!*

She is full of excuses, her main one being her pain, but then she'd spit out, "I don't know." Bloody grow a fucking brain and find out. And in the last year she's loved accusing me of panicking and to "stop panicking" even though I'm actually not. I had a go at her about it several times, and the last time she denied having ever said it before and so crapped all over me for accusing her of making stuff up. What a fucking joke!

I am over the bullshit guilt trips I stopped giving into years ago. I am over the controlling bullshit and way I am spoken to and treated.

I am over *not* being listened to because apparently I *do not* know what the hell I'm talking about and either she knows more or one of my sisters does. I am over her being more into phone calls from my sisters than what I'm doing for her. I am over being treated that way by people I don't know or companies I do business with on top of that.

I am over this bullshit life, this bullshit existence, this bullshit excuse of being.

When caring for a child you are in control as the adult, but when an adult is caring for a parent you become the child once more and are treated as such by the controlling parent. That means you, regardless of your age and being the adult carer, have no life because it's being controlled by the patient, the parent. It's hard to do anything, go anywhere, and have anything, because you *have nothing.* You *are* nothing. Because you became nothing from years of hell and bullshit.

We are shunted back to being a child with no brain, no capabilities, no thoughts or ideas about how things work and what things do and so they're always surprised when we come up with good ideas and ways of doing things. And it's like, *hello, I do have a brain in my head and can make things up just because you don't believe I can and refuse to believe I have a brain in my head and am an actual adult and not a five-year-old that you keep seeing me as.* I AM NOT FIVE

YEARS OF BLOODY AGE. And if you continue to treat me as such, then get yourself into a retirement home so I can retire to the GC! I am an adult with the brain power and rights to my thoughts and the way I express them!

Just shut the fuck up! Shut the fuck up and leave me alone.

I don't want this life. I don't want the abuse, the insults, the fights, the criticism, the anger, the hatred, the resentment. I don't want it because I know I am *so* much better and happier on my own or away from her. It's like a big fat dead weight is lifted from me.

And that's what I need to do. *Get away from her.* That's the only answer. The problem is, how? How do I do it? How do I manage it? A loan will cost too much to repay, and I wouldn't get one anyway. Lotto seems like a pipe dream. How do I live the life I want to live when I see no way out without help that just isn't there?

I didn't choose this. I didn't want this, and this has ruined what life I could have had. What I could have *made* of myself. What future I could have if only I had the actual help I actually *need*, not the help people *assume* I should have.

I don't know how many more years I can do this. How many more years I can take being treated like shit, spoken to as if I don't matter, as if what I say and feel doesn't matter because I'm no one. I may as well not exist. I may as well not be here. I don't want to do this anymore. I haven't wanted to do this for years, if ever. I don't know how many more years I can mentally, physically and psychologically do this or sustain any energy for this. I don't know how many more years I can keep going. I just do. It's not a matter of going back, I can't go back, not back to the nothing I had before. I had nothing before and I don't want to go back to nothing so I keep going,

I just don't know how many years I can keep doing this.

You don't know how hard this is on us. You have no idea unless you've been or *are* going through it. It's bloody hard, exhausting, debilitating, emotionally, mentally and our health, physical and emotional suffers for it. Doing everything and getting no help. No joy, only anger, hatred and resentment. It very slowly turns us into what we don't want to be. The very person we're caring for. Caring for someone 24/7 is a very sad, lonely existence because our environment sucks, and our life sucks.

But no one gives a bloody fuck.

In closing, if there's one thing that life, *my life*, has taught me, it's that old people shit all over you.

That *nice* gets shit all over.

I was *raised* to be nice. I was *raised* to not ask questions like, "where did you get that?", "how much was that?", and "who gave you that?" I was *raised* to stand in line and wait my turn instead of jumping the queue. I was *raised* to wait to be invited to sit at someone's table and not just sit down unasked. I was *raised* to not interrupt people's conversations and stand and wait for them to finish or turn to you and speak, because it was *rude*.

Because older people *are not nice. Older people can be absolute bitches and bastards who want to do nothing but shit all over you.*

That is what life, *my life*, has taught me.

People old enough to be your parent or grandparent do the majority of shitting. I find this quite strange considering the way they would have been raised. Back in their day, they would have been raised with the old adages, "children are seen and not heard", to "have manners at the table" and to "mind their own business". What makes "old" people think they can throw all of that out the door and just shit all over people now? What makes "old" people think they can just shit all over any young person who comes along?

I've been treated badly by adults since I was a teen, and because I was raised to be "nice" I tried to get out of situations or answer awkward questions as best I could while being "nice" and not saying anything or making something up. But the years have shown me that the older I get the worse people become. *Especially "old" people.* In my teens, twenties and into my thirties I had people treat me like shit because they thought they could.

Two of my sisters constantly asked, *"where'd you get that from"*, *"how much was that"*, or the classic, especially when I was a teen into my early twenties, *"did Mum buy you that?"* because apparently the very idea that I may have had enough money to buy it myself was far too overwhelming for them. *That. Was. Tiring!*

Not only was that tiring, but it was bloody bullshit and just one more thing I had to deal with in a list of millions that I've had to deal with in my life.

The woman at the post office, within days of us moving here, spoke very rudely to me when I went in. I had never met her before, so I have no idea who she thought I was to speak to me that way. The man at the post office not only spoke rudely to me, but to the woman beside me, even though she asked quite politely, *"may I borrow your pen, please"*.

I had an elderly lady in Target tell me off because she was so small I didn't see her when I moved my trolley. When I said sorry, she said, *"you should be."* Simply because I moved the trolley and it caught her in the wrist.

I've had women, mainly, say things with such critical, sarcastic, insulting tones that it's absolutely bloody ridiculous. And the women that come and go from my life on some sort of basis have shown they cannot be trusted or believed because of the lies they spew.

The list could go on, but I really don't want to go back over twenty-five years' worth. And on top of that I've had twenty years of my mother doing the exact same thing.

It's made me angry. It's made me hateful. It's made me resentful. It made me the person I am today. And now *I'm* wondering if I'm turning into a grumpy old woman!

If this is the person I am supposed to be, I have no idea what this person is supposed to be here on this planet living this life for.

My mother called me cold and hard because I didn't cry at Steve Irwin's funeral. I was not a fan of Steve's; he reminded me of a brother-in-law, and I didn't like him, so it rubbed off. So what! I don't need to like or be a fan of everyone's. Just because I don't cry at everyone dying does *not* make me cold and hard, although she still says I am because I don't show any emotion over other people and their problems, or other things. I'm not cold; I just refuse to get involved in their problems because they're adults and can sort out their own shit. I've got way too many of my own to deal with to piss away my time and energy on theirs.

Besides, I blubbered like a baby at Diana's funeral. And I still blubber over TV or book deaths. Death sucks. It's horrible and painful and absolute shit.

I'm not cold or hard when I'm on my own. But when I'm

around users and abusers I *am*. I *have* to be. I *have* to be that way to deal with and sustain myself through it otherwise I would have either been driven bonkers, killed myself, or someone else years ago. Although I think I have been driven bonkers living with her. How I keep on keeping on I don't know.

You need to be *like them* to deal with them otherwise they walk all over nice people. I am a hard person on the outside. I am a softie on the inside. Like Shrek! Okay, bad example.

I still have insecurities, but I keep them to myself because they are mine to deal with and something that's in *my* head and only *I* can deal with anyway. And of course there are parts of me I just don't like. I also *do not* believe there is one person in this world who loves one hundred percent of themselves the way it was naturally given to them.

Would I like to change my outside? Sure.

Would I like to change my insides? *Of course.*

I also know that away from this life it will be *so* different. I know I am fine around happy, outgoing, "normal" people. I am hard and uncaring around angry, hate-filled resentful people because that's what rubs off. Whenever I've spoken to some business people or councillors I'm told how intelligent and with it I am. I'm well-spoken and well thought out and know what I want and how to find out about it. I'm enthusiastic and charming and know how to plan things out. But she doesn't see, think, or say the same thing. Nope, not about me.

I know I get pissed off when the person I'm talking to doesn't actually listen to what I'm saying but *assuming* they know what I'm saying, *assuming* I'm saying something completely different to what I actually *am saying*, or just not listening at all.

I *hate* having to repeat myself. *A lot!* Like ALL THE BLOODY TIME!

I *hate* having to explain things time and time again because people *don't listen* the first time, or just don't care to understand or comprehend, wasting my time and energy when I could be putting that time and energy into something worth my time and energy. Like my writing, jewellery or designing. I don't want to spend the rest of my life explaining time and time again how things work or what things do when people can't even be bothered showing enough respect by actually listening to me. It's bloody tiring.

I *hate* having to live my life for someone else and wonder on a daily basis what my life is even for if it's not for me. I have no idea *why* I'm here. I have no idea *what* I'm here for. I have no idea *what* my role or job on this planet, in this life, *my life* is supposed to be, live up to, or do. *How the hell am I supposed to know that? How the hell am I supposed to know what I'm here for and what I'm supposed to do with the rest of my life since the last 40 years of it has been wasted by other people and the Universe.*

What I *do* know is that I *am not* living the life I want. The life *I need* to feed my body, mind, soul and psyche, and I can't get or have that life here.

I have not been jealous of anything or anyone since my twenties. I look back now or read articles and I have melancholic sadness. *Loads of it!* I'm sad that I did not get the support from my parents or family to pursue my hopes and dreams that other artists and creative people have received that helped them on their way up their career path. I'm sad that everything I wanted to achieve has not been achieved even though I have technically achieved a lot. I'm sad that the things

I desperately want more than anything else in this world may never come or happen. *All because of this life I exist in.*

It's funny, I look at everything I've done, run businesses, albeit badly, written, typed up, formatted left, right, and centre, made my own covers, and self-published my novels and e-books, set up all of my blogs and social media pages and decorated them myself, made some incredible jewellery and couture clothing pieces from beads, findings and components. I have an amazing wardrobe full of clothes, jewellery and accessories, acquired a huge Nancy Drew collection, have some *great* stuff, and yet, everything I've done doesn't seem like so much. Even though it's a *huge amount* of stuff that I've done that not many others could actually do, or say *they've* done.

While *my stuff* makes me happy, my life does not. Because my stuff fills the hole that lies empty and is the only bright spark in what could be considered the black hole of my life's cosmos that destroys it all.

And I really don't see that everything I have done and achieved as being something I've done and achieved because these days *anyone* can write, publish or produce a book. These days *anyone* can make jewellery and set up an online shop. These days *anyone* can do the exact same things I do. There are no niches in these areas because the world is full of people filling them by the millions.

I don't really feel pride for all I have done, probably because my life has not given me the feelings *to* be proud. I just think, "Meh, whatever, just one more thing I've done."

Zip, zilch, nada! Nothing. No feelings of anything, especially good.

What does pride feel like? I don't know anymore because

I haven't felt it in a long, long, long time. If I ever felt it at all that is.

I could write about this forever. Over forty years so much has happened, and so many people have treated me like garbage that I could probably write a proper book about it, a several hundred plus page book as I haven't really covered this particular topic in this simple e-book. Forty years' worth of life! *It doesn't even begin* to cover everything.

Caring is bloody hard, and it takes everything out of you, especially when you are the only one doing it 24/7 for over half of your life and the recipient is ungrateful and uncaring.

It sucks everything out and leaves nothing but a shell of the person you used to be, leaves nothing for the person you may have wanted to be, or could have been, and empties you of everything that could have been good, emotions, feelings you could have or did feel at some stage that is no longer there because it was shit all over and discriminated against.

It's because all of that has been sucked out of me, and I know when I get to live the life I want on Queensland's Gold Coast, in my own little apartment, with my own little car, zooming around doing what I want when I want and *how* I want, that my life will be so freakin' fantastic! Yes, it will be and then everything else will come into my life. My life will be a billion times better than it is now. I'm forty as of this writing, and have nothing but my stuff and my dreams so life *has* to get better; it just has to, unless I'm *meant* to have nothing besides my stuff and my dreams to get me through the rest of my hateful angry life.

*****

It's amazing, how in 2024 as I put this memoir together, everything I wrote in that book, now essay, still happens, except it's worse.

How I feel, how she treats me; it's all worse.

She's become even stingier with five times as much money as me, and I know as I'm the signatory so I can pay the bills. She could afford a new electric lift chair but whined about it. Could afford that new bed years ago, but whined about it, could afford that new car in 2015, but whined about it and wanted me to pay half. Like that was happening. She'd already scabbed half of the last car out of me, costing me almost $10,000 of money I didn't have, leaving me a petty amount in the bank. She hates forking out money for things she needs and refuses to update anything she has, constantly demands I pay more towards the household when I already pay the most and have more general bills than her which she denies and still claims all these years later that she pays for more, and has more bills, when she doesn't.

For my fiftieth birthday she kept hounding me about getting a present. What do you want, have you found something yet? Every week that I went shopping in May she asked if I'd found something. I finally did and told her it was a bottle of perfume. She asked how much, and I told her $80. She said, "oh, well, that's more than I expected."

When we finally got around to sorting the money out, as I'd booked it up on credit when I got it, she was so busy flapping around trying to sort her money out, exchange big notes for little notes, that she handed me fifty and said that's for the perfume. I said, "don't worry about that for the moment, deal with exchanging the money and paying for lunch first."

She did that and then said, "where's the fifty for the perfume?"

"I said, it's here."

"But you took it."

"No, I didn't."

"But you must have."

"No, I didn't. We hadn't done that yet."

She created such a goddamn argument out of a fifty dollar note I told her not to worry about it because the perfume was $80, not $50. And so, she didn't pay for my present after all, which is nothing new. But how stingy is that? Tells me she'll get me a present for my fiftieth and then didn't want to pay full price for it. It was only $80, and even though we're on the lower end of the finance scale, she has the money for it.

Here in Aus, we live in a government rent controlled home, but every six months the rent goes up in accordance with the rise we get in our benefits. We hate it, and sometimes it's a good chunk of money, but in 2023 she started demanding that I pay half of the rent.

I scoffed at her demands and thought, yeah, right, and kept on with what I was doing. Once I finally went through my budget, I just couldn't pay it on top of the $300 a fortnight I was paying for the food, the monthly internet/phone bill, and the quarterly gas bill. She only had the quarterly electric bill, and a fortnightly $150 for food, on top of the rent. Because I couldn't afford another $250 on top of the $300, making it $550 a fortnight that I'd be paying, in turn, dropping her fortnightly bill down to $400, I chose to add another $100 to the fortnightly food bill.

When I explained it to her she didn't get it, even though I spoke in plain English. I told her she hadn't even bothered asking me if I could afford another $250 and I told her I couldn't, so I'd added another $100 to the food. She still demanded half the rent.

This happened in 2023 and I finally realised that she was financially abusing me. She probably had done since I was twenty-seven when my money had been in her bank account. I don't remember how that came to be, but after years of her ripping off my money, I finally asked for it so I could put it into my own bank account. She hated that. She tried the guilt trip, the lies, the manipulations. But I stood firm and got my money. And she still has five times more than me, so it's not as if she was hard done by. If anyone is, it's me. And I stupidly gave her half my $1200 lotto win, just as I stupidly let her keep my money from selling some furniture to go towards our move to Queensland decades ago, just as I stupidly allowed her to harass me into buying shoes from her. My lotto and furniture money are long gone.

These days, I'm threatened with having Centrelink take me away, or FedEx will get her out of here. Yeah, she said that, clearly not having any idea what FedEx actually does. She's always threatening to call up someone, like our local council, and have me removed from the house, or she's going to leave, and I'll be left on my own. I wish she would. She's verbally abusive more than ever, financially abusive more than ever, and emotionally abusive more than ever. She tries guilt trips, lies about me to everyone who listens, says I don't let her do anything, even though she physically can't. It's clear her brain, or memory, or thought patterns, are deteriorating, and that's not a good thing.

I tell her all she can do at this stage is tidy up her stuff and dust, and yet she refuses to do either of those things, and her stuff has piled up and become too much to deal with, even though I suggest dealing with a few bags, or one corner of her room, at a time. But no, she doesn't want me doing anything or touching anything, regardless of how bad her hips and back are. She's been on a walker since 2012 and she's not coming off it if she doesn't get her hips done. But now she's refusing to have that surgery and didn't want to pay for it because she's stingy and thinks it costs $50,000 per hip. It doesn't.

When I suggest that I'll clean out her room she gives me excuses, "you always put things where I can't find them", "no, no, I'll do it", yet she never does, because she has an issue with throwing things out, or donating, and so the piles get higher, the windows get mouldier, and the dust gets thicker.

The excuses have got to go. She used to be house proud; now she's not. Now it's all about excuses. "I'll pay #1 or #2 to come in and do it", yet in the same breath she says she doesn't want anyone touching her stuff, and my siblings don't come to see us in general, and they'd just tell her to throw it all out, anyway. She's no better off. She even keeps up with the "I'll get someone in to clean up" routine, yet the cleaning crews have already told us they don't move furniture and don't do certain other things when cleaning houses, so no, they won't. Does she believe anything I tell her? Nope, not a word, yet I'm the person dealing with everyone, and it's been that way for decades. Apparently, everything I say is a lie and she doesn't believe me, so tells on me to three of my siblings, or lies about me to them and then says it's nothing and not a big deal. Yeah, it actually bloody is.

For some reason she has a hatred for me, and when I pull her up on her lies and tell her to stop lying about me she doubles down. Everything is my fault, I took her stuff, I need to give it back, blah, blah, blah. I keep telling her to look for it, to find it, but she gets the narrative stuck in her head that I took it when I didn't. The arguments we get into are screamers. She starts arguments and then blames me for starting them. She puts it all back on me, turns it on me, takes it out on me. She wants to harp on instead of move on. It's incredibly hard having a decent conversation with her when all she wants to do is repeat the same narrative that's stuck in her head and not move on with the conversation and thought process. She gets stuck, and that's when she harps on and then blames me for not being able to have a conversation and accuses me of not listening and understanding. I understand all right; the problem is, I move on with the conversation, she doesn't, and so we go round and round in circles and nothing ever stops. And then we get into another screamer of an argument. So many times...

And when she does bother looking for the item she claims I have and finds it, does she apologise? Of course not.

How do you like being lied about to your face? I deal with the bullshit, the abuse, the lies, the hatred, the anger, the rage, the garbage, the household, the bills, the everything. She sits or sleeps her days away and does fuck all, or picks fights when I ask a simple question, or even when I don't. She picks fights over anything and everything with the bullshit in her head, and it's fucking exhausting on every level.

Typical narcissistic behaviour.

It's one many of us daughters of narcissistic mothers have to deal with on a daily basis. Especially when we're the carers.

She used to tell anyone we'd talk to that she did everything in the house and I did nothing. She did all the washing, the cooking, the cleaning. Meanwhile, I did half of that, but she didn't want them knowing. She had to make herself look big, look better, and do so by putting me down in front of others to the point I couldn't look at anyone and would go bright red and embarrassed as hell. A classic narcissistic trait.

Her health problems are worse, and my health problems are worse. Life is worse in general and I'm not happy. I haven't been happy for decades, since I realised how my life was going to be. I may never be happy and that's something I have to deal with because this life is unhappy.

I have arthritis, psoriasis, skin conditions, nerve issues. My body has deteriorated exponentially since 2014 and I truly believe that my health issues came on twenty years early because of all the stress of my life. The bags under my eyes have turned into full, and very heavy, luggage sets, and there are days I feel five hundred and fifty and look five thousand and fifty. That's how much being a full-time carer sucks out of you; it sucks everything until you have carer fatigue and burnout. I can't leave with no money, and no one else even bothers to help because they know that I'm here to do it all, so, they go about their life as they always did.

And on top of all of this shit that I have to deal with, I also have to deal with the raging arseholes called my siblings.

There was a year, can't remember when, when #2 had come for a visit on a Sunday or Monday, and had Mum's arm through hers as she led her outside because she was leaving. She automatically let go of Mum without thinking. Mum didn't have her balance or a walking stick, and down she went. I was opening the driveway gate, but sprang into action and rushed back, telling Mum not to move and just take a moment. We ended up calling an ambulance. They checked Mum out; Mum didn't want to go to the hospital and #2 left. Within an hour #1 was ringing because #2 had rung her the moment she got home because she was all upset. For me, it wasn't a big deal, but #1 was all bossy and dictatorial. "You should have rung me I would've dropped everything and come down, blah, blah, blah."

Yeah, sure. As if I hadn't dealt with Mum falling before... so many times that I had it down pat. It's not as though #1 and 2 come over any other time, so why would they come down then? And why would I bother calling someone who's nearly two hours away just to deal with something I'm perfectly capable of dealing with?

Regardless, by Thursday, Mum's inner ears were playing up and she was dizzy. It was something to do with the tiny crystals on the inner ear hairs. While we were waiting for an ambulance, #2 rang and we ended up telling her, then when we got off the phone she rang #1, of course. She is the gossipy resident switchboard operator constantly telling people everyone else's business because she's unable to keep out of it and has to be the one in the family who knows everything like the resident know-it-all, except she doesn't...

And then #1 rang us. Of course! Because I wasn't expecting that call, I said, "Oh, #2 rang you did she." And #1 went off her face. Telling me she had a right to know and to be concerned, and I should've done my job and sent her to hospital days ago, blah, blah, bloody blah.

I hung up on her. Don't fucking ignore your mother for years, and then fucking dictate to me, the *actual* person caring for her, what to do. It won't work and I'll hang up on you because I don't need that fucking abuse. So, fuck off, grow up, and do better as a human being and a daughter, and actually give a shit about the only living parent you bastards have had for the last sixty plus years instead of obsessing over the selfish cunt who killed himself and made your lives a living hell.

Jesus. I really don't know why the Universe is making me suffer so badly.

Karma's a bitch and she's been slapping me down ever since. I have no idea how long she intends to make me pay, but it's long pissed me off.

I really don't know where I went wrong in life to end up here in this abusive hellhole. When I should have gone left instead of right, forwards instead of backwards, said yes instead of no and vice versa.

It could be karma for something really dumb that I did in school. I skipped it with my then-best friend and went to Rundle Mall for the day. A teacher saw us and reported it. Our parents got a call and I got into trouble like never before. Unfortunately, that day, my mother was vacuuming and "accidentally" knocked a folder off my cupboard, seeing the notes I'd been writing to my friend in class calling my mother some pretty bad things. Things weren't great after that, and I've been treated badly since. It could also be karma for ruining her uterus as she had fibroids after having seven kids, the last being me, and had it removed.

I have no clue what the lesson is in being abused; in staying in an abusive situation. I know I don't have the ability to leave. If I could, I would, believe me. But the how is so damn hard to answer. *How* do I leave? *Where* do I find the money to pay for packing my stuff up, transporting it, storing it, paying for accommodation and transport? I don't have support. There is no one to help except myself and it's beyond exhausting trying to survive in a shit life I can't seem to change no matter how hard I try. I'm all out of ideas, so if anyone's got any…

But that's life, isn't it? We suck it up and deal with it while others coast and skate through with no problems whatsoever… never having the health issues, the physical issues, the money and housing issues.

Many therapists say something along the lines of, "*we all have something from our childhood that we have zero control over. You can't control someone else's behaviour, but you do control how you deal with it for the rest of your life.*"

Yeah, great, which is why I desperately want to get the hell out of Dodge and have my own damn life, so I don't have to actually deal with these dickshits. But the Universe has other plans. And clearly these therapists never had to deal with mentally lacking adults who just wanted to treat them like garbage. But then again, maybe they have. Believe me, this is shit you can't deal with or live with for your entire life, because it sucks the living life and soul out of you. No one else is going to fight my fight for me. I have to fight it myself, and that's damn hard, too. And what's the cost to me? Everything!

They also say things like, "*you get to choose the type of relationship you have with said person.*" Well, I don't want any. Because you can't have a relationship with someone who is so deep in their own head they don't recognise you as an equal let alone a person. I need to be away from this person and this family, and desperately want it to happen.

Life is worse for Australians, and for most of the world, thanks to that wretched disease that sent the world into a spiral in 2020 and locked us all down as a whole. We've recovered from that, but there will always be a new issue to deal with. New housing crisis, new finance crisis, new relationship crisis, regardless of what type of relationship it is. Many countries still treat women like shit, many men still want to rule over women's bodies, and spaces and life, and I could say so much about that, too. Such as sick men pander to sick men from the very top down and in all aspects of day-to-day life.

As women, we not only have to struggle against our personal circumstances, but those of the world as it, and men, try to screw us over time and time again, and other men let them get away with it.

Life, as a whole, sucks a lot worse than in 2014, and I have to wonder if it will ever be okay again. If I will ever be okay, period. I certainly won't be the person I used to be, as she has often whinged. "What happened to the little girl I used to know?" Bitch, that little girl grew the fuck up because she had to thanks to her family hating her and had to become cold and hard just to emotionally survive. And that's still fucking hard.

Sadly, life will never be okay as long as it stays the same. But how the hell do I change it?

I AM A KING

I am a king, not a queen,
refuse to be somewhere in between.
I am sparkly, I am tarnished,
I am both, and I am garnished.
I am brilliant when I dazzle,
shine brighter than a diamond.
I hate diamonds, I hate tarnish,
I am covered in smothering varnish.
I am both, and I am neither,
but I am a king and I will never
conform or deny my true self.
I will never shine bright like a diamond,
because I am a king, and I will shine brighter.

♛ ♛ ♛ ♛

My Sparkling Obsession

I'm not exactly sure when my love for jewellery started; there's a photo of me at six or seven wearing plastic jewellery from the one and two cent machines outside supermarkets in the '70s and '80s. Plastic was enough at the time. I was a kid; it was all I needed.

As I grew so did my collection, although not until I left high school and had some money to spend. After 1994 my collection grew bigger, going from being hung on a pin board to being stored in a tallboy and now, thirty years later, living in two huge five drawer roller cabinets, two large and one small glass cabinets, two decorative wooden boxes, and one massive blue Caboodle.

I wish I had the space to display it all, but unfortunately that's just not possible. I'd set up a room of glass cabinets and shelves and buy a hundred busts to display all of my favourite pieces, but I also know that wouldn't be the best for them.

I have no idea why I'm obsessed by sparkle, bling, jewels and gemstones. It could be the rainbow spasms of light that flash in shafts of lightning around the room as surely as a disco ball. The colours and shades catch not only my eye but my attention and capturing it, hold it for those few milliseconds of time in my never-ending dull day. Sparkle makes me happy, whether it's from jewellery or disco balls, or simply watching a double rainbow appear in the sky outside my window.

I've occasionally wondered if my deceased grandma had something to do with it. I was told she had left each of her granddaughters a tapestry and a piece of jewellery. I ended up with the tapestry, one I didn't choose but which is nice enough, and never got the piece of jewellery as it was stolen from me due to selfishness and disrespect of the dead. I have no idea what I was supposed to have received. I was a teenager when she passed and never got to go to Perth for the funeral or the reading of the will. I've often wondered if this was her way of making up for me not getting the piece she wanted me to have. She pushed me into buying, making, and creating so I would have more than enough to make up for it.

I love it to obsessive death and really don't get how people who design it barely wear it or wear just a couple of pieces. I love drowning myself in it when I get dressed up and I'm never without a big pair of earrings and big funky watch even if I'm just running to the doctor.

If you love jewellery, then go ahead and live your life drenched in it! It hurts no one, let's you live like a disco ball and is an easy way of getting sparkle into your life.

*****

I think I made my first pieces of jewellery at sixteen but didn't dabble much after that, and I certainly didn't start creating to set up a business, in fact, it was the farthest thing from my mind as a teenager. The internet, eBay, and online stores for selling certainly weren't around then for new designers and creators. There were more markets to have stalls at but none in my area.

It wasn't until my late twenties that I really started making big fancy pieces that people, especially in my area, noticed and started commenting on. The women in my local book shop suggested selling on consignment in a jewellery store which had been bought by the woman who ran it and had had a name change. Since my local shopping centre refused me a stall because of the "new" jewellery store I ended up in her shop to see if I could sell on consignment. I took in my African Safari range and even though the girl who worked there was enthusiastic about my jewellery and oohing and aahing over it, the owner had quite a sour, uninterested look on her face. It was so obvious that I felt I, knew it, and saw it. She was uninterested and said no. No wonder she closed about a year later.

After signing up for a business name and ABN I jumped into getting a website done in late 2008.

The woman who did my original site took my money for doing nothing, told me everything I *should* be doing, and couldn't even work out how to use the hosting site I'd signed up to. She used Yahoo for the websites she designed, and I had no clue.

Times have certainly changed concerning that.

She couldn't even tell me how much to pay her when she rang. She complained that I owed her and needed me to make a payment but couldn't tell me how much to pay her. As I said, "I can't pay you if I don't know how much to send."

That was a bust and I needed to sign up to a real company who then charged me $1500 for a website as they had to redo everything. Between paying that off each month, and paying for the hosting fees, it took me two years, from memory, to pay it off.

While all of this was happening, in July 2009 I started a companion jewellery blog, Jewel Divas Jewellery, along with multiple social media sites. Before the original jewellery website even went online, I was emailing magazines and TV shows about getting my jewels in *and* on them. I blogged about it, put flyers up in my local shopping centre. I was on the local talk back radio, I tweeted and Facebooked the normal magazines, plus beading magazines. I was in a beading magazine that year with some of the *African Safari* hair bobbies and ties and have since had some of my own personal pieces feature in another beading magazine in 2012.

While I did get my designs into bead magazines, getting them into normal magazines was another thing. Being a designer with one-off pieces was never going to get into a magazine unless I sent them pieces to keep, and even that didn't guarantee getting into magazines. I've looked at sending to TV show hosts, and other places, all to no avail. Clearly it was all against me and so I gave up trying.

And in 2012, I decided to transfer my jewellery blog over to WordPress, so I needed a new hosting company as the old one was screwing me around by now and I needed to keep blog posts going, plus set up the new blog for migration. I closed down my old jewellery website and set up shop on MadeIt instead to ease some of the emotional and mental burden it was all becoming.

If I had known about this website back in 2008 (it started in 2007) I would have signed up immediately instead of wasting money I didn't have on people who wasted my time, money and energy.

It was one of the best decisions I made at the time, after thinking about it for over a year mind you. It was all done for you, the set-up was easy, uploading was easy, and filling out your details was easy. All I had to do was make my photos look real and natural and pre-write my details so I could copy and paste it all in.

But one irony in all of that was, I didn't like selling or giving jewels as gifts because I didn't know where it would end up or with whom. I needed to distance myself from making for others and selling because of this. It would be different if I made and sold in bulk as I could have a couple of everything as most designers with big businesses do, but I don't. I make one-offs, or in the case of AC, different colours in the same style. It's just a very weird feeling knowing that the person who buys it may not keep it and hand it on, or, if it breaks, it could end up in the bin. All that hard work just for it to end up in the bin or lost really freaks me out.

It's a weird thought, isn't it?

*****

I've faced a lot of issues with trying to make my business happen. One of them happened back in 2009 when I first set it up. I filed for the trade mark of the name and the issues I came up against were astoundingly ridiculous.

After I filed for the trade mark of the name, I received a letter from patent and trade mark attorneys informing me that my trade mark was being opposed by a large overseas corporation that carried on under a particular name here in Australia.

A long list of oppositions followed, some claiming the

following: I wasn't Australian, the lady who issued my trade mark didn't know what she was doing (what an insult), I filed my trade mark in bad faith, amended it after the issue date (which I hadn't), that the people at large would not be able to distinguish between our names and logos, that the whole world would be confused, and how dare I use their name in mine!

Besides being overly dramatic, they assumed idiotic things when they hadn't bothered finding out the truth.

I was a little online shop, not a massive chain store conglomerate that was going to take over the shopping centres and malls of the world. They bought en mass from China. I handmade my stuff right here in Australia.

I loved this particular chain store and bought regularly from them. I was even registered on their website to receive newsletters, but that soon stopped.

If only the issue had.

A week on and I received more papers from the same corporation.

This time, the lawyers claimed they wanted to negotiate with me and come to a settlement.

That sounded good, except for the fact that they sent a paper for me to sign and send back giving up all rights to my business.

Yes, that's right, they wanted me to cease trading as my business.

To me, that's no bloody negotiation. That's telling me what to do and when to do it and not giving a stuff about what I wanted.

They expected me to give up trading under my business name, deregister the name with the company I registered it with to trade under, give up my domain name and anything to do with that, agree to never use the name and logo ever, and never start another business with the name again.

I went to the trade mark data base and looked up all trade marks containing the name they wanted for themselves and found quite a few in Australia. I was one of them. This company had opposed most of them. Any that traded in bags, jewellery, or accessories, have copped an opposition to the trade mark.

Any companies with the word in it, trading under any other class besides 14 and 35 have not been opposed. And even some that do trade under classes 14 and 35 have not been opposed.

The company used bullyboy tactics on people that wanted to use a word in their name. And surprisingly, they don't always win.

But then the story continued…

My trade mark opposition was dragged out for another month.

It would seem the company loved doing it for the hell of seeing who shut down first. It wasn't going to be me.

They dragged it out and then I received a letter from them saying they'd asked for one more month to get their evidence together.

I didn't know what evidence they needed; they were clearly trying to get dirt on me, but there wasn't any.

But I did learn of one low-down and dirty thing they did.

They printed out my logo on a survey and put it in their stores in other states, and asked customers a series of questions about the name and image. Did they think it was owned by their store, what did they think when they saw the logo, and so on. Half the people thought it might be something to do with them, half didn't. I know this because the bastards sent me a copy of it.

It proved nothing. To me it was inconclusive that every person was confused about it being attached to their name. My logo was not theirs by a long shot, my name only had the word Diva in common with theirs, and that was it, and I have no idea if these customers were coerced, or led to specific answers, or not.

I thought it was a pretty low, illegal thing to do. I had an appointment with my local business centre to get legal advice, and they made photocopies of every page to go over. She did ask permission if they could use the case in an upcoming meeting, but I don't even remember if I was supposed to attend because they didn't get in contact with me after that. Thanks for nothing and nothing is what I got out of that meeting.

I could only hope the whole palaver ended by the next month.

And then finally, the whole trade mark controversy came to an end. Not because they dragged me into court and wasted my time, no, it was never up to them to live my life.

I stopped the whole process because, quite simply, I had outgrown my logo.

The photographer of my jewellery had done the graphic image of three dolls with the word Jewel on the left and the word Divas on the right. By this time, I realised I had matured, my logo hadn't.

The trade mark process had finished, but that's not to say they'd won. They hadn't. I still have the trade mark in category 35, and I might trade mark my name at a later date in class 14, as I still own the business name, but then again, they still have their trade marks, and all these years later, I don't want to go through that again.

A few years after this happened; while following small business owners on social media, I came across other small jewellery businesses who were taking this company to court for theft. The company was selling products that were knock-offs of the pieces made by the small jewellery designers. Many took legal action, many didn't, but the company pulled the pieces from the shelves. The bigger problem was that the mega-corp had stores throughout Asia and England and bought their goods from Chinese manufacturing plants. Of course, they were going to have knock-offs in their stores. The company buyers wouldn't know any better. They removed the items and apologised yet dragged everyone wanting a trade mark through the courts.

Eventually, they closed their Australian stores, but their trade marks still stand as their sister company, another jewellery store, is still going.

Not sure if there's irony in there somewhere.

*****

After setting up Jewel Divas in 2008, I did a silversmith course to see how gold and silver jewellery making worked and whether making it could be a part of my business, but then in 2012 I considered styling courses to add to my repertoire and my jewellery business. I was going to go into people's houses and clear out wardrobes and help women find the right colour and style clothing just for them.

I scoured the internet and somehow, and I'm not sure

how, came across the *Academy of Professional Image* recognised by AICI, the Association of Image Consultants International.

I chose the two styling courses *Personal Stylist and Image Mastery for Men* and *Personal Stylist and Image Mastery for Women,* and the colour course *Personal Colour Analysis Theory.*

Unfortunately, due to the consultant having personal issues, I was left for months without my video conferences and final exams, which happened towards the end of the year, even though I did the courses in January and February. I also didn't get my final assessment for my CEUs, but looking back, I would've had to work at it to keep them and that was obviously not going to happen.

When I planned out my business and how it would work, I chose to go with wardrobe and accessory styling as I love to organise and colour co-ordinate clothing, jewellery, accessories, and wardrobes. And really, women are quite capable of sorting through their own clothing and throwing out what they no longer want or need; they don't really need someone else to do it.

But, sadly, with everything else going on in my life, especially at that time, all of that never came to be. And it got to the point where I was left feeling empty and annoyed at the time, money (it was a lot), and energy wasted on the courses. Not only because what I learned I already knew thanks to an old '80s styling book I had, and of course, Google, but after it, I didn't have the time or energy to do anything with it because 24/7 caring doesn't allow you to do anything outside of the home. I wanted to do it as an extra part of my jewellery business, but that wasn't going to happen. And still isn't while life is the way it is. Except for my own closet, I won't be wardrobe styling anyone else's any time soon. If ever. In my lifetime. Ever. In retrospect, I still think it was a waste of time.

*****

This story originally came under the MEN section in the LIFE chapter, but I moved it here because it had to do with my jewellery business.

I saw a business expert a few times to ask about setting up the jewellery business and the blog; whether I needed to make it a company, needed this, that, the other. He was very nice and gave me some ideas to think about. Months later, he sent me a link for a two-hour social media conference. If I went, I could get four hours of free mentoring.

I wanted to meet with that mentor to see what I could do about my blog and business and whether I could streamline it and make it bigger and better.

On the day of the appointment, he arrived a few minutes late and I made a joke about it, but his response was anything but polite. He also had the handshake of a limp fish.

During the mentorship it was all about his negativity. He constantly checked his phone for the time, laughed at and mocked the way my blog and website were designed with the colours and logos, talked and didn't listen, banged on about all the things I had done that were wrong or didn't work, and barely had any good ideas on how to actually help me or my business. All of this reduced me to tears in an hour and a half. He told me I wasn't the first one to cry, and told me three times during the appointment, "believe me, I'm not attacking you", and he mumbled something about, "if you don't want to change anything then I'm wasting my time".

Believe me, it wasn't your time that was wasted, and yeah, you were attacking me. Why the hell else would I cry? Because I was being attacked. Typical fucking arrogant, misogynistic, sexist shithead.

He also had no freakin' idea about what a carer actually deals with because I could see the lack of comprehension on his face when I talked about it and how it meant not being able to go to many places because Mum was on a walker, unable to travel to a lot of places, and needed daily help. He also didn't care that there were no markets, stalls, or shops in the area to sell at, and said I should have been travelling to get to them. Yeah, with a bad car that conked out when you went around corners, and a bad mother, he still expected me to do it all.

I could not wait for him to leave and sat at my desk in my bedroom. Three hours later, I stopped crying at the complete overwhelming emotion of it all, and the word that came to mind to describe him was brusque. I don't think I've ever used that word before in all of my life, but that was the one word that came to mind and suited him perfectly.

All of this happened on a Wednesday.

I thought about things, and the three decent ideas he actually had in those two hours, for the next four days. I did some googling and researching, and on the Monday rang up a new hosting company. I set things in motion that week, so I left my sale site alone while changing hosting companies and setting things up.

Ten days after he'd been and gone, I received an email from him telling me he'd checked my website and I clearly was not going to change anything because it was still the same and hadn't changed since he'd been at my place.

The fucking arrogant prick! He knew fuck all!

I emailed back with a list of things I'd done and achieved that week showing him I had been quite busy. It was my "fuck you" to the arsehole who thought berating women was the way to get his shit done. It isn't. And God knows how many other women he had reduced to tears. I'd like to know if any complained about him. He probably never did that to men, or they were "man enough" to take it. The cold hard fact is, he was a knob who had no clue, had no empathy, and sure as hell had so sympathy. And he never emailed me back. So yeah, fuck you!

I never asked for my other two hours and have never been asked to offer my opinion on the mentoring, which wasn't actually mentoring because I certainly don't call negative shit and harping on all that has been done wrong as mentoring.

Mentoring is supposed to be positive, manoeuvring people into the direction they need to be going. Not dumping your shit on them and tearing them down.

That's not what mentors do. At least, not the kind I know of.

*****

In December 2015 Mum became quite ill. She was in and out of hospital three times across three weeks and the hospital's treatment of her was abysmal. They even dropped her in the car park and chipped her hip the second time, because their policy was to let patients fall so they didn't hurt their back. Yep, their backs came before the life of patients. I couldn't cope between dealing with her, trying to run Jewel Divas, and releasing my new kids' stories that I had written.

I closed the store for a holiday over Christmas, but in January 2016, I reopened for a couple of weeks before realising things still weren't great. I closed the store again, for what ended up being a permanent holiday. I was hoping to get back to it at some point year after year, and year after year I kept writing and publishing, and every January when doing my yearly to-do list and figuring out what I wanted, I would always say to get the Jewel Divas store back up and running.

Sadly, that wasn't to be, because in late 2019 I hit burnout and ground to a mental halt and needed a break. I mention more of this in the writing chapter.

After years of small ideas percolating in my brain, in September 2021 I wrote copious notes over a three-week period. I came to the decision I would change how I did things moving forward. I came to decisions about my life and my businesses.

I wanted things to be easier, and in trying to come up with an idea, a plan, a clue, I came to the realisation that I wanted to go back to *before*.

Before things became hectic and a million things needed to be done. I wanted to make life easier again.

But that meant changing EVERYTHING moving forward.

And then things changed again.

One of those decisions was to potentially close down the jewellery business.

I sat on that idea and let it percolate away under the surface of my brain and another idea came to me in a weird way. I buy Art Union house tickets from Queensland. As a process, I think about moving into these houses and where I'd put the writing room, the library, the office, and so on. I was doing it about the Christmas apartment building, and how I'd lay out my jewellery findings, charms, work pieces, and realised that if I had jewellery parties to sell it all off, I wouldn't make any more. I thought about that idea and was pretty okay with it.

In December 2021, I decided to close the business because enough was enough. It would move into being a label, the pieces left would be sold off at some point, and only the webstore would remain until that happened.

Come January 2022, I put a message up on the Jewel Divas socials saying the business would close at the end of the month and the socials would be closed down.

They were. The Facebook, Twitter, Instagram, and Pinterest accounts all went, with all pictures of the jewellery being uploaded to the Pinterest accounts of Jewel Divas Style and Tiara King, and its own page on the Jewel Divas Style website.

And then, a year and a half on, the Universe gave me another sign.

MadeIt, the website I had my store on, had new owners and the business had a makeover in 2023. I would have to pay a monthly subscription fee just to keep the store open, even if I didn't sell anything, and that would cost me almost one hundred dollars for selling nothing. They also only sell in Australia, so I couldn't make overseas sales.

The Jewel Divas webstore closed on October 2023.

It had been ten years since I joined MadeIt in 2013, and I think the Universe was sending me a message. Time to close and fully concentrate on my writing.

I asked for them to take me off the list for migration, but as I own the business name and trade mark, I would be keeping an eye on who set up a store with that name.

I know there was probably more I could have done to sell my jewellery and myself as a jewellery designer and business, but there were no markets out this way and no stores that took on designers wholesale, so it was a bloody hard slog to get myself known.

I'm sure the Universe had other plans for me, not helping me make my business a success was the start. But then we never know unless we try. It's been statistically proved that many first businesses don't work; one in three new ones I think the last statistic was. We don't know what we're doing, so it all goes to pot and after ten years, my poor business did.

*****

As I leave this chapter I'll end with a couple of stories about sparkle.

As any sparkle lover would know, regardless of whether it's ridiculously priced big name designer pieces or a chain store or eBay bought article, stones are bound to fall out of jewellery.

Some of the biggest criminals are rings as they are bound to take more wear and tear as we do just about everything with our hands. Hands open doors and bottles, pick up bags, open car boots (trunks), put on clothes, take off clothes, try clothes on, wheel shopping trolleys (carts), delve into the nether regions of our massive handbags to dig around bottomless pits for our purse or keys, hand money over, get money, get waved around when we talk.

Bracelets and bangles are also part of the usual suspect gang, when reaching into bags or trolleys, when hitting your hand on something, or when the bracelets are pushed and rubbed against something else. I've had crystals drop right off my bracelets and land on the floor in front of me. Piece saved and fixed! Others have disappeared into the nether regions of the shopping centre universe.

For those of us who love our rings, rings take a battering in daily life and so it's inevitable they will lose stones. This has happened to me countless times where I have been unable to find the stones to re-glue, but this time was quite something.

Mum and I had pulled up in our local centre and I got out to start loading up the trolley with our shopping bags and handbags. I was wearing my Pink Flutterby set, and when I flipped up the boot with my right forefinger knuckle, it slid off and the ring hit the metal. I took one look and knew what had happened. A big stone had come out.

Once I'd got Mum out of the car, even she looked. I figured the sun would shine off it and I was looking around the car, in the boot, all over the ground, but I knew all may have been lost.

I switched the ring to my left hand, so it wasn't noticeable and we spent the next few hours shopping. I hoped that when we got out the different angle of the sun would help shine a light. We got to the car, and I unloaded both of the trolleys, got Mum in and then started to look for that pink sparkle, and lo and behold, there she was lying on the ground close to the car, surprisingly decent and not trodden all over by foot traffic. I was surprised, but not overly shocked. I had hoped it would be there and the sun shone its way to me finding it. I tucked it safely away and glued it back in later.

That's what I call, *The Miracle of Sparkle!*

And there are so many more jewellery stories I could tell you.

Like the story of how I was at the shopping centre with my mother one day and my double layered blue bead leaf necklace broke right off my neck. My right hand flew to cover it, saving most of the beads from falling. But I saw a few bounce across the tiles and under peoples' feet. Two young girls managed to grab a few and I quickly grabbed my big Nancy Drew bag and opened it, letting my necklace fall into the bag as I couldn't do anything else at the time. Later, when I counted the beads at home, I found there were about ten or fifteen missing. And, as there was nothing I could do about that, I remade it bigger and better.

Then there was the tale of two rings, a few years apart.

There's the time I was shopping when I heard a metallic clink and looked around, realising I had lost my black and white art deco ring, broken off the shank. It cost about $3 from a chain store, and I knew it wasn't worth worrying about, so after searching around the register, and even getting help from the two young guys who came through behind me, I thanked them and walked off.

As I was unloading the groceries into the car, I finally emptied the trolley and found the decoration on the bottom. I thanked the Universe and took it home, where I glued it back together. That was able to be saved, but many are not.

One ring I didn't notice was missing until I was in the post office. The decorative top had broken off the shank, and I went in search of it, retracing my steps to the newsagent, the chemist, and back outside the way I'd come in.

And I found it, crushed on the ground in the driveway just outside the centre. It wasn't able to be repaired, and luckily, I had only paid about $30 for it, so it was easily replaceable.

And then there was the earring that broke off and flew across the car while I was driving to the library.

I didn't know what it was, but was able to pull over and

felt my ears. Realising it had broken, I quickly searched for it and found it in the passenger side foot well. I removed the other earring and took them home, turning the unbroken one into a pendant on a red bead necklace.

But what happened to that? The first time I wore that necklace with the earring pendant, it broke.

Yep, the second earring broke and now I don't have a pair of red crystal earrings.

Bugger!

Needless to say, whether it's chain store, high-end, or real gold and silver; whether it be rings, bracelets, earrings, or necklaces, crystals are lost, pieces are broken, and all you can do is repair it, repurpose it, or put it in your jewellery tool box in case you can make it into something else such as a hairpin, or brooch.

It can be sad to lose a great piece of jewellery, but you also realise that chain store jewellery can be replaced with something better, and real jewellery can be repaired at the jeweller.

Blog It!

Brain dump your thoughts onto the screen,
    tell a story, weave together a scene.
Liken yourself to a great writer of old,
    whip out the one-liner, truth be told.
Onward and upward reveal all to the world,
    or reveal very little, be it boy, or be it girl.
Go where it takes you, tell your life story,
    show what it makes you, no matter how gory.

It can be therapeutic to tell your tale,
    as much or as little, it's your place to sail.
Today or tomorrow, blog it now with intent,
    blog it and log it, make it all your content.

Keyboard Warriors

I did consider putting this section under the writing chapter, as blogging is writing, but these stories are about the abuse of people online and what they think they can get away with. And more than likely it's why I came to write my teen/young adult book *#Teenblogger: To Follow or Not To Follow?* which I released under my real name.

Blogging is an access to like-minded others from around the world with whom you can converse. Although it's changed in the years I've been online, and social media has taken over as the primary source of interaction, millions of us still have blogs, more than likely on a website as we converted the blog into a site for more of a professional look, unlike some of our blogs when we first started. Remember how bad some of those looked in the '90s and '00s? Oi!

Blogging is writing on a grand, and very public scale, and was probably the next logical step for me to take after writing songs and setting up my jewellery company. I'd already written two novels, and I was going to use my blog to promote myself and have an online presence for when I was picked up by a publisher and made rich and famous.

Right from the beginning I knew there were things I

wanted to do and did not want to do. I never wanted to monetise any of my blogs. That's not what I started them for, and I will never do so because I still don't want to. My blogs are about my businesses, my author names, my books, and the awesome things I buy, and what I think about things.

When I had the T.K. Wrathbone website from 2015 to 2023, I only blogged once a month with an update on how my writing was going, and the books when they were published.

On L.J. Diva, I started blogging on the 1st of January 2009, and went from blogging whenever I felt like it to multiple times a week, to five days a week, down to three, down to two, down to once a week, which I did for about five years, and then to once a month in the final few years. Posts were mainly book updates, and soundbites of what was going on in the world of books such as copyrights, trade marks, legalities and all things writing, plus updates of what I had planned for the coming month. I did that until it was migrated over to my websites in 2023 and closed down after fifteen years.

Jewel Divas Style also started in 2009 and will continue to have posts about the things I buy, books I read, what I'm doing, and will be my primary site for blogging about my life. After migrating over many of the lighter LJD posts in 2023, that gave me a broader range of topics, such as movies and more literary fiction that I'd been reading.

And yes, I will continue blogging about all things fabulous at JDS and want to have fun doing so. Things are so much easier thanks to the overhaul of 2023.

My primary blogging site is my own at Tiara King. I post about my latest book releases, all things writerly, and anything else I want to talk about that has nothing to do with the fun and funky clothes, shoes, and jewels I buy, or the movies and books I watch and read, unless it has to do with authors and writing, of course.

All of the T.K. Wrathbone and L.J. Diva posts that were migrated over concerning releases, publishing, writing, movies and books about writing, and my thoughts continue on writing, publishing, and being an author, and will do so for as long as I do this.

The following blog posts that I decided to add here, are just a few things that happened to me with commenters on both of my blogs. Unfortunately, some people love to hide behind being anonymous, while others just name themselves outright. But abuse is abuse, and abuse online is just as bad as abuse in real life. Some people can't help themselves, because they choose to behave like animals in order to bring others down and make them feel bad in order the make themselves feel good. They are bullies, and bullies only learn when they are stood up to and shot down.

It's an abusive cycle, and not going to stop while people are online, and social media owners don't pull the websites into line, and parents don't get tougher on their kids. There should be multiple levels of people and safety trying to prevent this garbage, and that starts with parents because they are the first line of defence in raising their children and allowing them to use phones, tablets, and computers and be on social media in the first place. Parents are followed by schools who should not allow phones and tablets in classrooms, and which should have been doing free classes on internet safety from the moment they allowed electronics with internet into the classroom. These are followed by the platform owners raising the age limits and banning people who whore their children out to social media for money, banning perverts and paedophiles from being on the website, banning children from having accounts… followed by politicians, lawyers, and the police actually getting off their backsides and charging the people abusing. Law makers need to keep up, but they're not.

Here are a few stories of what I dealt with.

*****

On January 1st, 2009, I started blogging on Blogspot, as it was known then, as *Bitchfest!* under the domain of jewelsdiva.com.au. Over the years, it grew by name, to *A Bitchfest! Lovefest!* to *Lady Jewels Diva*, with the same domain of ladyjewelsdiva.com.

When you're blogging, you have so much to contend with. One of the first things we had to deal with, for those of us who started in the late noughts, was those leaving their comments as anonymous. They were the bane of our existence. As were those who felt the need to insult.

Those were weak and insipid cretins who didn't have the balls to back their shit up with their own name, who came in like a criminal in the night and thought they could drop their bombs and slink away.

And shit it was. Some of the abuse I received was full on and warning them I'd remove their comments did no good, so I did it, depending on which words they used.

We bloggers retaliated by attacking back, and most times it worked. Many never returned to keep commenting on those particular posts, but many more came in their place.

One post in particular at my author site became heated with fifty plus comments from people just attacking each other. I had to delete and block, and fortunately, that post is long gone.

I'd gained 25 followers by the end of my first year and we all commented on each other's blogs. My blog was colourful and designed in a way that most would have thought I was in my 20s or 30s. But I wasn't. In 2009 I was 35 and followed many twenty-somethings because I was young at heart, and jokingly think that I was emotionally stunted at twenty-five. We fitted right in.

Unfortunately, I didn't fit in with everyone.

Much like high school, really.

Over the years I had quite a few who would come on to my blog and dictate how I needed to be. I always knew none of them had any clue how old I was, and I always knew they were in their twenties. Their language, their word usage, the way they thought they had the right to tell me how to be, what to write and what to post showed their age.

In many cases, I would attack only if they posted vile comments as anonymous, calling them out for their shit. In some cases, they would email me and attack, so I emailed back. There was one email exchange that went on for some time, and the poor girl got so confused that she forgot what she'd said to me, and I needed to remind her that she had attacked me and told me to shut up. She said she didn't. I showed her the receipts. Her emails. She finally gave up and blamed me for it all, even though she had emailed me to attack in the first place.

Sheesh, some people!

And then there was the exchange on a post I had written about a young woman who had killed her sister.

I had two anonymous posters who attacked, and when I attacked back and called them out for posting anonymously, they signed in with their real names, and their profiles from another website, feigning that it was so hard to out themselves.

One told me she was going to make screenshots of the post and send it to all of the publishers, so my book was never published, and labelled me as homophobic.

My post was not about lesbians, and I made no mention of anyone being gay because I had no clue if they were, and the post wasn't about that.

Her friend copied with the same tropes.

I clicked on the links in their names and went to their profiles, and then posted them to the comment section. The reason I did this was because poster 1 told me I had clearly done no research and had no clue what I was talking about.

I thought, *I'll do my research then.* On them. And neither was happy. They both attacked because I'd put their details in the replies. Considering their profiles are public on those sites, I have no idea why they were so upset... *massive eyeroll*

Unfortunately, narcissists love to attack people, and then when you pull them up, they continue their attack while also playing the victim. They weren't victims of anything except their own bullshit.

It was about a five-year period where all of this happened. Around 2012 to 2017, though 2009 to 2012 had been pretty good, with regular posting and comments, until everyone moved to Tumblr or WordPress and stopped blogging at Blogspot. From 2017 to 2019 I was blogging once a week, and only one or two were regular posters.

In late 2017, eight years after I'd started blogging, I opened the brand spankin' new L.J. Diva website, along with the Porn Star Brothers website. It was everything the blog wasn't, and I kept both the blog and website running for two years before making a decision once more about cutting and culling.

I had my Blogspot blog migrated into my WordPress website in early 2019. I cleared out some of the older posts I no longer thought were worthy of being in existence or which just embarrassing and hideous and I no longer wanted around, to make it easier to move over. And I started thinking about what to post moving forward. I'd blogged about a lot of things over those years, but over the five or so previous years, I'd toned down and written more about publishing, writing, books and movies I'd read and watched. I also talked about authors, and the many legalities concerning authors. I rarely feel the need to comment on everything in the world anymore. Doing so for years had been exhausting.

By then, no one was actually leaving a post because I was now on WordPress. And even if they did, it was usually on years' old posts which always surprised me. Why would you comment on a five-year-old post when time, the person who posted it, and the people mentioned in it, had moved on?

In early 2020, I deleted another hundred posts or so to clean up the backend, and then came one final comment. It was via Facebook, to my then author page, and it was from the daughter of a woman I had blogged about ten years earlier. The daughter was angry at me because I said the woman didn't deserve a second kidney. She had destroyed her own kidney with drugs and alcohol, and then did the same to her donated kidney. She had then pleaded on TV and in magazines that she deserved a second donation. I said she didn't, as did many others did on TV and socials, as she'd had her chance and squandered it by going back to drugs and alcohol.

The daughter was older now, but not happy. I wondered if she'd tracked down everyone who'd written something about her mother just to attack them, to redirect her anger onto people who still existed because her mother didn't. She was the person the daughter should be angry at, not everyone else.

It did make me wonder though if I still wanted those types of posts to exist. I had long moved on from those posts and what I used to be and write about, as many bloggers do. We grow, we change, we get older and do other things. And then, in 2021, I deleted another couple of hundred simply because they were no longer who I was.

Was that move because of the daughter? No, but it did narrow my focus even more about the type of posts I wanted to write and leave as a legacy.

And then, in late 2022, when I decided to close down my author sites and move it all over to my own website, I deleted and cleaned up more. So much was written, and joked about, and criticised. But it was time for them to go.

Right before I had my two author websites migrated in April 2023, I culled even more, and cleaned up the categories into a neat and tidy batch. There are 385 L.J. Diva posts on Tiara King, and 334 on Jewel Divas Style. 719 posts. That's all that's left from between 2009 to 2023.

By the time it was all migrated over, I had culled a good 3000 posts from my 14 years of posting. Had I had kept posting consistently, and kept all of the posts I'd ever done, I would have been heading for 4000. If not over.

Cripes!

Moving forward under the L.J. Diva name, I will always release my adult novels under that name and post about them at my website under the category of L.J. Diva. The posts will grow, slowly each year, but as for blogging about anything else, that will come under my name on my website, or under my style site Jewel Divas Style.

I've corralled all of my posts, websites, and socials to make life easier, and I talk more about that when I discuss having burnout in the writing section.

*****

Something happened on Jewel Divas Style in August/September 2014.

On four of my posts, a girl, and I call her that because not only did her name give her away, but so did her language, made comments that made me disgusted by their viciousness.

On one MY STYLE post, the comment was only three words. *One. Hot. MESS!!*

I never did like that term; I think it's stupid and an insult to most and told her as much.

Second, when I did a blog post on how the great bargain of $3 Kmart leather gloves turned out to be a style failure because they were both right hands, she got more insulting and not only trashed me, but Kmart as well.

She thought the Kmart gloves weren't the only style failure on my blog and didn't think the words "$3 k-mart gloves" and "style" should ever be used in the same sentence.

Clearly, she had a HUGE problem with Kmart for some reason, and clearly didn't know what style actually was.

Thirdly, she attacked my couture jewellery, leaving the definition of couture as the comment, probably from Google. She claimed my jewellery was not couture but *a hot mess*.

God I hate that phrase! And how rude. She clearly didn't

understand that couture also refers to jewellery.

Fourthly, she got absolutely vile on a cancer post I did when I had my mole cut off. I spoke of my personal experience, but it clearly wasn't bad enough for her.

Her comment was gross, and quite frankly, *she* should be ashamed that she even left it. The anger she spewed…yikes!

First, she told me that my blog post was one of the most appalling she'd ever read about cancer, that I was incredibly clueless, and could not compare my tiny skin cancers to all the other cancers out there. Which I didn't, I was simply talking about my mole removal and how I deal with having cancerous moles.

She then spewed on with details that left me thinking she had either been through cancer herself or knew someone who had. But that was no excuse for spewing hatred at me. She made a lot of assumptions about my experience with cancer, and we know what assume means.

She went on to tell me I was in no position to pass opinion or even advice on this matter, which I wasn't doing, that it was bad enough I spoke the way I did, but to publish my post was absolutely woeful and that I should be ashamed.

I'm not. Not then and most definitely not now.

Second, she went on to attack my jewellery and style, calling them both horrendous. She claimed that she was embarrassed for me, which I never understand when someone says that and think it's a stupid thing to say. She said she'd never seen anything as disgusting, cheap and tacky as what was displayed on my blog, I shouldn't be using the terms couture or fashion designer, and that I was buying cheap crap online & mashing it up together into a hideous mess. She then went on to say there was a reason barely anyone acknowledged my social media posts.

As if she'd know!

And last but not least, she added a P.S. and spewed to me that if I kept eating burgers & chocolates for breakfast, or all that ice cream, or quarter cheesecakes or hot chips, or packets of chips that I'd end up with more than a few tiny skin cancers.

Fuck, I hate some people!

Seriously! I had no idea why she'd be embarrassed *for* me or be worried about what I ate.

Normally I don't call people jealous unless you can really hear it or see it, and you can definitely see it in her comments. You can tell when jealousy is afoot because the attacks get personal.

And she assumed a lot. There's a saying when it comes to the word, assume. "It makes an ass out of you and me". It's supposed to be the easy way of remembering how to spell it. But I've changed it to "it makes an ass out of the person doing the assuming". Never assume from one or a chain of photos because it's never the whole picture. The saying, "don't judge a book by its cover" works well here. Never judge a situation by one photo.

She assumed a lot about my personal life, including that I don't know about cancer because I haven't ended up in ICU or had therapy. No, but my mother and father both did. Skin cancer is not a tiny cancer; it can lead to death and is one of the biggest killing cancers in this country. Had I not caught it in time then yes, I would have been in the ICU, losing a limb or worse. I have been in and out of hospitals with my mother since I was ten when she had her cancer cut off; a gaping hole is still in her arm, and she had a skin graft from her leg.

My father had a brain tumour out when I was 20, something he could have had since birth. NEVER ASSUME you know about someone simply because they don't mention it.

She personally attacked everything, my style, my jewellery, what I wear, what I put in my blog posts, stated that my couture isn't couture, because she has no idea about what I have made, and called it all a hideous mess. Mind you, she even came back the night after to make another comment on another post.

Then she attacked me on the social media front. I follow a lot of people who may have a lot of followers but barely get any comments. So what! I'm not desperate for likes, likers or followers. I'm not into it for that. As long as my posts are seen in people's feeds, that's all I need because people will also comment on my social pages. It really shows immaturity when they attack you over the lack of response on your social media and shows they clearly have an addiction to being liked and needing responses from others to make them feel better, bigger, more liked and more powerful.

A personal attack means jealousy, and her comments led me to believe one of three things. She either cannot buy the amount of clothes and jewellery I do (regardless of it all being drastically reduced on sale) or make jewellery the way I do, and so has a problem with that and decided to take her anger and hatred out on me. Or else, she blows all of her money (or Mummy and Daddy's money) on big name designer duds and Kmart wear is so way beneath her. Or maybe, she doesn't have the confidence, looks-wise, to wear what I do. Is she the one dealing with cancer? No idea, but it could be one reason she chose to attack someone she doesn't know about their looks and one little blog they posted about being skin cancer savvy and seeing the doctor once a year.

Could it be that she's dealing with cancer and didn't come out well on the other end, so trashes anyone and everyone about their looks and cancer posts? If that's the case, I could not have been the only one she did it to. And she trashed a store for God's sake, and that showed her problem with Kmart. Regardless of what it is.

Her jealousy is eating away at her and makes her angry; hence she unleashed her hate fuelled venom on me. Couture does apply to jewellery, and I have no idea why she has such a hatred for what I buy. She clearly has no idea about designing either. I believe she would have read my side bar where I say I'm a jewellery, accessory and fashion designer, creator, collector and consultant and then wrongly believed that meant everything I had to wear had to be made by me for me to be considered a designer. But I'm sure even then she would have criticised.

I make jewellery, I buy jewellery, I have also made clothes, which I've posted in the past, and that MAKES ME a designer. I also buy a lot, which MAKES ME a collector. She has assumed and wrongly labelled me with her jealousy, ignorance, and arrogance.

Then she made it even more personal and attacked the few food photos I've posted to Instagram, wrongly believing that was the food I ate all day every day, and I would be getting more than a few "tiny" skin cancers if I kept eating that way. I'd posted 33 food pictures on Instagram from when I started in 2012 to the date of her comment in 2014, and apparently that's the way I always eat, according to her. She must have gone all the way back with some of what she mentioned. The quarter cheesecake was shared with my mother as were the corn chips and two litre tubs of ice cream. She clearly thought I ate everything myself.

Fuck! How freakin' rude! What I eat is no one's business. What I wear is no one's business. My style is my style, and I don't give a fat rat's whether anyone likes it. I was forty freakin' years old at the time of that post. I'm now fifty-one. I didn't care what people thought of me then. I still don't. I had no idea why she would feel embarrassed *for* me. That's rude too because she's *assuming* I'm embarrassed, or at the very least, would be embarrassed by what I wear. Never mind the millions of comments I get when I go shopping. Yep, they know style and individuality when they see it. And to attack me so personally shows her immaturity and insecurity in her own style, or should I say, lack thereof. The fact she cannot buy what I buy; or make jewellery like I do would have set her jealousy meter off.

You don't attack someone so personally, make a bunch of stupid assumptions and insult someone unless jealousy has set in. Jealousy fuels anger, anger fuels hatred, and hatred makes you rude. Insecurity shows immaturity and they are both a very big turn off. If you're jealous of what I buy or make, I don't want to know about it. They are your issues to deal with, not mine. I did not make you jealous, angry, or full of hatred. They are already within you and nothing to do with me, so keep them to yourself and off my blog.

After this, I received a reply from her on one post and deleted it, as I said I would, leaving this reply.

The person who I am speaking of has come back and left more messages for me across three posts, this one included. Since she clearly could not be bothered reading my answers to her previous shitty comments where I told her I would trash all future comments of hers, she won't be getting any more space on this blog.

I then received a comment from someone who I suspect knows the original poster. They told me I was being very unprofessional, and that I should take it on the chin, ignore it, and move on instead of fuelling the fire.

My reply was this: *I find it inherently funny that I get attacked and my reply is called unprofessional by not one, but two immature children.*

It's actually NOT unprofessional to reply to someone dumping their crap on you. I laid out her answers, laid out my replies and discussed what her possible issue with me was for her to be so personally critical about me, and what I wear and buy, so unless it's you under a different email, clearly you have no understanding of right of reply or the right to defend oneself against vicious bullshit. My blog, my right to reply to a poster who was rude and insulting, just as I'm replying to you now, TWO MONTHS after posting this blog post. God knows why you bothered on a two-month-old post unless it is you and you're using an alias.

I'm not fuelling anything as this post was two months ago. I moved on until she replied to it, and as promised, I deleted her comment and left my reply to it, and now here's you with the same ignorant, immature understanding of defending oneself against personal attacks labelling it as unprofessional. By whose standards is my reply unprofessional, only hers and yours clearly? She said the same thing, and just goes to show how immature the two of you are because I don't actually have to take abuse on the chin or ignore it simply because people think they can shit on me and expect me to not reply. I have EVERY right to defend myself and reply to it and if you don't like me or others turning garbage like that into blog posts, then don't bother commenting.

If you're this immature and insecure in your daily life that you don't understand that people have the right to defend themselves against bullshit from others any way they see fit, then you have no airspace on this blog. Don't come back.

That happened so long ago. I blocked them both and have had no replies since. I really don't understand why people go onto someone's blog and leave such shitty comments about them. People they don't know. Making personal attacks on their looks, what they eat, what they wear.

I've seen it a lot in the years I've blogged, and many young women talk about the comments left on their socials. It's become a lot worse in the blogger sphere and social media since I received those comments in 2014, and some of the comments I've seen are just vile. Why the hell would you threaten someone you don't know with rape and death is beyond me and I'm glad I never received such shitty garbage. But even now, if I did, I would unleash the beast and let it out, because I have no time or energy for cunts.

*****

A follow on post from the previous came from a comment that I thought about, and realised, yeah, I am. Let's blog it!

Can you still call yourself a jewellery or fashion designer if you buy jewellery or clothes?

Of course, you bloody can!

This is following on from the post where I was accused of hideous things by a very rude, insecure, immature child.

She called my jewellery and style absolutely horrendous,

disgusting, cheap & tacky. That I really shouldn't be using the terms "couture" or "fashion designer", and that I was buying cheap crap online & mashing it up together into a hideous mess.

I gave my opinion on designing and being a designer.

The definition of designer, be it jewellery, accessory, clothing, household furnishings and what not is this: A person who devises and executes designs, as for works of art, clothes, machines, etc.

So yes, anyone designing, making, and creating jewellery or clothes is a jewellery or fashion designer.

This doesn't prevent or stop you from BUYING jewellery or clothing. If you make your own clothes or jewellery you don't have to refuse to buy or wear any other designer or even store bought.

Just because I buy most of my clothes doesn't mean I haven't designed clothes before and therefore can't call myself a designer. The same with jewellery, just because I buy a tonne of it doesn't mean I'm not a designer.

The person was clearly confused. Does she believe that because I show the clothes I buy, I must be claiming to make them? I don't and never have as I leave the details of where I buy them from and how much the article cost. The same with jewellery. I've always kept my jewellery that I sell separate to what I buy or make for myself. That doesn't mean I don't make it and therefore can't call myself a designer.

I'm a designer because I design, make, and create jewellery. I do this more so than clothes, but I've also done that over the years. Abusing someone and telling them they really shouldn't be using the terms couture or fashion designer because I buy online and mostly in store is rude and shows a lack of maturity and security in your own self and own style.

Attacking someone about their style is also not on. Style is what you make it. Just because it's not "on trend" doesn't not mean it's not style. I dress in what I like. I don't dress for anyone else, least of all immature, insecure children like her.

I AM a jewellery designer because I design, make, and create jewellery, for myself and for sale.

I DO make couture pieces because couture also refers to jewellery.

I AM a fashion designer because I've made and decorated clothing for myself in the past.

I have style and flair because I'm not immature or insecure in my looks, the way I dress or what I wear. I dress for no one but myself, I buy for no one but myself, and know what I can and can't call myself.

I CAN call myself a jewellery, accessory, and fashion designer because that is what I am. Whether anyone else likes it or not in their jealous hate fuelled anger.

I've only made three articles of clothing; my Hawaiian print dress and skirt which I cut out, sewed up, and decorated with sequins by me; and my jumper that I made, from scratch, in high school, cut out, sewed up and decorated by me.

I made hair accessories when I had long hair and still make hair sparklies in my collections for sale.

I've made pocket kerchiefs and scarves. I may not be a pro, but I can sew the basics.

I've made hair combs and hair clips. The combs are painted or have Swarovski crystals, as are hair clips, to which I added blue pieces with crystals.

I've also designed many pieces but had them made by someone else. My mother knits everything I have, so my cardigans and jumpers are by her but my design. My line dance shirts and rock 'n roll jacket was done by a local seamstress back in the late '90s when we danced. I designed everything and drew up the pic, and she made them. She worked just down the road, so it was easy enough to go there on the way out or on the way home from somewhere.

So yes, after all this, I CAN call myself a designer!

The Creative Artist

I am an Author, a biographer,
a composer, a creator,
essayist, fictionist, littérateur, lyricist,
novelist, opinionator, pen,
putting pen to paper
to be a poet, a publisher,
a rhymer, a reasoner,
a storytelling woman of letters,
a wordsmith with a need to be better.
From A to W, author to writer,
I am always me, the inventive designer.
The Creative Artist.

Writing on the Wall

I read my first Nancy Drew in 1984 from the school library. It was the cream UK Armada print of The Haunted Showboat and I loved it!

Then I read every Nancy Drew in the library and our local suburban library. Then Mum bought me some, and then as I got older, I started buying them from book exchanges, and bookshops when new ones came out and I could afford them and then eBay came along, and Amazon, Abe, Awesome Books and suddenly my collection amassed of well over 2000 items across 40 years.

Yep. I've been collecting since I was ten. And believe me when I say, I really wish I was a minimalist and didn't love stuff and have countless collections, but I do and I have to deal with it because I love pretty, and sparkling, and have to have stuff. If it's because it fills the emotional black hole inside of me, then it fills the emotional black hole inside of me. No harm, no foul. But damn, what a lot of money over the years. On all counts.

Because, of course, one must also buy the sister collections of The Hardy Boys and The Dana Girls, who were also published by the Stratemeyer Syndicate which owned Nancy.

Plus, I bought other book series, Trixie Belden, Susan Sand, Connie Blair, Linda Craig, Kay Tracey. That branched into collections of Murder, She Wrote, Castle, Crimes of Fashion, and when Jackie Collins died, her entire catalogue in hardcovers and paperbacks.

And they weren't the only books I collected. I also collected books on fashion, style, jewellery, accessories, home design, Barbie, and whatever took my fancy.

But going back to that very first year of finding Nancy, in 1984, at the age of ten, little did I know what was to come.

I read a lot of US teen series for the next eight years, and then at eighteen I turned very adult and started reading the Harlequin Mills & Boon red Desire books.

God knows why; probably because I had turned eighteen and, I guess, wanted to read romance books. I read them for four years before suddenly doing a one eighty and starting on horror.

Not sure why, but along came my brother from another mother, Stephen King, with Dean Koontz, Johnathon Kellerman and many, many more weird-ass stories like The Beast House. But then they were all weird-ass stories. The Beast House will make you want to glue your legs together. God knows why I read it. Such schlocky '80s fare.

All of that lasted for four years each. Four years for romance, four years for horror.

And amongst all of that was R.L. Stine's Fear Street...

And then along came Jackie Collins...

I realised many years later, probably just four or so years ago, after writing so many stories of my own, that they were probably setting me up for the stories the Universe was putting aside for me to write in the future. The adult romance;

the young adult horror. The Jackie style of glamour, hot men and women, and Tinseltown. The Stine style of death, bad boys and girls, and even worse creatures.

It had all set me up for what I ended up writing, and that's a little bizarre in itself.

*****

The introduction I wrote for my *Poems of a Musical Flavour* series is perfect for putting here because it explains everything beautifully about how I came to write songs and then books.

My writing career can be traced back to primary school, year seven to be exact, when I wrote and published my first book. After that I wrote and published a second and third for school and then for some reason, fancied myself as a song writer. I wrote lyrics, more on that in a moment, and wrote "songs" because I wanted to be a singer. But after seven years I stopped and that was replaced ten years later by longer "songs" called novels. That's when books and short stories came. Then came the idea to write out and print up these lyrics of mine into books…

It took me three weeks to write out 639 sets of song lyrics and I was definite that I had 700…maybe I need to add to that 639…I even wrote songs about child abuse, heavy lyrics by my standard back in 1994 when I was 20, and probably still very relevant today. There are also a few things I realise now, at the ripe old age of 43 (at the time of printing), that I would not have realised back then.

1 - Most of the songs had the same lyrics, so I seemed to plagiarise myself a lot.

2 - The lyrics were incredibly young-sounding at the beginning.

3 - I wrote the way so many teens did back then.

4 - I was way ahead of my years and the time because of the topics I wrote about, and surprisingly, they are still very and incredibly relevant, if not more dominant, now.

My lyrics were young because I started writing them when I was 15 in 1989. It was year ten in high school, I played the drums and piano, wore a funky blue knitted jumper with a stave on it with the first line of Funky Town and thought I was hot. I also wanted to be a singer...

I wanted to be Australia's version of Debbie Gibson and I'm listening to her first album, *Out of the Blue*, as I write this (I love '80s music more than anything). I loved everything about her. Her funky clothes to the Swatch watches she wore. And when she moved into her new mansion, I wanted *it* and everything else. That's why she inspired me with her lyrics and melodies. She did it all. It also didn't hurt that the only time she ever toured Australia was with my favourite Aussie band, Indecent Obsession. I also wrote many a song about them. She even had a thing with the lead singer.

Debbie Gibson was huge, along with Tiffany, Kylie and Dannii Minogue, Indecent Obsession, Yazz, Kim Wilde, and an abundance of others in 1989. There was '80s bubblegum/pop blasting from every radio and TV. Even Jem and the Holograms got a go (gotta love the '80s). Debbie was the inspiration for my lyrics, so the early ones are very similar in a young teenage style of the '80s. They aged as I did, but I stopped writing after 7 years as I'd moved on, but did write one song in 2002. But Debbie is very much in there, in inspiration for song titles, or lines or phrases, as are so many other artists who gave me the idea for a funky tune or romantic ballad.

When going back over the decades of music, lyrics were incredibly simple, be it '50s, '60s, '70s or '80s. Come the '90s it changed. Grunge came in and lyrics became down right weird, and you'd read them and go 'what were they on when they wrote this?' These days it's different again. Between Kelly Clarkson, P!nk, Lady Gaga, Taylor Swift, and so many other females and males, not to mention bands, lyrics have become harder, edgier, and downright far too sexy for the teens singing them. I occasionally wonder how they come up with such adult stuff.

Back in the day, lyrics were young and innocent, now, they're far too sexual. I definitely don't know if I could write any now; the lyrics would be older, more mature, but writing books gives me a longer platform to get the story across. Not sure I could do it in four verses, a chorus, and a bridge anymore. But you never know. Writing them all up gave me inspiration… And you know I can't *not* write something… with everything else I already write and the books yet to be written…something is going to come out at some stage.

I wrote from 1989 to 2002 then that was it. Four years later I wrote my first novel, and I think my lyrics made way for that. I even wrote song trilogies which have stood me in good stead for writing the book trilogy I wrote in 2016. Lyrics were clearly my training for bigger and longer stories, which songs are. They are stories of love, pain, hurt, heartache etc. Just listen to country songs. The dog dies, the wife leaves, and the ute breaks down. Songs are full of it and many times lyrics are simple.

Remember all those really poppy songs from the '80s? Try

Stock, Aitken and Waterman songs, Kylie Minogue, Jason Donovan, Bananarama, Sonia, any UK '80s pop act had one of their songs and they were all done to formula. Two verses, chorus, two verses, chorus, bridge, chorus to end. The music was what sucked you in, it was up tempo, poppy and danceable. But analyse the lyrics and they were the most teenager-ish ridiculous things around. Yet they meant so much at the time when we were young but reading back over them as adults they are just silly and childish. Remember B*Witched's *Rollercoaster* and Kylie's *I Should Be So Lucky?* Enough said!

But that's what makes a pop song, and that's what I wrote. Young pop lyrics from a 15-22-year-old that didn't know any better and wasn't experienced at anything we call life. Like now.

Did my lyrics get older and more mature? Sort of. You can see the progression into '94-'96. Around this time Alanis Morissette came out and I desperately wished I could write a song like her. I didn't have her angst, but I tried. I'm not sure I succeeded. There are a few good sets of lyrics in the last years and some of my song titles were freakin' awesome, like *Brunettes Look Best in Red*, *Ginger Elle*, *Cool Fred* and *Firenze*. A line from someone else's song, or an Impulse body spray name (big body spray label over here that's been around forever) was all for the taking.

I did songs about politics, the world, generation X (the Spice Girls ripped me off a few years later with that one, lol). No topic was not written about…that I remember.

But for me, life took a turn and here we are, nearly 30 years later, and I still don't sing or write song lyrics. Instead, I write books and short stories under three names and maybe these songs, these lyrics, were the beginning of my ability to come up with unusual titles and strange stories (although I'm sure all of my English teachers at school could attest to the fact I did that even earlier), and writing a trilogy of songs as I do a trilogy of books.

Thank you to all the muses, guides, helpers, inspirational musicians and singers that gave me the lines, the titles, the ideas for these songs. I honour you and dedicate these books to all of you.

*****

I wish I could be like Jackie Collins. She wrote bonkbusting novels about people she knew, the gossip she overheard, the stories she was told. The glamorous life she lived in London and Hollywood all while wearing animal print and the most ah-maze-ing jewellery. That's definitely something I want to do, and she's someone I want to be when I grow up. Here's what Jackie means to me in an essay I wrote. The full piece is on my website on a page devoted just to her under my L.J. Diva author name in the menu.

THAT ONE MOMENT

We all have that one moment, that one day, that we remember a particular event happening.

I do.

It's Sunday the 20th of September 2015, at one o'clock in the afternoon, Australian time. I was working and listening to the radio in my office when the news came through that Jackie Collins had passed away.

I cried out in disbelief and my head spun to stare at the

radio. How could she possibly have died when she didn't look sick, hadn't said anything. I was checking her Facebook, Twitter, and Instagram pages, and had only just answered one of her questions a week before. I went into shock. How could Jackie be gone?

I turned on my phone and checked Facebook and there they were, a plethora of posts about her passing. I shed tears. Lots of them.

It's hard to describe the feelings one has when they lose a mentor. To lose someone you look up to. Someone that means the world to you even though you'd never met them. Business experts tell us to find a mentor, whether they know you've made them your mentor or not, and to follow the things they do that work, and ignore the things that don't.

That's Jackie for me, because there will never be another Jackie Collins. There will never be another ball-busting, bonkbuster writing, rollicking author such as Jackie. Her sense of humour, her knowledge, her…everything.

She didn't take bullshit, lived her life the way she wanted, had husbands and lovers (now there's a book title), and wrote what she wanted without giving a damn. She was strong and gutsy, ballsy and rollicking, a fabulous dresser, and a woman who made her heroines tough, fierce ass kickers, and she is who I aspire to be when I grow up.

INSPIRING

A scene from one of Jackie's books was stuck in my head, and I kept thinking I wanted to write a book with a character like that in it. It inspired me to write my first novel, The Road to Vegas, in 2006.

Jackie was an inspiration for those of us wanting to write

and be writers. She inspired me to write shorter chapters than the normal 20-25 pages dictated by publishers, and to write how I wanted instead of how the publishing world expected me to.

I loved a lot of things about Jackie. Her saucy secrets, her books, her vast collection of blazers she designed herself, her house, and the amazing adventures she had. I can only dream of having a gorgeous house with seven writing desks and a huge, decorated office with rows and rows of my books in hardcover and paperback.

I also put a dedication to her in The Road to Vegas, and spoke of her in my second novel, Hollywood Dreams. Jackie loved putting Australian characters in her books, so I reciprocated by talking about her in several of mine. She'll also have her place here on my website, because as my inspiration, she's not going anywhere.

In 2007 when she was here in Aus on morning TV, and I was struck with the idea to write her a letter on her website. She answered on her site and subsequently answered a second question. I didn't get to take a screenshot of it as I didn't know how on my old laptop, but did manage to copy/paste her replies into word.

In the years following those inspirational comments, I continued writing sexy, sassy, kick-ass romances the way Jackie did, with Falling for London and The Billionaire's Dirty Little Secret following Hollywood Dreams and The Road to Vegas. Jackie had a way with words, and wrote the type of stories I wanted to be immersed in. About A-Z grade celebrities and Hollywood elites, alpha male bad boys and kick-ass good girls, and the glitzy, glamorous world they all lived in. They were the type of books I wanted to produce for myself and put out to the world as my own.

And in 2014, I did. I had the vague idea for a porn star book before the ideas grew in early 2015. When she died, I knew I had to get it out of my head and onto paper, then out into the world, which I finally did, in 2016. Her death urged me on to write the initial novellas of Carlos, Pedro, Tomas and Retribution, which I rolled into one fabulous omnibus novel I called Porn Star Brothers. Then came the novels Forever, Love Never Dies, Stefan: The New Generation (a nod to Jackie's Hollywood Wives: The New Generation), DeLuca, Spiros & Jenny, and And Always. Seven massive novels of a family saga consisting of 1,088,563 words, and full of salacious celebrities, glamour, money and power, all run by the kick-ass Stephanopoulos matriarch, Jennifer. The whole series is dedicated to Jackie because SHE IS the original LADY BOSS! And I believe the series is my best work when it comes to my adult novels. Not even my stand-alones come close.

Since that series, I've written, along with my kids' horror stories, more novels. Anything for You is about an Australian author who falls in love with an A-list Hollywood actor who has a bitch of an ex-wife actress who's dating a toyboy singer, and how their obsessions change their lives. The next novel to be released, on September 19th 2024, is about three hot, sexy people, a club owner, a band manager, and a detective, and the tragedies that brings them together for some hot sexy nights. Very Jackie-esque!

BEING SOCIAL

Before she passed, she liked two posts on my Jewel Divas Style Instagram page. After her passing, her account liked a Jewel Divas Style Instagram post, and a L.J. Diva Facebook post for Forever, my Porn Star Brothers series book, as I'd written in the post that the series was dedicated to her.

In January 2020, not long after I posted on my L.J. Diva Instagram account about some of the Jackie Collins books I'd recently acquired, which seemed to be incredibly rare, Jackie followed me.

I felt incredibly honoured and chuffed, but weird that my writing mentor and inspiration had followed me on social media. Honoured, because it's an honour to have your writing mentor and inspiration follow you, and I'll always treasure the posts she liked, but weird because she'd been gone for over four years.

I know it wasn't actually her who followed me, and I wished it was, but her daughters who are running her social media. It's hard to deal with when she still seems so very much alive, and yet so very much gone.

I have since closed the social media accounts for my pen name, L.J. Diva, in order to make my business life simpler, but I most definitely took screenshots before doing so.

A PARTICULAR EVENT HAPPENED

As I mentioned above, Jackie was here in Aus in May 2007. During this time, our TV awards, The Logies, was on and she appeared on a morning show called 9AM with David and Kim the morning after. She spoke about watching the Logies and loving Kim's earrings, which Kim had borrowed for the awards and was still wearing. It was later revealed that Jackie bought those exact earrings while she was here.

During that conversation they talked about it being carer's week. Jackie spoke of caring for her husband and fiancé during their cancers, and subsequent deaths, and how everyone's so busy looking after the person who's dying, that everyone forgets about the carers. And the carers are the ones dealing with the anger and resentment, as I related to as my mother's carer. She'd also lost her mother to cancer, so it was a triple blow. And then she herself dies from cancer.

Her daughters had known for years, but she only revealed all to her siblings, Joan and Bill, when she visited London for a book tour the week before her death. After looking at the pictures from those last few weeks, it was clear to see Jackie's face had become gaunt and thin. You could tell she was sick, and I assume she knew the end was possibly coming fast.

And Jackie worked until the end, with several books on the go, including her memoir. I'd love to read it, but sadly, that hasn't been published and may never be. But I have the documentary, Lady Boss, to weep over, with never-before-seen images and videos of the ballbuster as she was.

I wish I'd met her, but never had the opportunity all of the times she was here in Aus. I always dreamed and believed that when my books hit it big, I would travel to America and meet her, but dreams are not always meant to come true. I'll never get the chance to see her, talk with her, or to even visit her house. If I'd had the millions, I would've bought her house just for the sake of it being Jackie Collins' house. Imagine all of the inspiration oozing out of the desks and walls that I could have soaked in to write my own books. But sadly, I'll never do any of it. That's why I've downloaded all of the videos I could find on YouTube, so I can keep watching her, watching her life, watching her write her ballsy strong women.

Many times, when watching a video or ten, it seems as though she's still here and you forget that she's not. And every now and then, I have a little cry about her being gone.

I'll treasure the Jackie goodies I find online, and the fact my writing mentor and inspiration followed me on Instagram, liked several of my posts, and answered my questions on her website.

Jackie, you are so, so, sadly missed, but forever on the highest inspirational pedestal I can find. I celebrate your rollicking ballsy attitude and pretend that on another plane of existence I am you. But if I'm not, can you please send your inspiration my way so I can write and produce many more novels like yours.

Forever and always, Tiara.

*****

For years I knew I wanted to write a book. I'd had a few dreams and written them down, had a vague idea of what it was going to be, and had one scene in particular where two of my main leads meet.

But, like so many people, I kept saying "one day". And then "one day" my muse, guide, helper, whoever it was up in the nether regions of the cosmos, laid two hands on my back and pushed me across the hallway into my then bedroom, now office, and said in my right ear, "get that notebook out of your desk and start writing". I pictured that notebook in my mind because I knew the exact one she meant. I also did the usual, "yeah but I don't have the right notebook", and she repeated herself.

I got the notebook out and started writing.

First, I tried to start the book from what would be the beginning. But it just wasn't working because I had no idea what the beginning was. Then, I flipped twenty or so pages ahead in the notebook and started from that scene. The scene where two of my main leads, Tahlia and Vegas, meet, and on she rolled like a bullet train doing double time.

That was 2006, and I called the book *The Road to Vegas*. I desperately wanted it to be published and sent it to publishers all around Australia and the world. Little did I realise it was not the masterpiece I thought it was.

After two years of schlepping it around, I wrote what was then called *How I Won Lotto, Moved to L.A and Married Michael Weatherly*, not exactly a fetching title, I know, and after some advice from another author who suggested I didn't dump the book and title on the poor guy, I changed it to *How I Won Lotto, Moved to L.A and Married a Really Huge TV Star*. Because that title was so much better. *eyeroll*. Finally, in 2019 I changed it to *Hollywood Dreams*.

I knew that I would need an author name, or nom de plume, for writing under, especially when I found out about blogs and decided to start one of those as well.

I didn't want to blog under my real name, as no one knew that I had written two novels and I wanted to keep that to myself. I also knew that my writing was going to be a business all in itself, away from Jewel Divas, my jewellery business that I also set up in 2009. I knew I needed to make the website about my books and so it would need to be about my author name. I chose one.

Jewels Diva.

I have no idea why or how my muse decided to mess with my head where the names of my two businesses were concerned. It's just what happened when it popped into our head. I mean my head.

And so the "s" changed from my business to my author

name. Jewel Divas to Jewels Diva. Confusing, I know, and I still don't get why I picked it. I started my blog on January 1st 2009 under a witty title and as my first author name, Jewels Diva. I first published under the Jewels Diva name in 2011, and then bought the very royal title of Lady and scored a one foot square piece of Scottish Highlands to conserve for my trouble. I trade marked my name for the sake of standing out from the crowd, a gimmick to make me different.

I changed my author name to Lady Jewels Diva in 2012 and released novels under that name until 2014 when I released two non-fiction books I'd written alongside my fourth novel. One about positivity, *Why Positivity Can Be a Bad Thing!*, and one about self-publishing, *Dream It, Write It, Publish It! An Australian Guide to All the Hard Parts No One Tells You About Self-Publishing.*

In 2016, I adultified my name and became L.J. Diva (the L.J. being Lady Jewels). My next adult novels, my family saga series the *Porn Star Brothers* series, came out under that name. After they were released I started reconsidering the non-fiction books I had put under my author name, and proceeded to add my actual name to them as well.

As the new decade of the '00s came upon us, I decided to unpublish *Positivity*, and it has now been delegated to my essays folder on my computer. I did the same with that book I wrote about being a carer. My book *Dream It, Write It, Publish It!* lasted a few years longer before I unpublished it due to it being old and out of date, as everything had gone ahead in leaps and bounds. I decided I was going to update it.

This time it will be re-released under my own name.

My adult author name has been L.J. Diva since 2016, and that's where she'll stay.

I believe my muse chose those names for a reason. I'm a Taurus with Gemini tendencies, or a Gemini with Taurus tendencies. Whichever one I actually am, it would explain so much about me and my businesses and why the names arose. My name is Tiara King, my jewellery business, which I chose first, is Jewel Divas, and then for some reason, I kept coming back to Jewels Diva for an author name.

Tiara = Jewel/Jewels, King = Diva/Divas.

A weird play on my own name and I'm glad I turned it into L.J. Diva. That's what my muse did to me, and I guess I can't really blame her. But then she kept going…

*****

In 2013, I'd been following a lot of bloggers for a few years, many of them mummy bloggers, and quite a few were getting book deals. I realised, as I had dabbled in jewellery making for twenty-four years at that point, that as a jewellery designer I could write a book about the thing I loved most and am actually good at, so I could release a book too and do it under my own name.

I'd been writing and releasing under the name Jewels Diva and then Lady Jewels Diva for years at that point and had done a bunch of posts under my style site, Jewel Divas Style, a blog I'd set up as the second tier of the Jewel Divas jewellery brand. I had the basis of many subjects that I could put in the book.

I began with word docs of posts and started laying out the chapters and topics.

But a jewellery book wasn't the only one I wrote. I decided to write the book, *Carers Need Help and Support Too: One*

Woman's Personal Journey through the Sacrifice of Caring, and the majority of that is now the chapter on caring.

I released my first two books under my name in 2014. *Carers* came first and was soon followed by the e-book version of *How to Be a Jewel Diva: Tips and Tricks to Buying, Wearing and Caring for Your Costume Jewellery*.

Writing and releasing under my own name had begun!

In 2015, I released *Closet Confidential: How to Audit Your Wardrobe and Update Your Style*.

In 2016, I released a six-volume set of my song lyrics, *Poems of a Musical Flavour*, and my first YA/teen fiction story under my name, *#Teenblogger: To Follow or Not To Follow?*

#Teenblogger was initially written for my horror name, but I soon realised there was no horror involved so I decided to release it under my name.

Carers has been unpublished since before 2020, and in 2023 was delegated to the essay folder, along with *Positivity*. At this stage, I'll be releasing all non-fiction under my name moving forward, including the updated *Dream It, Write It, Publish It!* There are a couple of other fiction stories I have in mind, such as a couple of children's picture books, and two jewellery themed series that aren't adult romance. All adult romance will be kept under the L.J. Diva name, and anything paranormal will be under the name I talk about next.

*****

In 2014, while getting my fourth novel and three non-fiction books done and published, my muse decided to bombard me with another idea.

How about getting those stories you wrote in school out and rewriting them to publish?

I thought about it, and because I was already doing so much that year with releasing the fourth novel and three non-fics, I decided to sit on it.

A year later, the idea came back, and this time I ran with it.

I pulled out my school stories, photocopied them, typed them up in a word doc, and printed them out so I could read it better.

Stories came thick and fast. I started coming up with ideas on which ones to expand, which ones would be good to use, and which ones wouldn't. I also sat down and tried to come up with another author name.

Following on from the whole, "each of my names is a version of my own", thing I went with my own initials for T.K., and wanted some horror paranormal type name for a surname. I came up with Wrathbone, similar to Basil Rathbone, best known for his portrayal of Sherlock Holmes. And so, T.K. Wrathbone was born.

I started the first stories in the second half of 2015 and out they poured. They weren't adult sex and romance; they were kids and teens delving into paranormal horror. Ghosts, ghouls, witches and goblins, haunted places, books, and magical islands. I even gave them the spiffy title of "paranormal with a light twist of supernatural horror crocktales" because they're all a crock. Hence, "crocktales". My stories had it all, and I decided on three long stories, and five short stories I could put into an anthology e-book. Eight stories per year, and each year, I released four new e-books under the T.K. Wrathbone name.

Until 2020.

I hadn't realised yet that I was suffering burnout from everything I was doing between three names, social media, writing, and releasing. It had become hard, and I had to get a Porn Star Brothers book out and then I tried to write the Wrathbone stories for the year. But they just wouldn't come. I fobbed it off and blamed Covid.

I was exhausted, worn out, and dead to the world of creativity. I needed a break.

I concentrated on getting the large prints and hardcovers finished and released in 2021, and in the second half of the year, I got back to completing the last round of books. Set six. I had forty-eight stories total across twenty-four e-books that were later published in 6 anthology print editions.

I've written one story since and have two more that I started in those years to finish off. But I also have another forty-eight stories to write if I want to get to the magical twelve anthologies, and then there's the special edition thirteen I want to release. But just the thought of writing that many more is exhausting.

As of now, the stories for T.K. Wrathbone still aren't coming, and I think that's because my brain wanted to just concentrate on adult for a while, which it has. Who knows what will happen in the future? They're on the to-do list, along with a very long twenty-four book series and a six-book spin-off, but even the thought of writing those makes me run in the opposite direction. Things will be taken easy for now, and I'll write what I write when I write it.

*****

When I started writing I had no idea I was going to self-publish. It wasn't even on my radar because I'd never heard of indie or self-publishing. I wanted my book on store shelves and that's all there was to it. I believed it was *so* good that publishers were going to want it and publish it, putting it in every bookstore, chain store and on every shelf they could find. I was going to be famous. I was going to be a published author.

Then came reality…

Then came the rejections from the big publishing houses of Australia, then the world. I couldn't believe they had rejected me. *Me!* And my fabulous novel that was so fantastic. *Me!*

I scoured Google and found my local writing centre. I borrowed every book from my local library and learned as much as I could about writing, formatting and submitting. I joined Romance Writers of Australia, and the world I was living in came crashing down around my head. I soon realised why I was rejected. *My book was crap* (apparently all first drafts are, regardless of how famous the author might be) and that's what I had sent out.

That book, *The Road to Vegas*, I wrote in July and August of 2006 and started sending out submissions in January 2007. I spent that year submitting, being rejected and submitting again. It was all to no avail, and I soon knew what the first lesson was.

Lesson #1 learned, BIG MISTAKE to send out first drafts!

Did learning Lesson #1 stop me from writing though? Of course not, as I wrote *How I Won Lotto, Moved To L.A. & Married A Really Huge TV Star!* now called *Hollywood Dreams*, in February of 2008. Let me tell you; you *could not* go past Michael Weatherly at the time as inspiration. He was very…inspirational!

An author from *Romance Writers of Australia* assessed my first three chapters and let me know what was wrong with them. I took her notes and scrapped the prologue and first three chapters and made them what they are today. A hell of a lot better! I entered writing competitions and took the year to edit it. I moved on to my third novel, *Life and Death Adventures in London,* now called *Falling for London,* in November of 2010, submitted *Lotto,* and finally, a publisher wanted it. Because I received a call. *That call.* The call that could have changed my life.

Back in November 2010, *How I Won Lotto, Moved To L.A. & Married A Really Huge T.V. Star!* captured the attention of one publishing house here in Australia called JoJo Publishing. I sent them the full manuscript as directed on their website, full of typos I'm sure since I have found some since, and they rang me. Yes, they actually rang me. That's how come I have the honour of saying "I got the call".

Because I did.

They wanted my book. They called me several times in November/December, sent me paperwork to think about and sign after I asked them to send it, and told me it would take two years to get it up and running. I had already been online since 2009 and had a platform and didn't want to wait another two years. I know publishing houses can take anywhere from 6-24 months to get a book out, so it wasn't unusual, but I didn't want to wait that long.

I didn't know about self-publishing, and desperately wanted my books to be out there. The only other alternative was to pay them $12,000, half of the $24,000 publishing fee, and then I would get 50% of the royalties.

I remember crying for weeks. I so desperately wanted to

be published like so many other authors and have my books in stores like so many new authors, and I emailed back and forth with one of my followers. I even asked for advice from the Yahoo group that I belonged to.

But when push came to shove, I didn't want to wait two years, didn't have $12,000, and didn't want to give up my rights to my book.

I thanked JoJo for the offer, but rejected it in December and went into 2011 with a heavy heart, even though I somehow knew that something was coming. Then I received a call in early 2011 because he hadn't received my tear-filled email. I thanked them for their offer once more and rejected it again.

At that time, I followed Nathan Bransford, an ex-agent and published author. He blogged about Amanda Hocking and how self-publishing, money, and fame had suddenly shoved her into the world's spotlight. I read her blog and found Joe Konrath. The advice, suggestions and links to informative websites and pages he had convinced me there and then to self-publish my own books. In March 2011 I decided to do just that and signed up to Smashwords.

I had discovered self-publishing and didn't look back.

I haven't bothered with publishing houses since, except to read about the Big 5's shenanigans where Amazon is concerned, and the lawsuit that the DOJ (Department of Justice) in America brought against Penguin Random House when they tried to buy Simon & Schuster. Because that's my business now. Writing books, releasing them, and learning my craft by reading stories about publishers and their feud with Amazon, and reading what other authors are doing to move ahead and make sales.

While searching for something on Google in 2017, I decided to look up JoJo for a book cover I vaguely remembered and discovered something almost hilarious. Hilariously ironic. Or is that ironically hilarious?

JoJo Publishing had been accused of ripping off its authors and had been placed in voluntary liquidation in 2015. It had published books by hundreds of authors since being founded in 2002.

The business charged some authors a fee to publish their books, which is referred to as vanity publishing, a different model to traditional book publishing. However, more than 50 authors were owed money, and more than 30 authors said they had invested between $9000 and $35,000 of their own money in having books published.

I'm so glad I didn't go with this company. I would've lost all rights to my book and been unable to publish it anywhere else. And in 2017, I read, by fluke, about what they had done to their authors. I'm so glad I kept my rights, and my head, and that my muse guided me away from them.

Even though the road to self-publishing is a long and tiresome journey, it can be well worth it, especially when you hold your book in your hand and think, damn, this is what I created.

*****

By the time 2016 rolled around, I was writing and releasing under three names, and about to release another plethora of books. I decided to think about setting up an imprint name to put them all under.

But I did nothing except self-publish. I had my own little

logos on the back of each paperback, a crown for my name, a director's chair under a star for L.J. Diva, and a skull for T.K. Wrathbone.

In 2017, I finally decided to do something about it, bit the bullet, and bought a business name. I spent many hours and long days and weeks setting up a website, and then decided to change the name to Royal Star Publishing.

Some legal issues arose with the original name's trade mark, as I mention in the next story, but I had to close the old website and start all over. More long hours, across more long days, across more long weeks. It turned out to be a valuable lesson in learning how to set up websites, and I was happy with the end result.

Royal Star Publishing was born.

But that also meant I had to go back through all of the sites I published on, unpublish the books, and re-publish under the new logo with newly bought ISBNs under my brand spankin' new publishing house name. Oi! Another time-consuming business thing that needed to be done. There are so many of them.

And RSP, as it's affectionately called, keeps on growing. It's updated with the release of a new book, and generally sits there on show.

Every time I publish a book; I use the name on sales sites, so it looks more professional. Because that's the whole point as an independent author/publisher. Having something that looks professional on your sale page and not the name Amazon or the words "independently published".

The website had a theme refresh in 2023 and looks even better than it used to, with pages for series, kids, adult, and non-fiction, our imprints, and about us. Plus, each author has their own page, and there's a Spotify page for the playlists connected to the *Porn Star Brothers* series, and the novel *Anything for You*.

I've surpassed 60 stories, non-fictions, novellas, and novels and there is so much more to come. We currently have five in-house imprints and there are a few more in the wings.

Chances is the fiction imprint for sexy and adult novels for women. Covering romance, it's for more in-depth genres, and features more sex, and mature adult themes. Chances was named in honour of Jackie Collins' book Chances. It suits this imprint perfectly as it's about women and men taking chances on life and love.

Love Beats is the fiction imprint for light and lovely romance novels. Whether they be sweet, comedic, fun or lightweight, these romances will make you laugh before they make you cry. With more love than sex, these will get you through a wintry day in front of the fire, or a lazy day on the beach.

Skull & Bone is the fiction imprint for children, tweens & young adults. It covers horror, paranormal, occult, fantasy, myths, folklore, fairy tale adaptions, and all other genres with a slightly twisted edge.

Dream Star is the fiction imprint for children, tweens & young adults. It covers light and bright themes across all genres, and it brings a little fun into their lives.

Notes on Life is the non-fiction imprint that covers poetry and song lyrics, and now this memoir as I couldn't be bothered trade marking another imprint for it.

Pen to Paper is the non-fiction imprint that covers writing and publishing in all forms and styles. It will make its debut when I republish my book on publishing.

Royal Star Publishing is not open for submissions. It's purely a name only business for myself at this stage. But who knows, maybe when I'm rich and famous and can afford to turn it into a company and publish other people…it might happen.

*****

While September 2009 was my first foray into being opposed when it came to trade marks, it happened again nine years later.

Then, it was about me using the word "Diva" in my jewellery business, Jewel Divas. In 2017 it was about using the word "Crown" in my publishing house name.

When I set up my publishing house, I came up with the name Royal Crown Press. It, like everything I do, was a play on my name.

I bought the business name, the domain name, started setting up the website, and set about trade marking as one does. But a couple of months into doing the website, I changed my mind and changed the name of my publishing house. A press is not for jewellery or blogging; it's for book manufacturing. And since the process was already in motion, I wasn't going to stop it, so I let it go. All was going swimmingly until it was objected against.

Crown Casinos here in Australia opposed my application.

Personally, I thought it was bullshit. The only thing we had in common was one word.

Crown.

My name was Royal Crown Press. Theirs is Crown Casino.

First round, they lost. IP Aus didn't accept their initial

findings and told them to give a more detailed reason why they opposed the name.

They did, and I received the paperwork in a timely fashion.

Most of it is the same old, same old garbage, as always, blaming the public for their lack of comprehension in separating the two companies. Claiming that I have not used the name, claiming that on my website, Tiara King, it states I'm a lifestyle blogger, author of non-fiction books (only half right), jewellery designer, and because I hadn't yet used the name for any of those things, clearly it was my intention to not carry on with the name.

It was a case of another big multi-corp conglomerate beating down the little people.

I did consider hiring an attorney, but with what money?

Letting it go probably made the big boys think they'd won. That I wouldn't fight. I didn't use the name because I had changed the name and let the trade mark process run its course, a course that cost me $250 to let go of, (after having to give up on two other trade marks I had previously applied for, costing me $500 I didn't have) money I do not come by that easily.

I let it go, for one, because I'm the bigger person, two, because I really didn't need that shit in my life along with the shit I had to clean up caring for my mother, trying to run a business and make products, and deal with arsehole companies, and three, because it wasn't my business name anymore. It was just going to be an imprint of the company, which, I guess, I'll have to change now.

You didn't win because there was never a fight *to* win. I just didn't need one more arsehole in my life to deal with.

*****

In 2020 I kept reminding myself to ask the local librarian if there was a writer's group or author group in the library. And finally, as I was walking out the door one day in August, I remembered, clicked my fingers, and walked back in. I asked her and she immediately put me on the phone to the digital literacy office for the library.

We had a conversation, she got excited, and that was the start of many phone calls as we organised what the writers' group would look like, what days we'd do it, and when we could do it.

Unfortunately, again with that shit disease we were all dealing with, the launch was postponed until April 2021 when the writing group started.

We got off to a bumpy start, and a very slow one. The library didn't advertise in the normal promotional way, so word getting out was slow. Throughout the year we had a couple of people join and then leave.

In 2022, we had more join and were quite packed one night with fifteen people. Not a lot, you might be thinking, but many writing groups aren't that big. Several of them left months after starting, but a few kept on into 2023, and many more came and went through the year.

Since the beginning, the only constant has been me. I was there before the group and have attended all but three nights the entire time. One per year. We start in February each year, and end in December, meeting every Thursday fortnight. We have a two-tiered start time. 5 p.m. for those who are carers, retired, unemployed and so on, who can turn up early for extra time, and 5:30 p.m. for those who work and need time to come along. And don't worry about coming at the later time, we rock up at all times of the hour.

I've led the group at the table since late 2022 and we give newbies time to talk about themselves and where they're at with their writing. We offer a lot of advice and help where we can. Don't be afraid to join; there aren't many writing groups north of Adelaide.

Writing groups also extend to online. I'm in several Facebook writing and self-publishing groups, and one day I replied to a post with, "writing is just one more thing that I do".

A person replied to my comment and was shocked by me claiming that writing is just one more thing. He took it out of context, as is the issue with emails and social posts, and I explained it to him like this.

"Writing is just one more thing that I do in a list of many. I've drawn, created, designed and made jewellery and clothes, so yes, writing is just one more creative thing that I do on a list of many."

For those of us who create, we don't always stay in the one lane. We draw, make, create, design, sing, dance, paint, sculpt, model; do all sorts of creativities. We don't just do one thing. That would be starving our creative need. Our brains want and need to learn more things. We are sponges; we want to learn, not just be stuck in the one field forever.

Not that I'm saying that doesn't work for some, especially those who need a stable creative lane for their brain to work in; it just doesn't work for all. We need to spread our wings and try new things.

So yes, writing is just one more thing that I do. I don't love it, I don't have a passion for it, I don't *need* to do it. In fact, during burnout, which I discuss later in this chapter, I grew to hate it and my ability to write fast slowed right down. But regardless of arthritis making it bloody exhausting, it's something I still want to do. I have a drive, not a passion, a hate, not a love, but I need to write these stories. I need to get them out of me and onto the page.

And if I didn't have a drive and need to write, then I wouldn't have done countless writing courses, and read countless writing books to better my knowledge of the field I am now so deeply entrenched in. I am a sponge; I have a constant need to learn about the craft of which I partake in. On every level.

But again, writing is just one more thing that I do, and I have no problem saying that.

There are so many aspects to being an author or writer, or both, as many of us are. So many things we go through; psychologically, emotionally, and even physically.

There are myths we need to combat, and non-existent syndromes we need to dispel.

I've written a lot about writing at my website, my thoughts on imposter syndrome, writers' block, right brain creative, inner critic, compare don't despair, flipping the switch from negativity to positivity, knowing your worth, and niches to name a few. So much has been written that you can use it as a resource.

I could go on to talk about how I don't suffer from writers' block and imposter syndrome and don't believe in either. I could talk about all of the author myths being myths for a reason— because they're rubbish— and tell you not to believe in them. I could talk about my routine, but all of that would be as boring as bat excrement.

I could talk about how writing is harder than editing for me, that you don't need permission from anyone, including yourself, to write, because you're free to just do it, that I have all kinds of feelings on writing, but I'll just tell you to go to my website and read it all. They're incredibly productive posts.

So many negative words, phrases and myths surround authors, artists, and creative people in general that I've become really sick and tired of reading, hearing, watching, and being accused of having or suffering from them when I don't.

We all suffer from imposter syndrome. We all deal with writers' block. We're all tortured souls. We're all dramatic. We're either self-loathing or self-righteous. Writers must write every day. The clichés are all true…

No, they're actually not. Neither are the myths.

The conclusion I've come to, after reading and researching these idiotic author myths for my blog posts, is they're negative connotations that have been passed down to current authors from elder authors and artists of bygone eras. They smoked, drank, drugged, and allowed their low self-esteem and insecurities to plague them to death. For some, sadly, mental illness was a big contributor, for many, low self-esteem and insecurities reigned supreme.

What's still sad, is that the monsters our fore-authors and fore-artists created are still very much alive and in the heads of authors and artists today. Many people in the creative arts cannot think and form opinions and ideas for themselves, and cannot understand that they truly do not need to suffer from age-old insecurities simply because of the job they do. They choose to live in the myths long ago created because it's easier to do or explain. Because, hey, that's just being an author or an artist and everything that comes along with it. Isn't it?

Change how you do things and be inspired instead of comparing.

Flip the switch and spin the negativity into positivity and abolish all of those nasty negative myths from your mind, and your writing.

Don't worry about finding your niche. If you want to be in multiple niches, go forth and create in every field and niche you can find, be multi-creative.

Don't worry about finding your tribe. Remember that saying from a decade ago? If you can't find a tribe to join then make your own. Sometimes we aren't meant to be a part of a tribe, sometimes, we're meant to be leading our own and being our own and there's nothing wrong with that. Be a tribe of one and go forth and be you.

Deciding if writing is even right for you is important. It's all well and good to say "I'm going to write a book", but it takes a lot of damn hard work to make it happen. And if you find along the way that you just don't want to, then that's okay. Because it's not for everyone. Maybe your creativity lies in another field of art, like painting, sculpting, dancing, or learning an instrument. There are so many fields to choose from, so it's okay if writing is not the one for you. It really is okay to quit it.

A lot of people believe the word quit is negative or has negative connotations. But quit isn't negative and means several things. To stop, discontinue, give up, leave, depart, set free, cease.

Whether you call it letting go, clearing out, spring cleaning, doing inventory, or hitting delete, it's all the same thing. Stopping. Quitting. Deleting.

Whether it's your wardrobe, job, interests, or online presence. Sometimes, it's a good thing to let go of something, or, to quit it.

I know it's been mentioned in a romantic movie somewhere, or from some expert on some show talking about knowing when to quit a relationship.

We see the ads online, on the TV, in magazines and newspapers about quitting smoking.

We quit jobs, school, hobbies, social media platforms. Even book outlines and ideas. And there is absolutely nothing wrong with it, or with using the word quit.

There's a mental and emotional attachment we form with the things we own and the things we do. When you invest blood and sweat and tears into it, and realise it's just not working, or it might be time to give it up, letting it go becomes the hardest thing to do. That's why sitting on ideas and decisions can be a good thing. If there is no rush to quit, then think about it.

Ask yourself every question you can think of, even if it doesn't seem to have anything to do with what you're trying to quit. It doesn't matter; you never know what answers you'll get, and you never know, those answers might lead you in a completely different direction.

The next time you come to the realisation that something isn't working anymore, whether it's not working for you, your life, or the situation, it's okay to consider quitting it. To stop it. To delete it. The world won't end, it'll keep spinning, and you'll be just fine if you bring something to its natural end.

Up next are a couple of things I do want to talk about at length because I think they're important. No, it's not about imposter syndrome or writers' block. Seriously, you can figure that crap out for yourself, because it's all inside your head, and only you know what you're thinking and feeling about yourself.

One's about burnout and how I struggled through four years of it and what I did to abolish it. The other is something I'm very strongly against, and that's stealing as an artist and author. These are two very important things for an artist.

My website has a plethora of good posts to read; just hit the link in the left top menu titled blog.

Go forth and happy hunting.

And for those who desperately need to know my opinion on writers' block, here it is.

In and of itself it does not exist. It's just an empty umbrella phrase that doesn't specify the *actual* problem. From my observations online and in real life, the issue comes under three areas. The writing itself. Do you have an outline, do you know your character, do you know your beginning, your end, do you know what the hell you're even doing? Did you even bother sitting down and coming up with anything? None of that is a block, it's lack of preparation. Either you haven't figured it out yet, or you're figuring it out in a step-by-step approach as you do write, and you work each step through to the end and then you sit and let your brain figure out the next step. There's nothing wrong with doing it in steps.

The second area is insecurities. Too many people allow their insecurities to stop them from doing anything. Stop it. Get out of your own damn way and get over yourself. The field of writing has no space for ego, insecurity, fear or arrogance. If you want to write a book, get out of your own way and write the damn book.

Also, don't say you want to write a book, but you're scared no one will read it, hence stopping yourself from writing it. It's an arrogant thought. Are you psychic? Can you predict what complete and utter strangers will and won't read? No, you can't. No one can read what you haven't written, and besides, not one author on this planet can guarantee that anyone will read their book after publication.

And who are these people, anyway? Your family, friends, and network of people? Or do you mean complete and utter strangers that you don't know and who don't know you even exist? Stop putting your time and energy into worrying about people you don't know, and who don't know you. It's weak, and quite frankly, pathetic.

The third area is everything that comes under the umbrella word of life. Being exhausted is not writers' block. Having to care for elderly parents, partners, children, is not writers' block. Losing a job, working at three to make ends meet, dealing with losing a loved one, is not writer's block. Sadly, too many now arrogantly label everything in life as a block. It isn't. The Universe doesn't give a flying fuck if you want to write. It's going to throw shit at you to clean up. It's testing you to see if you're still strong enough and want it enough to deal with what was heaped on you, and then come out the other end and sit down and write. Life takes precedence, writing, dancing, singing, painting, and every other creativity, does not. The Universe is trying to tell you that something else is currently more important, so listen to it and deal with what's happening.

If life *isn't* throwing shit at you, and you have no reason to not write, then you either choose to sit and write something when you have the ability to, or you don't. Writing is a choice, plain and simple. You choose to put it aside to deal with shit, or you choose to do it. If you have a migraine and want to rest, do so. Your health is important and comes first, so make the time to write some other time. If you're just procrastinating, or as I call it, making piss weak excuses to not write, then clearly you just don't want to write at all. That's when you need to be asking yourself the question, "why don't I want to?". And if that's the case, and you don't want to write at all, fine, there's nothing wrong with turning around and deciding writing isn't for you. That's perfectly okay, and it's okay to change your mind.

Lastly, if actual experts, either those with degrees in psychology, or those with degrees in writing who teach writing and have done so for decades, are telling you it doesn't exist, you might want to believe them and not everyone else.

*****

I've briefly mentioned burnout throughout this book. It's a bugger of a thing to deal with and here's the essay I wrote for my website in 2023 as it might help others. I haven't updated it; just left it as is.

Back in 2022, on my L.J. Diva website (now migrated to Tiara King), I did a post about getting back to *Before*. I've mentioned it in previous posts, and some of what's in that post is also here, but I've expanded greatly on it with what's happened since, especially concerning burnout, which is what this post is about.

Burnout can last for weeks, months, or in my case, years. Here's what happened to me...

From late 2019 to early 2020, I had brilliant ideas for a

novel, or two, but pushed that insane inspiration aside to try and focus on writing other stuff, namely the final Porn Star Brothers novel, And Always. It was an overwhelming effort to write it from April until August with a September release. The book only came about after deciding, in 2019, to not write the 40-plus short stories about certain characters in the series, which meant not leaving Spiros & Jenny as the last book, but to wind up the series with a book of stories concerning the last five grandchildren who were yet to find their forevers.

I also had to deal with companies not doing their job, continue to run multiple websites and sets of social media, and then try and do other things. A LOT of other things! I finally ground to a mental halt and knew I needed a break. From EVERYTHING!

By January 2021, I hadn't even attempted to write those new novels as I was battling to get my hardcovers and large prints under my three names finished after they were delayed from 2020. They were finally released in March, April, and May 2021. They, for the most part, were finally done. But I also had leftover kid's horror stories from 2020 to complete and release, adding more pressure.

It was around this time that I concluded that I had burnout, and it had taken me two years to figure it out. I don't remember how it happened. It could have been a blog post, a social media post, or something I read in a book. It made a lot of sense because I was mentally and physically exhausted. My brain had been screaming at me to not write, that it didn't want to write, and that it needed a break. Hell, at times, it didn't even want to write anymore. Ever!

Not that I'd known I had it, after writing over one million words in The Porn Star Brothers family series and releasing a book every six months from 2016 to 2019 when I not only had to type up an extra 15,000 words and then write an extra 67 pages for DeLuca, but then write Spiros & Jenny as well, all under my L.J. Diva pen name. Plus, for every one of those years, I was also writing and releasing horror stories for kids under my pen name, T.K. Wrathbone. And in 2016 I'd also released my Poems of a Musical Flavour series under my name. Nope, I didn't know I had it at all. Until I did.

But even realising I had this thing called burnout didn't stop life from happening because other issues were also bubbling up.

In September 2021, I had *another* awesome idea for a novel but had to put it on the back burner for other things, thus extinguishing the inspiration for it. That novel is something else; it made me rub my hands together at all of the twists and turns my brain was coming up with. That has *never* happened with any other book I've written.

And, after small ideas had been percolating in my brain, simmering away under the surface like a volcano ready to blow, I knew something else was bubbling along with it. I took time off from the gym I'd started at in April, wrapped up a few other things, sat down at my desk and wrote copious notes. Thought upon thought poured out of me, mainly about why my writing life wasn't working anymore. How could I get back to the way things used to be? What the hell was happening? Was it just burnout or was it something more?

The answers were that I wanted to get back to before all of the pressure of everything I was doing, and that I was creatively stifled by the hours spent going to the gym. I decided to leave, as my most energetic hours of the day were being wasted there. These were hours I could be writing and creating. Hours I could be getting back to before all of the stress when I wrote filled with excitement for my characters and my stories. I made the decision to change how I did things moving forward.

But, as is life, things had to become harder before they became better.

In November 2021, I saw a movie called Colossal and had another idea for a novel. But I still had those pesky kids' stories to finish off; something I was forcing myself to do because I'd put them off in 2020.

Then, over the last month of 2021, I had more thoughts, because the thought train had gathered speed. And that train wanted to change *everything* as it moved forward into a new year.

It was time I stepped back and made more time for myself to once again be creative. I needed to once again write what I wanted, when I wanted, how I wanted, and not set myself ridiculous deadlines that I couldn't possibly meet, because that had been a big problem. I'd set myself deadlines for writing and publishing and could no longer meet them. I'd spread myself across too many outlets and the inspiration and motivation had disappeared.

I made the decision to close my jewellery business and delete its social media accounts. I made the decision to close multiple social accounts of my two author names and go silent on the rest. I made the decision to post more often to the accounts in my name.

I've written millions of words across three names, multiple genres, stories, non-fictions, stand-alone novels, and a family saga that burned me out, and it was now time to go back to *before*. *Before* having all of that, before doing all of that, *before* when I wrote with no stress and no publication date.

That is what I wanted to get back to. It was just a matter of letting myself write whatever my muse gave me. I wanted to get back to writing freely.

But, another problem, from conversations I'd been having with myself from 2020-22 and after the end of the PSB series, was that I didn't want to write long novels anymore because they're time and energy-consuming. I was physically exhausted from handwriting those novels and wanted to ease back into it, creating shorter works of around 75,000 words so I could produce more.

And I thought I could do it in early 2022, when I started the novel from the idea in September 2021. But eight pages in I had no idea what I was doing because it was going to be the first book in a duology, and I'd never written a duology where events in one coincide with events in the other. I had no clue which way I was going to write them. I chose to write a stand-alone novel instead.

Anything for You was an arduous labour of desire and love that my mind fought against. It wasn't ready to get back to writing. It was throwing up roadblocks to stop me from doing it. The main bugbear was my arthritis. I looked for easier pens to write with, I bought rubber pen grips to make gripping easier, I baulked and reared at the actual physicality of writing. I didn't want to write long novels because it was going to hurt. But I still didn't want to write in general.

Even as I argued with myself over Anything for You, I realised that maybe the argument was moot. Maybe I was just destined to write the books I was meant to write, the ones I was given by the Universe, or by the muse, and I just had to stop arguing and do it.

I went on to handwrite one full notebook and three pages of a second, and then decided to eliminate handwriting altogether and typed up the rest, sucking it up until I finished it. The novel's not as good as I originally wanted, but it's done and released and I'm happy with it. It's far longer than 75,000 words, a trend I saw coming from a mile away.

It was clearly never going to be possible to write short novels. But I still bucked against it. I even made the decision to never handwrite again, just type up every book I was ever going to create. I went through my notebooks and pulled out stories I'd started and typed up what there was. But, one year on, I went back on that, too.

In 2023, I bucked against it all again, wanting, and trying, to write a 75,000-word novel. I started handwriting that novel in March, and made the decision to not publish this year, removing the pressures of the deadline and timeline I usually set for myself. But then I stopped on April 11th to migrate blog posts from my two author sites to this site and my style site in the lead-up to closing them in September to eliminate even more stress from my life. Plus, I updated both sites along with my publishing house website.

I didn't get back to that novel until June 11th, and even then, it was a struggle. I pulled out an old trick. I read a Jackie Collins novel and voila, that night, off I went and wrote about twelve pages. It wore off the next day, but my mother had been sick, and I was still a bit all over the place, so I amped it up and put in a heroic effort, got some excitement going in me, and it was done and dusted in July.

But, during those weeks of writing, I had kept asking myself, *why am I still struggling after four years? What are the real problems going on here? Why can't I do this anymore? Why can't I do it the way I used to? Do I even want to do it anymore?*

I didn't know, but I damn well wanted to find out.

And I realised one night, when I had sat down to write, that besides the freezing cold weather wreaking havoc on the arthritis, I just didn't want to do it because I was bored. I was bored with writing in general, bored with the book, and bored with writing this particular story which had started four years ago as an idea. It was four years too late, basically. I had no interest in it, no excitement for it.

And when I said to myself, it doesn't excite me anymore, I have no excitement for it, ten seconds later my brain said, then you need to get excited. You have to get excited about writing again if you want to write the stories on your list and to finish this book.

Because the cold hard fact was none of it excited me. Between having so much to do all the time and the old arthritic body, writing had become a pain, a physical, emotional, and mental one. It wasn't exciting and I wanted the excitement back, so clearly what I'd been reading in the books from the library had sunk in, and that led to many more questions.

What was I going to do about it? Could I get the excitement back? Where was I going to get it from? Was writing just a decade-long thing? No, it's been a sixteen-year-long thing and ongoing, and I'd been writing for eleven years straight, and publishing for nine. I wanted to keep doing it. I had so much more to write, and stories don't write themselves. But how was I going to do it?

And it wasn't just excitement I needed to get back; I wasn't inspired by any of it either. But I guess excitement and inspiration go hand in hand when it comes to writing.

Plus, my plotlines were a mess compared to the neatness of previous book outlines. They were a confused mess like my brain, unable to be laid neatly one after the other in order of how they needed to be. What I'd once been able to do with novels had escaped me and left me with a hodgepodge of scenes.

I gave it the analogy of a dot-to-dot puzzle. I had once been able to start at number 1 and hit every dot in order as I went around the puzzle to get a complete picture. But with the last two novels, I started at dot 2 or 3, and lurched back and forth, jumping ahead and falling back, until I made it around in a mess of missed dots and scenes I'd thought of, but not written down in the outline or the book. The book I wrote in the first half of the year is a disaster I know will be fixed in the editing, but that's not the way I used to do it and it's annoying me. I can categorically say it's a short novel, 200 handwritten pages long, but who knows how many words it's going to end up when I attack it with a set of steak knives and create a viable product.

As I come to the end of this post, do I have any of the answers now at the end of the fourth year of burnout?

I believe it's finally over. For now.

My thoughts have been, that I can keep guessing and keep asking myself questions, keep reading books about writing, keep making decisions about blogging, websites and social media, and maybe, one day I'd find the answers in a paragraph on a page. But maybe I've had them all along and didn't know it until I had a lot of thinking and figuring out to do.

I'm my mother's carer, and my health has declined year after year. Both have contributed to the hideous all-consuming burnout I've suffered after writing over a million words in a short amount of time. All of that meant I needed to cull and restructure my business to be smaller and better and remove as many pressures from myself as possible. If that also means posting less to social media, and being on socials less, then so be it.

I was also bucking against the obvious, not wanting to write long novels anymore, but maybe that's just the way it is for me. I need to get back to writing out clear plotlines and having everything ready before I start. I need it all to flow again. I need the time and space, not pressure and constrictions. I need to get the excitement and inspiration back, the way it was when the Porn Star Brothers series poured out of me. It was pure magic waiting for its time to happen. Just as when my first four novels poured out of me.

I need to read my Jackie Collins books again and get my Jackie Collins on. I need to let my characters lead the way and take charge. I need to give my muse the reins again instead of keeping them to myself, holding them tight against my chest.

I want to go back to the good old days, in a better way, and I'd say I'm pretty much there after starting a second novel in October and actually being excited about it enough to write most nights. And thanks to daylight saving and warmer weather, I've had more energy during the day and I started compiling next year's to-do list as well as lists for things to do over December and January which I've started early thanks to more energy. At this rate, I'll have a lot of things done and dusted by Christmas on top of my stories, so I'll see what happens moving forward into next year.

Throughout all of this, the goal was to make my life easier. To get back to before the write, edit, publish, repeat cycle. This year, I just wanted to get a good stock of stories and get ahead of myself, and with luck, I've done enough by getting everything done and over with in the first half of this year and then closing my two author sites in the second. As I write this now, I can say that burnout feels as if it's over after four years, and I now have the freedom to write freely once more.

As I read that post, and write this extra paragraph in 2025, while looking at my production to-do list for the year with the twenty or items I have to work on for the first six months alone, I think, hell yeah, I got my groove back. Hell yeah, burnout is long gone. But I also know, if I'm not careful, it can come back any time. So, for the first six months of 2025, I worked on a couple of things at a time, per week, per month while everything was in motion at different points of their production schedule. Twenty or so items. For the first six months. But again, hell yeah, I got my groove back!

*****

Apparently, it was Picasso who said something about creativity, how good artists copy, but great artists steal.

I feel very adamant about stealing, and you should to, especially if you choose to be an artist.

Stealing, whether from others, or via AI software, won't make you an author. It will just make you a plagiarist and too damn lazy to actually write something. And don't even think of making money out of it.

I have spent too many years slogging my guts and brain out, and my fingers to the bone to condone stealing.

As an artist, which is an umbrella title for many job descriptions, we work hard to create different and unique art for sale. When arseholes come along and steal it, or when arseholes think they can take other peoples' ideas and stories to use for themselves, it pisses me off.

There is a very big difference between taking inspiration, and directly taking the idea, but sadly, many do the latter.

There are so many stories of authors coming up against people who pirate their books. Some authors have found people that fully, or partially, plagiarised their book to sell on Amazon. Artists have had people they know print their art out and put it on their wall.

People don't care about stealing because they don't believe they're doing it. People don't have a clue about copyright theft and fraud, and theft and fraud in general.

The whole concept of "if it's on the internet it's free to use" is a lie. There is no such law in Australia. Read Owning It, by Sharon Giovoni. She's an expert, so she knows. Unless the law has changed in that concern, it's still illegal to steal other people's belongings. And that's what books are. Other people's belongings. The author made the book; they spent days and weeks and months, and sometimes years slogging their guts out to create what they sell. You don't get to be the arsehole who steals it for yourself to put on your shelf, or on Amazon to sell under your name.

There are a lot of people who believe wholeheartedly that you can steal. I will not and cannot be on the side of people who pretend to write books or create something they don't.

I will never be on the side of a writer who blatantly steals other authors' ideas, or who uses AI to write a dodgy book and then call themselves the author or writer.

Be honest, be upfront, and be true. Write and create your stuff your own damn self.

*****

There have been many factors against me and both of my businesses from the get-go.

It's clear the Universe had other plans for me; not helping me make my jewellery business a success was the start. But then we never know unless we try. The statistics prove that many first businesses don't work. Basically, we don't know what we're doing so it fails.

I've struggled, more so with the weight of my mother and her care, which is why I'm surprised I even found the time to make jewellery or write books.

I'm tired. Emotionally, mentally, physically. I'm tired of my life not being mine. I'm tired of doing all of this shit on my own.

All of this has been a factor in my slowing down, and I talked about that in burnout. I've been thinking that the Universe is testing me and how much I can take. But it has made me tired and on the verge of a breakdown. Nobody cares about my mental health in all of this, or my physical health either. Nobody wants to help; not family or health care professionals.

I've debated whether to give up or keep going. The conclusion I did come to is that I *want* to do this, regardless of it not making me rich and famous. I most certainly want to be rich—who doesn't—as it would afford me the money to buy the house, the car, and a bundle of goodies that would make my life complete. I could help out others, and charities, and try and fulfil my life that way, and fame would come with that, because I'd be going around to the opening of every envelope.

The opening of an envelope is an old saying, but I would, in order to get my name, my jewellery, and my books out there, go to the opening of every shop, restaurant, cinema, movie, the opening of anything and everything. I would try and get my photo in the paper every week, go to all of the local markets and author stalls, and try and get myself and my books onto every TV and radio show in the nation. If I had the opportunity to move to the Gold Coast, I'd most certainly be doing all of that and then some, making sure to be a constant on the local scene, and getting myself in the coastal magazines to be seen. And yes, I meant to rhyme that. I absolutely know my life would be different if I had that freedom.

Unfortunately, when there is a health issue, or physical issue, such as looking after someone, we can't just jump into the car and go to all of these places. That means we have to find what we can within our area or do everything online.

We might send our books to media and celebrities. I've sent *#teenblogger* to Ellen DeGeneres, *Anything for You* to Jason Sudeikis, *Hollywood Dreams* to Michael Weatherly and Aussie TV hosts Karl Stefanovic and Larry Emdur.

We can do videos for socials, as I do, to market and promote online as much as possible and yet that's not always possible.

Do we spend thousands on advertising just to make that back and a little bit more? Do we hire a publicist and give them a try?

We do what we can, when we can, and hope something comes from it. Of course, many are more successful than most, and good for them, but it's a damn hard slog and I feel that being on my own would get me into a lot more places, and in a lot more media, than what I'm doing now.

I have exerted more energy in the last twenty years writing, making, and trying to run a business than I probably exerted in all my previous years—except maybe for when I was line dancing because that was a lot of energy. But then I didn't have the health issues, the business, the blogs, or a crippled mother to look after way back then.

Whether we market our books to death or not, it comes down to what our plan actually is. Do we write and sell to make money, or do we do it because we have a want, a need burning inside of us? Do we want to be rich and famous, or do we really just want to produce work we can proudly hold up and say, "hey, I made this"? You can't always market that.

In the meantime, there is so much more on the to-do list to come, so I'll stay on and try and make it more fun.

Yes, fun is what I need back in my life.

*****

The end is not so nigh!

As of May 1st, 2025, I've written 653 songs, 21 poems, 144 essays/opinion pieces, 7 novellas, 14 novels, 4 non-fictions, and 70 short stories.

I have a running tally on the About page on my website and update it every six months, in January and July. I also have a yearly list on the timeline page. While I originally only counted songs and novels, as that's all I'd written, I then added stories, and before I knew it, poems, essays, op-eds, and non-fiction. I think it's fun to add together everything you've written; it's a list of what you've achieved, and you should be proud.

As for what I've published; that's always a different number as the e-books will be a higher number than the trade paperback editions.

My 639 songs are in a six-volume e-book set along with two e-book box sets, but six print books along with an omnibus.

My kids' horror stories are published as single e-books, but each set of four are in one paperback. Twenty-four e-books, but six print anthologies in four print formats.

I have single stand-alone novels, but the Porn Star Brothers series has the first four collector's edition novellas, Carlos, Pedro, Tomas, and Retribution. They're singular e-books, but also rolled together as one e-book box set, or one print omnibus novel titled Porn Star Brothers. It has a hot dude on the cover wearing nothing but a pair of tighty-whities.

I've written and published six non-fiction books as of this memoir. Out of those, I have unpublished two and turned them into essays, one of which then ended up in this book. A third was unpublished and rewritten and will be released this year, along with two other updated non-fictions, the "Blue Bloods" novel duology, a horror guide, and who knows what else.

With luck, I've already written a novel or two, multiple children's picture books, and a plethora of others by now, and there's more to come in the second half of the year.

At forty-three, I once joked, under my pen name of L.J. Diva, that I needed to get a hurry on and finish off the novels I wanted to write so I could retire by the time I was fifty.

Fifty's been and gone, and I'm still writing and publishing, so stay tuned for everything else I release under my three names as the future reveals itself.

My Reflection

I look in the tidal pool all craggy and dark
and see my reflection.
It's not the same as the one I see in the mirror,
it's pure, clear of pain.
The one in the mirror shows the horror,
the story my life has told
all there on my face
to show what the future holds.

Reflections on 50 Years

We're now at the end of this book, and I'm sure many of you are thinking, *but you've done so much.* Yes, I have, to a degree. But it was in two different stages.

One, everything that happened when I was younger.

And two, all of the books and stories I've written and published in the last two decades.

I'm going to repost a section of a blog post I did at the beginning of 2020 about the decade I'd spent online, writing, and making jewellery. It was not only a new year, but a new decade. And yes, I know that's years ago now, but it shows the mindset of one living this kind of life. One with a life unfulfilled who strives to do something for themselves, while not actually getting anywhere.

"I started the decade one year into my author blog with two novels already written, and a jewellery business at the beginning of its life. I had no idea what the hell I was doing, or where I wanted to go, but I knew I wanted to do something.

As the years progressed, I wrote more novels under my author name, which I matured and adultified, blogged weekly, set up a website for my jewellery business, bought multiple domains, trade marks and copyrights, and had legal issues. I then started writing under my own name and progressed to a third author name. Not only did my own health suffer greatly during this decade, but my mother became so sick and crippled that I had to put my jewellery business on permanent holiday just so I could focus on my writing. And then I lost my writing inspiration, Jackie Collins.

I continued writing so much that I not only set up multiple websites to cover all of my names, but decided to set up a publishing house to publish all of my books. I bought my own ISBNs, bought everything that I would need, such as pictures, and gave my cover designer mock-ups of what I wanted for my books.

I've dealt with shit, literally, that no one should have to deal with. I resent myself, the Universe, and my enemy, for what has happened in my life and have no real idea how to get out of it. My life is not where I thought it would be, nor where I want it to be. And how that will evolve over the next ten years I don't know. I cringe at the thought that I'll still be here, in this exact place, in ten years; living the same life, dealing with the same shit. Because sometimes, it just ain't that easy to pack up and leave. But that's for another time.

And yes, all of this is a weight I've borne by my own hand.

As I ended the year, and decade, I looked back at all the crushes I'd had, the love I didn't experience, the children I didn't have, the things I did, and saw nothing but insignificant achievements that meant, quite frankly, not a fucking lot. Although, setting up a publishing house and releasing a whole bunch of books IS a lot, it just didn't feel like it.

I ended the decade with two rooms full of clothing and accessories, books, collections, and knick-knacks that I loved and wanted, but which I had no place to properly display or store. I also ended the decade with seven more novels, four novellas, eleven non-fiction, and forty-two short stories under my name and two others, all published under my own publishing house, plus a thousand more pieces of jewellery than what I started it with and more kaftans and kimonos than I ever dreamed of having. I have multiple websites, domains and businesses, more business debt than I've ever had in my life (but can fortunately pay off each month), yet I own nothing except what I have in these two rooms.

While I ended the year, and the decade, with a whole lot more than what I went into it with, regardless of what I had actually done and achieved, it seemed like I'd done nothing at all."

Looking back at my life, I know full well I've done more than others. It's that weird balance of life. You know you've done a lot, but it feels as if you haven't. Maybe that's because I haven't achieved what I actually want to, so nothing else feels like an achievement of any kind. It takes a lot to write a book, but it came easily thanks to still being creative coming out of school. It also takes a lot to get your work out there, to get yourself out there, and to try and make something of yourself, and that's damn hard. And some days, you feel as if you've achieved nothing because the hard work isn't paying off.

I also know I haven't done as much as many others. I didn't get to travel broadly, or overseas, have a career, or move interstate on my own, or have kids or marriages, and at this point of my life I'd get married and divorced just to say I had.

In the general sense of the "average" life most have, with relationships, kids, careers, and travel, I didn't get to have it, and there will always be that part of me that regrets that. I hated kids when I was a kid. I couldn't stand my screaming nephews, but once I turned eighteen, all I wanted was a baby. A girl to be exact. I wanted the mini version of me, which so many girls seem to want. And every time I saw a baby girl, or toddler, out in public my heart panged for what I wanted desperately. And that desperation never left. It may have mellowed, but the pain is still there and sometimes I cry at night in the darkness of my bedroom about how fucking lonely I am and how I've missed out on the two things I wanted most. And still do.

And because of these emotional holes that are in my heart and soul, I developed a lower scale shopping addiction. Buying pretty things that I can sometimes barely afford, but want, fills that hole left in my life. I own pretty things; I have nothing else. It fills the hole, but not for long as the cycle starts again. I buy things to fill the holes. I buy things to fill my life.

Being single for me has only ever worked to get things done. Because in the scheme of things, I'm in a relationship with the person I live in the same house with. My mother. It's an emotionally unwell relationship, one that will last as long as this situation does and which won't stop until I can leave or get out from under it, and that can only happen if my life changes as I mentioned several times in this book. The usual winning of lotto or a house, or my books exploding in popularity and me suddenly selling and making millions.

For a lot of single ladies, they think, *great, I have the bed to myself, the food to myself, and the remote to myself!* There is a part of being single that *is* great, but for me, there's also a part that isn't. And it sucks.

We're constantly told by so-called experts that we need to learn to love ourselves before anyone else can love us, but

I'm calling bullshit on that.

It's damn hard to love yourself, especially when you have a shit life and when the Universe is telling you that you don't matter, that your life doesn't matter, that your thoughts, feelings, and actions don't matter. That the Universe is going to do what it wants when it wants to you, and you have no fucking say whatsoever in what happens. That's why I get so sick and tired of men, but women mainly, who get on their pedestals and dictate to us how we need to live life. Most of them have never had a bad life. Most of them wouldn't know what it's like to *not* have the ability to go after what they want in life. But many would, and many of them come from pretty shit lives. They understand.

I posted a picture of myself to my Instagram page on May 21st, 2024 for my 50th birthday.

The problem was, thinking about it months later, the me in that photo wasn't the one I wanted to convey. I took maybe twenty or thirty photos, trying to get the words on my t-shirt in, get my books in, but I smiled. Even though I didn't want to smile.

I didn't feel like smiling because I was miserable. I *am* miserable, with the way my life turned out at fifty. Who knew I'd be doing the same fucking thing in the same fucking place that I had done at 25!

But instead of showing me looking miserable, I posted a photo of me smiling. Why? Vanity! So, you didn't see my dark circles and bags, my acne scars and red veins, and my thinning hair, basically how shit I looked. Because that was the truth. I looked and felt like shit, but vanity took over and I wanted to look good without make-up. Jesus fucking Christ. So that photo of me smiling is not an accurate representation of where I was emotionally, psychologically, or physically. Just vanity. For the sake of looking good without make-up, and once I had this thought a couple of months ago, it didn't sit right.

Because being a carer stuck on the same goddamn treadmill of life for half of my life is exhausting, and I'm fucking exhausted.

As I move into the second fifty years of my life, I look back on these stories to try and see the lessons life has thrown me. The problem is, I think the lessons ended up being different to what life *thought* it was teaching me.

The lesson that no matter how hard you work, most will never have success. Success is left for those who are either touched by the hands of the gods of fame, success, and money; those who have other people working to make them famous, like stage parents; the people who get instafamous, are on reality shows, or OnlyFans. And let me tell ya, if I was half my age and shit hot, I'd probably be on OnlyFans too. They're making *millions.*

Obtaining success is damn hard, and no matter how hard you try, no matter how much shit life throws your way, you have to keep stumbling along, wading through the shit of life that keeps piling up and suffocating you.

I learned lessons like, *don't expect people to help you, and certainly not those who you believe are meant to. Support yourself because you're the only one you can trust and support.*

Lessons like, *family isn't everything, especially for those full of toxicity.* Or, *those who have gone through unexpected life loss have to struggle to raise themselves without the family they expected to be around.*

Lessons like, *rely on yourself and no one else because no one's your biggest supporter than you.*

Lessons like, *life is going to be damn hard, and you either give up, or redirect what little energy you do have into what you can deal with.*

You really are the only person you can rely on. I certainly couldn't rely on the woman who helped set up my jewellery business, or the two companies I then turned to in order to further the business. I certainly couldn't rely on my first cover designer to complete a couple of jobs after years of being a loyal customer. I certainly can't rely on my family to be supportive.

Life lessons are hard, and some of the people who know my situation constantly have their minds blown by some of the stories I tell them. They can't believe I have to deal with so much on my own, and there is so much I haven't told in this book. They've constantly told me they don't understand how I deal with it all and I must have broad shoulders to do so. Maybe I'm just strong willed. Or maybe I'm just too cowardly to try and change it. The way I see it, without financial or physical help and support I won't be able to. It costs money to move and that's something I don't have. Until my life does change, my life will stay the same. And the one big lesson I've learned in the last fifty years, is that the Universe doesn't give a flying fuck about me, and I have to suffer on through the hell I'm going through. That's a really damn hard lesson to accept. One I've had to accept every New Year's Eve when I stand in my backyard, look up into the sky, and ask the Universe to change my life this year. I've done it for over thirty years now, and nothing's changed. Ever. So I soldier on.

It pisses me off that I didn't get to have a life, or haven't got to have one, regardless of how much I try and change things. I also don't expect anything *to* change, even though I try and will it to, so in another fifty years I'll be talking about the same things.

Like being envious of others. I have no problem saying that. I'm not jealous, I'm envious. I envy what they have, and what they have is what I covet. The freedom to do what they want, go where they want, and have what they want when they want it.

That's what I want most. The freedom to do what I want, when I want, with whom I want, how and where I want. But that's not going to happen now, is it? And that's a really damn fucking hard lesson to learn because all of it, my whole life, and all of the lessons, have led me to here. A place I don't want to be. Here. Stuck in this hole of an existence not knowing what the hell to do to change it. I soldier on, suck up my lot in life, and get on with it. Because what else is one supposed to do? What am I supposed to do but suck it up and get on with it and keep on soldiering on through this shithole of an existence?

So as I rolled into the fifty-first year of my life, I decided to throw together this memoir, because, hey, why not. It's one more book I've written, using stories from my life, and may or may not have any relevance to you, the reader. But then again, it might. I didn't set forth to teach any lessons. That wasn't the point of this book. I just wanted to tell some stories about the things that have happened in my life that may be of interest to others. I hope you enjoyed it, and will pass it on to someone else for whatever reason.

See you in another fifty.

Not Free

After breathing all day
I walk through the loudness,
and drown among the whiteness.
No one knows where I am.
And then I hear it,
the sound of silence,
the sound of opulence,
drowning the world in hedonism.
And I am still not free, not free.
And still, no one knows where I am.

About the Author

Tiara burst into the world of publishing in 2011 and has blazed a trail ever since. Writing adult fiction as ***L.J. Diva,*** non-fiction and teen stories as ***Tiara King***, and teen and young adult stories as ***T.K. Wrathbone***, she set up her own publishing house, ***Royal Star Publishing,*** to accommodate all of her books and multiple personalities.

Tiara's been creating jewellery and accessories since 1990, turned her obsessive love for it into her label, ***Jewel Divas,*** and writes at her style site, ***Jewel Divas Style***, a one-stop blog for sparkling jewels, style, fun, and dancing under disco balls.

Tiara lives in Australia, has an obsession with colourful kaftans and kimonos, is a jewellery and sparkle addict, '80s music lover, and book collector.

Socials

You can find more about Tiara on her website; follow her on social media, or visit her lifestyle blog, Jewel Divas Style, or her publishing house, Royal Star Publishing.

tiaraking.com.au

jeweldivasstyle.com

royalstarpublishing.com.au

Sign up for Tiara's Newsletter...

Make sure you're always in the know and never miss free exclusives, the latest news, book updates, and so much more with newsletters from...

tiaraking.com.au

Have you read these?

AS TIARA KING

Series

Poems Of A Musical Flavour: Volumes 1-6

MG/YA

#TEENBLOGGER: To Follow or Not To Follow?

Non-Fiction

How To Be A Jewel Diva
Closet Confidential
Dream It, Write It, Publish It!
Unfulfilled

Or these?

AS L.J DIVA

Short Stories

The Body
The Perfect Plot
The Star of Your Own Crime Scene

Novels

Burning Desires
Anything for You
Falling for London
Hollywood Dreams
The Road to Vegas
The Billionaire's Dirty Little Secret

Illicit Things Series

Her
Him
Madam X

AS L.J DIVA

Porn Star Brothers Series

Carlos: Book 1
Pedro: Book 2
Tomas: Book 3
Retribution: Book 4
Porn Star Brothers
Forever
Love Never Dies
Stefan: The New Generation
DeLuca
Spiros & Jenny
And Always

AS T.K. WRATHBONE

Next Top Mannequin
Cinderfella and Princess Charming: Witch Hunters
www.badluck-youredead.com
The Bones Of Wrath: Changes
One Bone: Anthology 1

AS T.K. WRATHBONE

The Orphanage
Hantel and Gresel: Food Critics
Mirror, Mirror On The Wall
The Bones Of Wrath: Haunted
Two Bone: Anthology 2
The Howler
Shadow Walkers
Faded
The Bones Of Wrath: Ghosts
Three Bone: Anthology 3
I Spy With My Little Eye
Knock, Knock…Who's Dead?
It Creeped At Midnight
The Bones of Wrath: Monsters
Four: Anthology 4
Trick Or Treat
All Hallows Possession
They Rise On A Blood Moon
The Bones of Wrath: Horrors
Five Bone: Anthology Five
All Clowns Must Die!
The Demon Resides
Infestation
The Bones of Wrath: Terrors
Six Bone: Anthology 6

www.ingramcontent.com/pod-product-compliance
Lightning Source LLC
Chambersburg PA
CBHW030304080526
44584CB00012B/434